BASRA AND BACK

BASRA AND BACK

THE MEMOIR OF AN UNLIKELY INFANTRYMAN IN THE IRAQ WAR

MATTHEW OKUHARA

Pen & Sword
MILITARY

AN IMPRINT OF PEN & SWORD BOOKS LTD.
YORKSHIRE - PHILADELPHIA

First published in Great Britain in 2025 by
PEN AND SWORD MILITARY
An imprint of
Pen & Sword Books Limited
Yorkshire – Philadelphia

Copyright © Matthew Okuhara, 2025

ISBN 978 1 03612 965 1

The right of Matthew Okuhara to be identified as Author of this work has been asserted by him in accordance with the Copyright, Designs and Patents Act 1988.

A CIP catalogue record for this book is available from the British Library.

All rights reserved. No part of this book may be reproduced, transmitted, downloaded, decompiled or reverse engineered in any form or by any means, electronic or mechanical including photocopying, recording or by any information storage and retrieval system, without permission from the Publisher in writing. No part of this book may be used or reproduced in any manner for the purpose of training artificial intelligence technologies or systems.

Typeset in Times New Roman 11.5/14.5 by
SJmagic DESIGN SERVICES, India.
Printed and bound in the UK by CPI Group (UK) Ltd.

The Publisher's authorised representative in the EU for product safety is Authorised Rep Compliance Ltd., Ground Floor, 71 Lower Baggot Street, Dublin D02 P593, Ireland.
www.arccompliance.com

For a complete list of Pen & Sword titles please contact
PEN & SWORD BOOKS LIMITED
George House, Units 12 & 13, Beevor Street, Off Pontefract Road,
Barnsley, South Yorkshire, S71 1HN, England
E-mail: enquiries@pen-and-sword.co.uk
Website: www.pen-and-sword.co.uk

or

PEN AND SWORD BOOKS
1950 Lawrence Rd, Havertown, PA 19083, USA
E-mail: uspen-and-sword@casematepublishers.com
Website: www.penandswordbooks.com

Contents

Introduction vii

Part I – The Background

Chapter One 2
Chapter Two 5
Chapter Three 10
Chapter Four 14

Part II – The Build-up

Chapter Five 20
Chapter Six 23
Chapter Seven 28
Chapter Eight 32
Chapter Nine 38
Chapter Ten 42
Chapter Eleven 46
Chapter Twelve 51
Chapter Thirteen 57
Chapter Fourteen 61

Part III – The Wait

Chapter Fifteen 68
Chapter Sixteen 70
Chapter Seventeen 74

Part IV – The Deployment

Chapter Eighteen	82
Chapter Nineteen	86
Chapter Twenty	90
Chapter Twenty-one	93
Chapter Twenty-two	98
Chapter Twenty-three	103
Chapter Twenty-four	107
Chapter Twenty-five	113
Chapter Twenty-six	117
Chapter Twenty-seven	122
Chapter Twenty-eight	131
Chapter Twenty-nine	135
Chapter Thirty	140
Chapter Thirty-one	147
Chapter Thirty-two	153
Chapter Thirty-three	157
Chapter Thirty-four	161
Chapter Thirty-five	167
Chapter Thirty-six	172
Chapter Thirty-seven	177
Chapter Thirty-eight	182

Part V – The Return

Chapter Thirty-nine	188
Chapter Forty	192
Chapter Forty-one	197
Chapter Forty-two	200
Chapter Forty-three	208

Part VI – The End

Chapter Forty-four	214
Chapter Forty-five	219

Introduction

I was running towards the sound of gunfire. I don't remember how the contact started. During a traffic stop, a policeman fell away from the open taxi window he was speaking into. He crawled a few feet towards the pavement and collapsed. I thought I had heard a shot. Or maybe it was a burst of fire. As I ran, following the patrol commander, he turned and pointed to the wounded police officer on the ground. He was in a bad way. It was the senior of the three cops that had joined us on patrol, the Iraqi equivalent of a corporal or sergeant. He had been leading his team and spoke some English, which had made it easier for us to work together. I had met him before at a nearby checkpoint. I swung my equipment off of my shoulder and went into a side pouch. His shirt was red from the collar down. It was obvious where he had been hit – the projectile had reduced his shoulder joint to fragments and pulp. I ripped open a bandage and held it in place.

'I've been . . . sh . . . shot', he told me.

I could see in his eyes that he was looking to me for some kind of reassurance.

'You'll be okay', I told him.

Linking up with the rest of the patrol, there was more firing. I took cover behind the sturdiest thing I could find – a newspaper stand. I looked back to where I had come from and could see the blood and bandages that had been left by the casualties. I looked up, and saw that the rest of the section was engaging, keeping our assailants' heads down. We were being fired at from a rooftop. If I didn't move soon I would be in serious trouble. I scrambled over a tall fence and crashed down the other side as more gunfire erupted. The deep, rapid booming sound was in contrast to the sharp crack of the weapons that we were carrying. I took up a position behind a low wall and looked through my sights. There was a makeshift barricade on top of an abandoned building directly opposite. A figure emerged. It was dark, but his silhouette was clear enough to indicate that he was armed. Almost in slow motion, his hand rested on the barricade as he pushed himself up to get a better look at the situation below. Then, in an instant, he was gone.

Silence followed. It was soon broken by the radio communications coming through my earpiece. The patrol commander was checking up on us and ordering us to regroup. I took a few seconds to compose myself. 'This is a stupid place to be', I told myself as I checked my ammo pouches were closed. 'I could be at uni or enjoying some fine company and a weekend away.' I got to my feet and made my way to rejoin the section, who had taken up position in a deep river bank. 'But here I am, aged nineteen. A finance worker. A banker, but now a soldier. In Basra. How the fuck did that happen?'

* * *

The eighty-five infantrymen of Salamanca Company represented a unique deployment for the British Army. It was the first time in nearly fifty years that a formed unit of reservists had deployed in a ground-holding role. The last time the British Army's reserves, known as the Territorial Army (TA), were deployed in such large numbers was during the Suez Crisis of 1956. During the Cold War and early 90s, the need for a mass call-up of reservists for frontline operations had been nothing more than a contingency plan for World War Three, or another war in Europe. In the mid-90s the role of the UK's reserves was less certain. The collapse of the Soviet Union had delivered a 'peace dividend' that politicians were keen to make the most of. However, this changed in the early 2000s. With dual commitments in Iraq and Afghanistan, the diminished British forces turned to their volunteer regiments for the first time in decades, in order to fill the gaps left by years of cutbacks and shifting political priorities. Salamanca Company prepared for action. Uncertainty loomed over how they would confront the harsh realities of conflict. For most, the sound of shots fired in anger and the shock of combat was utterly unfamiliar.

Based at Basra Palace, Salamanca Company wasted no time in assuming its duties: providing security to the new coalition's provisional

INTRODUCTION

government and navigating the tense and dusty streets of the city. By now, Islamic militants had infiltrated Basra and were sowing discord amongst the population. Iraq's 'second city' was already grappling with shortages of essential resources like food, water, fuel and electricity. The soldiers understood the gravity of the situation. They braced themselves for civil unrest and worse, knowing that the deployment would draw them into even more dangerous territory. For six months in 2004, the officers and men of the Rifle Volunteers became reservists on the frontline. Now that the war had been won, it was time to win the peace.

Basra City, Iraq, 2004

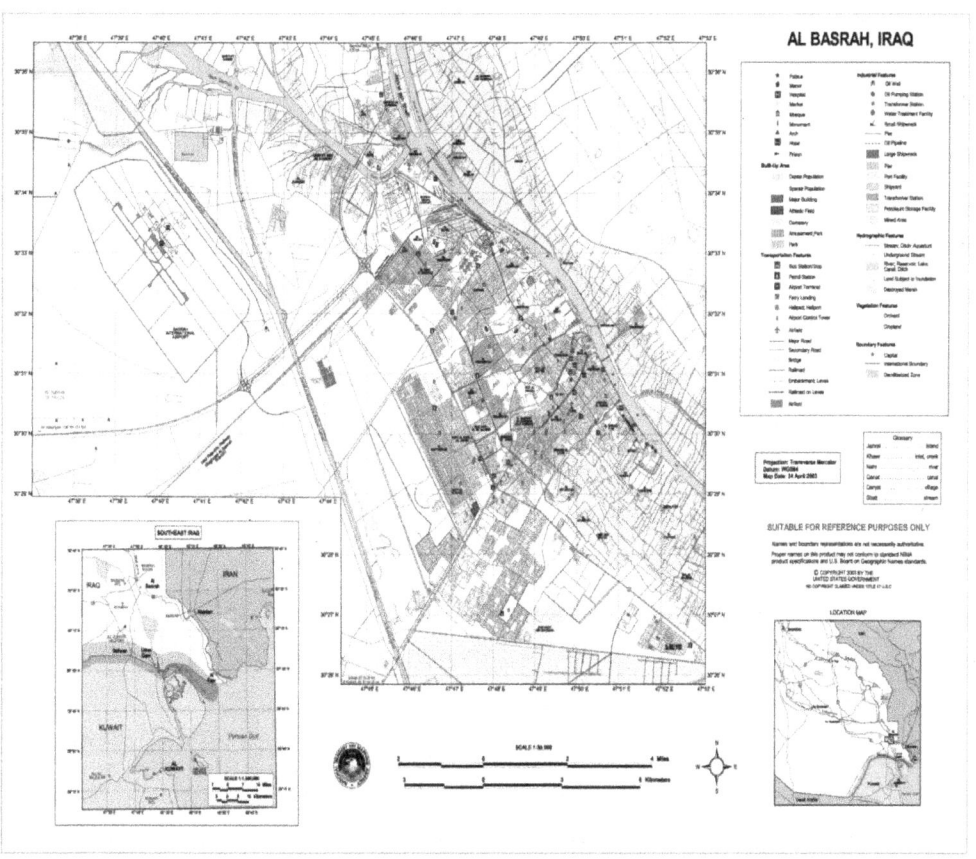

Part I
THE BACKGROUND

Chapter One

When Operation Telic began on 19 March 2003, to many it seemed like just another foreign conflict. British forces had already been deployed to Afghanistan since late 2001, and only two years prior to that, the Army and Royal Air Force had been operating in Kosovo. So when the headlines 'US and British Marines Invade Iraq' appeared in the following morning's newspapers, it seemed like business as usual. Within weeks, the Iraqi capital Baghdad had fallen – an event relegated to short sound bites on the evening news and articles buried between the Page Three model and the sports section in *The Sun*. But the conflict was only just beginning. After winning the war, the next phase was winning the peace.

Like almost every nineteen-year-old on Saturday mornings, I had no interest in getting up, so as usual I put it off as long as I could. Eventually, though, I made my way to the ground floor of the family home, picking up an envelope with my name on it as I walked past that morning's post. I made myself a coffee and turned on the TV, intent on finding some background noise while I had the house to myself. Life in rural Gloucestershire was relaxed and quiet. With nothing planned, I thought about ways to waste my weekend. I considered going to Bristol or Cheltenham with some friends, and also thought about doing nothing at all. At that time I worked in retail banking. It wasn't something I enjoyed, but it paid well for someone of my age and experience. I decided it would be good to relax from the stress and pressure of the financial sector for a weekend. It had been a long week.

Weekends off at that time were a luxury. I had been training hard with my local Territorial Army (TA) unit on Saturdays and Sundays for several months. I had joined the TA as soon as I was old enough –

CHAPTER ONE

at eighteen. The Royal Gloucestershire, Berkshire and Wiltshire Regiment (RGBW), also known as the Glosters, was part of the Rifle Volunteers, and it was my local unit. Growing up, I had always noticed their small base on Eastern Avenue in Gloucester whenever I passed it. I always noted the sign visible from the main road that declared, 'It's Part-Time but a Real Soldier's Job'. Fresh-faced and full of enthusiasm, I had attended an induction weekend the previous year, before going on to complete phase two of my training, which was a combat infantryman's course. Having achieved that in early autumn, it now meant that as far as the Army was concerned, I was a competent and efficient soldier, suitable for military operations both domestically and abroad. In reality, though, I was just a kid who knew very little about the world and even less about what it meant to enter a conflict zone.

Settling down, I opened the large brown envelope with my name on it. I rarely received any mail, so I assumed it was related to work. In a way, it was. Just not my regular work. I took out the covering letter. It was from the TA & Reserves MCM Division. Initially, I thought that maybe I was to go on a course. I had recently had an interview with the battalion commander about starting officer training. Now that I had completed the infantry course, I wanted to try and earn a commission.

Over a cup of tea and a biscuit in his well-appointed office in Exeter, the battalion commander had outlined what he expected of his officer cadets and casually enquired, 'How would you feel about being called up for Iraq or Afghanistan or such?'

Lieutenant Colonel Blewitt had recently deployed some of his battalion to Afghanistan. Thinking that this was just a part of the informal interview, I let him know that I would not have any problem with it, adding that perhaps I would volunteer for full-time reserve service in the near future. In truth, I had never considered being deployed but I wanted to make a good impression. Feeling as if I had given a strong account of myself with my up-for-it attitude, I left the interview feeling confident and hopeful. 'Maybe I did such a good job that he recommended me for an interview board,' I thought to myself as I drew the rest of the letter out of the envelope.

NOTICE OF COMPULSORY CALL-OUT. 25173850 PTE M OKUHARA.

'Oh shit!'

It continued:

1. As you know, the British Army is involved in supporting a number of international military operations, and the government has taken the decision to mobilize compulsory elements of the reserve forces in order to sustain these deployments. They will deploy alongside the regular army, in support of the UK's contribution to operations.
2. Under powers conferred on him by the Reserve Forces Act 1996, the Secretary of State for Defence has issued an order authorising the compulsory call-out of individuals from units of the Territorial Army and Regular Reserve.
3. A formal call-out notice is on the reverse of this letter. Accordingly, you must report to THE RESERVE TRAINING AND MOBILISATION CENTRE, CHILWELL, NOTTINGHAM, on 02 Feb 2004.

My morning lethargy had all but disappeared, along with my appetite for any kind of breakfast. I retreated to my spare room, overlooking the Gloucestershire countryside. It was a mild shock, to say the least. I needed a few moments to think about what I had just read. All in all, I had had around thirty days of military training – and that was a generous estimate. Phase one of my training had taken five weekends. Ten days. Phase two had taken fifteen days. At a liberal guess, and rounding up all of the Tuesday evenings I had spent with the Glosters, I estimated that I had no more than a month's experience. Had there been a mistake? Probably not. I read the letter again, turning it over this time to read the 'formal call-out' notice. It was not a mistake. It had been decided. Not by me, but it was decided. I was going to war.

Chapter Two

I sent a text message to some of the others in my platoon. Almost immediately, I heard back from Foz. Corporal Andy Foster was my section commander, and I had taken to him immediately after being introduced. He had guided me through many of the basics on those few evenings I had paraded with the rest of the Glosters. Everyone in the company seemed to get on well with him, from the company commander down to the newest recruit. He had joined the TA at eighteen, just like I had, but now, in his early thirties, he was as experienced as anyone could become as a reservist. Athletic and energetic, he was also extremely funny and mentally agile.

'Got my travel brochure too,' he replied to my message.

He had already been in touch with the company admin officer and was arranging for us to go to the TA centre to meet and come up with a training scheme before reporting for mobilization. Half a dozen of the company were already in Afghanistan, so at least there was a precedent for us to follow regarding deployment.

Instead of bombarding Foz with questions in a text, I decided to give him a call. He seemed to know a lot already. I guessed he had opened his post a few hours ago while I was still in bed.

'There are fourteen of us called up for Iraq,' he said.

I still didn't know all the members of the company and struggled to put faces to the names he mentioned. Most of my time had been spent training as a recruit, which didn't happen at the local TA centre but at a regional unit that served south-west England. He rattled off a few more names he could remember.

'Oh, and Broz is called up too.'

I knew Broz. We had joined around the same time; maybe he had been in for two weeks longer than I had. So at least there would be two familiar faces – Foz and Broz. That was reassuring. It struck me, when I hung up the phone, that I was more concerned at that stage about whether I knew anyone else who had been called up than worried about the current situation the British Army found itself in. There were frequent news reports about casualties in both Iraq and Afghanistan. In Iraq, a few months earlier, six Royal Military Police soldiers had been brutally killed in Mahar al-Kabir, in the south of the country. In Afghanistan, a member of the Rifle Volunteers, Private Jonathan Kitulagoda, had been killed, and others wounded in a suicide bombing. Maybe I should have been more concerned about the potentially deadly nature of what I had been compulsorily called out to do. But that wasn't at the forefront of my mind.

Not long after, Foz sent me a message letting me know that in the afternoon the fourteen of us would be expected in the bar at the TA centre, so that the company commander (or OC, Officer Commanding) could meet us for a chat and answer any questions we might have. I replied, letting him know I would be there. I felt a mild sense of unreality about being deployed.

I had never really been anywhere on my own before. The closest to independence I had ever experienced was a week-long trip to Switzerland as part of my school's music department. This was going to be completely different. The notification I had read did not give a fixed amount of time for the deployment. It just offered vague information indicating it could be up to a year. Until now I had been living a comfortable and predictable life. I lived in a decent-sized home in the countryside, surrounded by hills and farmland. I was never more than a few steps away from the peace and quiet of the great outdoors. I had a bedroom and a spare room. I had a job that paid well, friends to spend my free time with, and hobbies. Was this all really going to be put on hold? It appeared that it was. Had I really signed up for this? I supposed I must have.

I walked to the tiny station close to where I lived – nothing more than two platforms, a bridge and a smoking shelter – and rode the small train to Gloucester. It was only a short ride, but the easiest way to the city. Once I got off the train, it was a short walk to the TA centre. I figured that if I spent some time walking I could come up with some good questions to ask the company commander or Foz. But I found that I had nothing to ask. I was struggling to get my thoughts in order. But I was also starting to accept that things were just going to be that way, and that the best

CHAPTER TWO

thing for me would be to just get on with it. 'I'm not really sacrificing all that much,' I thought to myself. 'Nothing that can't be picked up as soon as I get home.' I decided it would be best to gauge first how everyone else was feeling. Surely the rest of the guys would be having similar thoughts and would probably end up asking the questions I was unable to come up with.

The TA centre, or reservist centre as it became known, is a small Army base close to Gloucester city. It did not have much in the way of facilities, so training usually happened at larger locations such as Dartmoor and Woodbury Common, or larger bases like HMS *Raleigh* and Beachley Barracks. The TA centre was, however, suitable for weeknight activities and classroom-based training. The vast majority of the base was designed to support a full infantry company along with some associated units. It had enough equipment, vehicles and weapons for three platoons of infantry, but in late 2003 the total establishment was less than half of that.

I joined the rest of the fourteen in the TA centre bar. We were waiting for the company major and the administration officer to give us more details. Having had no plans for the weekend, I now wanted to find out as much as we could about the call-up. Anything else could wait. Looking around, I recognized some of the others who had been called up, but I struggled to put a name to any of the faces. I knew the NCOs. I could see some of the other younger soldiers from my platoon, including Broz. As I walked into the bar and took a seat I remembered my induction weekend. It was less than a year ago, and just as now, I had been filled with a mix of enthusiasm, curiosity and doubt. Back then, a few of the other potential recruits and I had finished a host of problem-solving and team-building exercises and were sitting at the same table I was at now, when some of the company returned from a weekend exercise. Wearing their green DPM uniforms and black boots, some headed to the bar, while the rest sat down in their regular seats around the room. Clearly we, the potential recruits, were all in someone's seat, as we were soon joined by a trio of soldiers who put their pint glasses down on the table next to ours.

'Who are you?' the biggest of the group asked.

I noticed that he had parachute wings on his shoulders and a maroon beret tucked into his leg pocket. Everyone else's headdress was dark blue, almost black.

One of the other recruits answered him, 'We're looking to join up.'

'Oh, right,' he replied. 'Thought you might be cadets or something.'

It was a fair comment. We all looked young. Especially me.

'Does your mum know you're here?!' he asked, looking at me and laughing with the rest of the group.

I thought about my decision to join the Glosters a little more on that first weekend. Keeping a low profile, I looked around the bar and said to myself, 'I want this. I really want this.' It was not a huge ambition. Militarily speaking, it was about as small as ambitions get, but it was still something I wanted to be a part of. I saw the groups of soldiers laughing and talking; I saw the way everyone seemed to get along; I saw the unique badges of the RGBW berets, the history of the local regiment. My local regiment. It was entirely different to everything I had ever seen, done or experienced. For me, I decided, it was going to take a lot of hard work. I was a skinny 18-year-old. Just a boy. I was highly-strung. Easily upset. And a vegetarian. Not exactly infantry material. But I made my decision there and then. I wanted to be a part of the Glosters.

My mind snapped back to the present. I was sitting in what I considered to be 'my chair' in the bar, along with Broz opposite me. Broz was in his early twenties and bigger than me. His wide shoulders made it easy for him to carry enormous amounts of equipment during training, something I had struggled with. I was built more for speed and had been called a 'racing snake' by most of the staff at ITC (Infantry Training Centre). Broz and I had both completed our combat infantryman's course only eight weeks earlier and were trying to guess if any of the other guys we had met would be deploying with us. As if to answer that question, the company OC, Major Wood, and the admin officer, Captain Fry, entered the bar, each carrying a box of papers. Neither was in uniform. None of the troops were either. Mr Wood looked as if he had just finished a round on the back nine, whereas Eddie Fry was his typical scruffy self in a faded Gloucester Rugby top and even more faded jeans. Nobody got up, but the bar fell silent.

'Gents,' began Mr Wood. 'You will be deployed to Iraq on Operation TELIC IV as part of a force protection unit known as Salamanca Company.'

I made a mental note to ask Foz ASAP what a 'force protection unit' was.

'In total, eighty-five men and officers from 43 Wessex Brigade have been mobilized.'

CHAPTER TWO

He paused and reached into his box of papers to pull out a batch of freshly printed notes and began passing them around.

'RGBW will make up the smallest component of Salamanca Company. None of our officers or sergeants are going. Corporals Foster, Kavanagh, Bonser and Hill are going to be your senior blokes.'

I looked at the paper that had been handed to me. In a few short paragraphs, it detailed what we were expected to do as part of the pre-deployment phase.

'Your build-up training,' added the major, 'will begin a couple of days after you arrive at Chilwell. At the mobilization centre you will get equipment, health checks and an evening meal. After that, Major Evans from the Light Infantry will be your company commander.'

I made another mental note to find out if anyone knew who the OC would be. I liked Mr Wood a lot, and he had been acting as the adjutant for recruit training while Broz and I were on our infantry course. He always had time to speak to even the lowliest of his men and came across as very patient and fair.

He continued, 'Mr Evans has sent over his concept for forming up Salamanca Company and we're going to go through that in a moment. First of all, does anyone have any questions and does anyone need a fresh pint? The next round is on me.'

Nobody wanted to turn down the offer of a free drink, and as if in unison, the whole company began downing their drinks. Behind the bar, Corporal Hill, who had previously been in the Grenadier Guards, started to fulfil the drink orders as quickly as he could. No doubt he was just as keen to hear about the deployment as the rest of us. Mark Hill worked in the company stores and was older than the rest of those called up. In his mid-forties, he was something of a father figure to many of the soldiers in the company and a good friend to the rest. He had a lot of experience both as a soldier and a storeman, so it was good to know he would be coming along, especially as none of our senior NCOs would be with us. He was very easy to talk to and get along with. The tattooed guy he was serving at the bar, however, I did not know. In fact, I knew only three things about him. I knew he was in the assault pioneer platoon, I knew he looked like a heavily tattooed escaped convict and I knew that he had a piercing through the end of his cock, earning him the name 'Metal Mickey'. Someone had told me this. I assumed it was true.

Chapter Three

We sat in small groups around the bar, glancing over the papers the major had given us. In the top right corner of the letter were the three cap badges of the regiment forming the Rifle Volunteers: the Bugle of the Light Infantry (LI), the Castle and Sphinx of the Devon and Dorset Regiment (D&Ds) and the Sphinx of the Royal Gloucestershire, Berkshire, and Wiltshire Regiment (RGBW). To keep us fully informed, Major Evans had written a memo for everyone due to join his unit. To ensure there was no ambiguity, Mr Wood read it aloud for us all to hear.

He began: 'You have been selected to be mobilized for a tour of duty in Basra, Iraq, serving alongside eighty-four other TA soldiers from the battalion.'

He listed key dates: formation, skills training, build-up training, and the all-important days off, then continued: 'You will be part of Salamanca Company, the Rifle Volunteers. Salamanca Company will be integrated into the 1 Cheshire Battlegroup. This integration will culminate with a confirmatory exercise. The following weeks will focus on continuation training in specialist skills (driving, medical, etc.). The entire pre-deployment training package will consist of a carefully programmed period of robust military training designed to prepare you for all eventualities in theatre. It will not always be easy, but it will be progressive and demand 100 per cent commitment. I strongly recommend you start working on your fitness, as a little work now will help you greatly during the training.'

I looked around the bar. So did a few others, but nobody tried to make eye contact. It was as if a break from reading the letter would provide some respite from this very informal but life-changing memo. Many of the assembled troops were married men with kids. No doubt their wives and children would be asking questions. I knew that would be a difficult

CHAPTER THREE

conversation for many, if not all of them. I could see the look of concern on more than one face. I probably looked the same.

The major continued: 'This is a significant undertaking by yourselves and your families, and I am very much aware of this. There will be a robust support mechanism in place to support you and your families while you are away, and you will have access to welfare facilities in theatre that will allow you to maintain regular contact with your families back home. You will find this experience both challenging and testing but ultimately immensely rewarding. I am sure you will rise to the challenge.'

The letter was signed off with a blunt remark – 'You will be thoroughly briefed on all other matters before you deploy' – and a scruffy signature.

Everyone remained quiet for a while longer, re-reading the memo and confirming the odd detail with the person next to them. There were no questions for the officers, so they gave some concluding remarks.

Captain Fry said: 'We knew a deployment was coming, but we did not know who and how many were required. Major Evans is from the Light Infantry. His 2i/c, Captain Roberts, is from the Devon and Dorsets. Along with the Colonel, they decided who would be best to bring from the regiment, based on a lot of different criteria. But none of that matters. The simple fact is this: you are in the Army, and you are going on ops.'

Eddie Fry was a late-entry officer who served as the administrator for the unit. He didn't really look much like a soldier or act like an officer, but it was hard not to like him, even if he did have a fearsome temper that could detonate seemingly for no reason. He passed around some notes he had typed up, a checklist of things he was responsible for before sending us to the mobilization centre.

Prodding a chubby finger into the palm of his hand, he said, 'Check that list and let me know ASAFP if you're missing any kit or if you're going to have any problems providing documents.'

The major added, almost immediately, 'And let me know if you need help with anything. Anything at all. No matter how small.'

The two officers looked around as if to double-check they hadn't missed a raised hand. Satisfied, they left the bar so we could carry on with our drinks and talk behind their backs. Soon enough, the volume and pitch of the assembled men's conversation returned to normal, and the mood changed from concern to one of cautious optimism.

I was starting to feel excited. What had seemed unreal at first now started to become more tangible. It felt like I would be doing something with my life. In truth, I had not lived much of a life up until that point and had deliberately avoided going to university to gain some 'life experience in the real world'. 'I should have been careful about what I wished for,' I said to myself. Most of my friends were at university. My twin brother was as well. This was something completely different. Turning to Broz, I asked him how he felt about it.

'It'll be the experience of a lifetime, I guess', came the reply.

That was more eloquent than anything I was used to hearing from Broz, who usually spoke in three- or four-word sentences. But he seemed preoccupied with his phone, so I didn't push the subject and instead joined Bons, who was propping up the bar. Corporal Bonser, or Bons as he preferred to be called, was the company signaller – a radio operator. It was a role that suited him as he was a telecoms engineer by trade. Pat, another signaller, was with him. In all, three of our four signallers were on the list for Salamanca Company.

'I bet you didn't see this coming,' said Bons.

Pat nodded in agreement as he finished off a pint.

'How long have you been with us?'

'Less than a year,' I replied. 'I thought the call-up papers were an invitation for an officer selection board at first.'

He laughed.

'I got a bit of a shock when I read the first line.' I gestured with my hands, spelling out each syllable: 'Notice of compulsory call-out.'

Pat got himself another drink.

'At least you don't have a wife and kids to explain it to. What you having?'

Pat was rummaging around in his pocket for a fiver. He was right. I knew Pat had a wife and two kids at home. But I still had to tell my family and my employers about the deployment. I finished my drink. By now, it was late afternoon and a clear, dry day. I decided to leave the bar and walk the long way back to the station so that I could think over the day's events so far.

I knew nothing about the country we were being sent to. I couldn't accurately locate it on a map, recall its flag or name any cities other than Baghdad. Iraq had been in the news a lot around ten years earlier

CHAPTER THREE

when the war was won almost exclusively by Coalition airpower, along with some help from Bravo Two Zero. The first Gulf War had captured the media's imagination, resulting in numerous books by Special Forces soldiers, many television programmes, documentaries, and the occasional Hollywood blockbuster like *Courage under Fire* and *Three Kings*. The closest I had come to the Arabian Peninsula was either watching those movies or playing Aladdin in the school play. However, I suspected that these 'Arabian Nights' would be far less pleasant than the family-friendly version that Walt Disney had put together.

Chapter Four

'A' Company of the Rifle Volunteers drew its personnel from a diverse pool of men. All of the reservists lived in and around Gloucester city, and all worked locally as well: labourers, health workers, teachers, office staff and shop clerks. We had more than a few engineers from the local aircraft undercarriage manufacturer, Dowty's, and we even had a sixth form student in his last year of school. Being only seventeen, he needed parental permission to volunteer, and he was too young to join Salamanca Company for their deployment. The entire unit was badged as RGBW and, to a man, were very proud of the history of the regiment as well as the unique backbadge that distinguished the unit from all others in the British Army.

The unit was a successor to the Gloucestershire Regiment, the Glorious Glosters. The backbadge tradition originated during the Battle of Alexandria, in Egypt in March 1801. During the battle, French cavalry managed to get behind the British lines, forcing the Glosters' rear rank to 'about face'. This meant the regiment, surrounded by French forces, fought back-to-back until they drove off the enemy. In recognition of this action, the regiment was permitted to wear a badge on the back as well as the front of their headdress. Even as reservists, we carried that tradition on our berets and combat helmets. Of course, the rest of the Army joked that it was because the Glosters were drawn from country folk who frequently put their hats on the wrong way round.

As I walked to the station I contemplated what the major had said and began thinking about my short military career to date and my own part in the Glosters. 'How did I get here?' I asked myself. I knew the answer. It was obvious. I didn't join the Army by accident.

Nobody believed I could hack it in the military, even if it was 'only' part-time. Friends and family alike doubted my suitability for

CHAPTER FOUR

the infantry, the part of the Army intended to close with and engage the enemy. During my teens, I had been thinking about what I could do in the military and went to the Army careers office to find out as much as I could. My school seemed only interested in sending students to university and offered very little in the way of career advice. At Gloucester Docks, where the Army careers office was located, I sat down with a pile of leaflets and brochures. Full-time? Part-time? Army, Navy, Air Force? Probably not the Marines; apparently, they have to eat worms at some point in training. I did some interviews and tests. Eventually, I received an offer for a full-time role in the Army.

'You could apply to join any corps you would like, within reason', the recruiter told me, but suggested that the Parachute Regiment might not be suitable. 'Would you be interested in attempting the Army Officer Selection Board?'

It was a good offer, and even now I sometimes wish I had taken it. But in the end I decided to join as a reservist to discover what life was like in the fighting arms. I also didn't want to miss another opportunity that had come my way almost by surprise – a job in banking that paid a lot more than the salary of an Army recruit or officer cadet. I wanted to do both, so I decided that 'Gloucestershire boys join the Glosters' and arranged to attend the next recruiting event at the TA centre. I also knew that if I wanted to move up, move to a different branch or service, go full-time, or leave entirely, I could very easily do so.

The local TA centre also had Royal Signals and Royal Army Medical Corps detachments. When I mentioned my plans to my father, who lived in a large house near the city, he said, 'You won't learn anything in the infantry. If you're going to join, join where you will learn something useful.'

He had been online, investigating my plans as usual. It struck a nerve. I had deliberately avoided university, despite good grades, to get some 'life experience'. I didn't want to 'learn' any more – I wanted to 'do'. As I continued to walk I realized that the plans I had set in motion only a few months earlier were developing faster than I had anticipated.

My first full weekend in the Army was spent at a large reservist centre called Wyvern Barracks in Exeter. Arriving on a Friday evening before my first day of training, I wore a poorly fitting set of green coveralls and some Hi-Tec Silver Shadow trainers. The TA centre was full to capacity.

The large barracks hosted several TA units as well as a university unit. It seemed as though most of the South-West's reserves were doing something that weekend.

I joined the line for scoff and looked down to see what was on offer. Chips, of course, some steam trays with peas and sweetcorn, and then some pinkish-looking meat, probably from a pig. Then some fish.

I asked the uninterested squaddie behind the servery, 'Is there a vegetarian option?' and received a delayed but definitive answer, 'No.'

So I settled down to a very yellow meal with some peas for added colour. Clearly, the guy behind me had heard my request and asked when I sat down, 'Are you a veggie then? You can't be a veggie in the Army, mate.'

He could have been right. I wasn't feeling as confident and settled as the others at the table. Or perhaps they were better at hiding their discomfort. Between generous mouthfuls of his meal, he asked, 'What unit are you for, mate?'

I told him, 'The Glosters.'

'Oh, right. D&Ds for me.'

Beside me, a Cornishman added, 'LI,' although his broad accent made it sound like 'Eloy' at first.

Coffey, as I found out he was called, had been an Army cadet for years. He gave the impression that he already knew everything and would be an ideal candidate for Special Forces selection at some time in the future. He looked grey and sickly, though, as if he didn't sleep much and didn't enjoy natural sunlight. A spell in the Army would probably be just what the doctor ordered and would work wonders for his complexion. The other recruit, bound for the Light Infantry, appeared the exact opposite. Tall and tanned, he looked like a Mediterranean fisherman – only the accent betrayed his true heritage.

I smiled to myself while considering my inauspicious start in the Army. Despite it all, I had achieved what I set out to, and I was proud of that. It was the first time I had accomplished something on my own. I started to think about the positives of being called up. Were there any? 'The targets will be easier to hit!' I laughed out loud. Retail banking was a very mercenary industry as far as I was concerned. 'I'll be able to get away from all that for pretty much a whole year . . .' Most of my Army experience had been over weekends until that point, which meant there

CHAPTER FOUR

was no conflict of interest with my full-time job. The one exception was when I had to attend the combat infantryman's course, which was residential and held over fifteen full days. At the time, my manager was reluctant to let me go, arguing that it was 'simply out of the question'. I was looking forward to providing her with the compulsory call-out notice and seeing if that was 'simply out of the question' as well.

On the other hand, there were some obstacles to overcome which, as a teenager with very little knowledge of the world, seemed almost insurmountable: namely, how to tell those nearest to me that I was being deployed to Iraq in only a few months' time? Granted, I did not have to kiss goodbye to a loving wife and ask an infant son 'to be the man of the house while I'm gone'. Also, I did not have any commitments that would negatively impact my life while I was on operations. No business contracts, no essential connections or financial arrangements, for example. I realized that if someone had to go, then I was definitely in a better position than the vast majority, if not all, of the company.

Part II
THE BUILD-UP

Chapter Five

Salamanca Company assembled for the first time in a car park at the Reserves Mobilisation and Training Centre, Chilwell, Nottingham, on a cold, wet Wednesday morning. We had arrived on Monday, been checked out and kitted out on Tuesday and had now been brought together to hear an opening address from the officer commanding, Mr Evans. I can't remember what he said. I was feeling embarrassed about being the last to join the parade; keeping him and the entire unit waiting. The last thing I wanted was to be noticed, especially on the first day. However, whilst the rest of the company had been standing at ease, waiting for the Company Sergeant Major (CSM) to bring them to attention, I had been helping move some equipment onto a coach that was about to leave. The major had dispatched a very irate sergeant to come and find me and get me into the parade. Everyone saw it, everyone heard it.

'Get the fuck over there, now! Now!'

It seemed as though the entire company was staring at me. The major was definitely glaring at me. Somehow he could see me through all the assembled men. He started his opening address. It ended without my catching a word of it. The company second-in-command, or 2i/c, then stepped forward with the rest of the officers. Captain Roberts' main function was to run personnel matters on behalf of the major, so that the latter could focus on more strategic problems. We had yet to meet our officers, or even be put into platoons, so it came as a relief when the CSM brought us to attention and dismissed us. The NCOs now took over and started allocating us to platoons, indicating where we should wait for our officer to join us.

I was in 3 Platoon, along with Broz and my friend from the 'Eloy' whom I had been on the combat infantrymen's course with. It was good to see him again. I hadn't realized that Drewy had been called up as well,

CHAPTER FIVE

until that moment. The past two days at the mobilization centre had been hectic. Rather than doing everything together, most activities happened either as individuals or in small groups; activities such as picking up desert kit, getting a battery of injections, sorting out pay details, having a dental check-up. The only 'group' activities were the meals –but Salamanca Company was not the only unit of reservists being deployed, and the entire base was a hive of activity. Despite being surrounded by people, it was definitely a lonely experience.

Aside from some kit we were expecting to receive once we arrived in Iraq, the reservists at the mobilization centre had access to the same modern equipment and resources as the regular Army. Mostly. I was hoping some extra uniform would turn up before we deployed – as well as some body armour which none of us had yet been issued. At least my boots fitted. The idea was to ensure we were well-prepared for our roles in both training and operational environments.

'Matt', Drewy said, smiling and holding out his hand. 'Broz! Looks like we're going to be a threesome, right?'

He took a step back and turned around to introduce two other LI squaddies. 'This is Mick, and that's Matt as well.'

Mick was a tall, shaven-headed and powerful-looking guy who seemed to be always about to burst out laughing. He had a single stripe on his chest, indicating that he would be one of the platoon's lance corporals. Matt looked completely different. His dark short back and sides, along with a very square frame, gave him the air of a substitute PE teacher.

In order to avoid the confusion caused by having the same first name, his suggestion was that 'You can be Matt, I'll be Thew.' He emphasised his plan with his hands: 'Matt – Thew.'

The newly constituted 3 Platoon was standing in a few small groups, making small talk and introducing themselves. A sergeant and lieutenant soon made their way over and we all came to a loose formation and stood to attention. Mick threw up a salute on behalf of all of us for good measure. Military courtesy was still something of a mystery to me, so I was glad someone had the initiative to do things properly.

'Stand them at ease, thanks, Mick', said the sergeant.

Friends, then. I had seen a lot of broad smiles and back-slapping as we waited for our officer to join us. It seemed that a good number of the men knew each other and had more than likely been on exercises together in the past.

Our platoon was only fifteen-strong – including the lieutenant and sergeant. The other two platoons held double that number as far as I could tell. Along with the platoon commander and sarge, we had one corporal and three lance corporals.

'I think I've met all of you before . . . except you two', began the sergeant, waving a finger at Broz and me.

He didn't say anything else, so I spoke up first: 'Private Matt Okuhara', and was followed immediately by 'Private James Broslin, sergeant'.

He looked at us both. He was obviously an experienced and likely a very tough guy, but at least his gaze held a kind of warmth that indicated that he was probably a decent bloke.

'Gloster boys. Well at least you didn't show up in wax jackets.'

He was referring to the tendency of the occasional Gloucestershire soldier to wear a dark green wax jacket in lieu of DPM. I decided not to mention that such a garment was in my bergen, and made a mental note to relegate it from its spare uniform function to off-duty attire.

He smiled. 'Reg Derrick', he said, tapping himself on the chest, and turned to the officer behind him: 'Lieutenant Sherwood'.

Chapter Six

We now set off for Tregantle Fort, near Plymouth. Getting on a coach with an overweight driver in a short-sleeved shirt plus tie made it seem more like a school trip than the first step in a military scheme of manoeuvre. But it was a lot more comfortable than the fold-down benches of the four-ton trucks that usually moved us around the country. At Tregantle we would ease into our pre-deployment training through fitness and skill at arms work. I wasn't worried about either of these. I was looking forward to them. I knew that I was in good physical condition and that I was at least above average when it came to weapon-handling. But the hardest thing for me, and my only concern at that point, was self-reliance – in a domestic sense. My plan was to find someone in the same room as me who looked like they knew what they were doing. Then copy them. If they were polishing boots or ironing or cleaning, then I would be polishing boots, ironing or cleaning as well.

Soon enough I found my target: in the bed opposite me an efficient lance corporal, who was unpacking and tidying his bed space mere seconds after getting through the door to the billet. Another soldier from the LI, he had a fair complexion that looked like it might struggle in the desert sun. That seemed like the only thing that he might struggle with, though, as the guy was obviously very fit and very switched-on. I wondered why he wasn't in the regular Army or police or fire brigade, as he was clearly suited to that line of work.

The building was old, with a single heater near the door of our room to keep the thirteen of us warm. This would also be the only way to dry out wet kit, so I foresaw a damp start to Op TELIC. The sergeants and officers had their own accommodation somewhere else inside the old castle. My bed was almost at the back of the room – a plastic mattress on a steel bed frame that had doubtless seen service in the Crimea. I unrolled my maggot (sleeping bag) and put my kit at the end of the bed. There was only one window, and the thick stone walls gave the place a distinctly 'communal jail cell' feeling. At least the door wasn't locked. We only had a few minutes to unpack and get to the parade ground at Tregantle Fort to await the officers. We had spent most of the day travelling and arrived just as the sun began to set. On the parade ground, the cold wind blew in from the English Channel and whipped around the high walls that surrounded us. The fort looked old, and I discovered that it was indeed, having been built in 1865. Putting this in perspective, I realized that it was the same year that Abraham Lincoln met his untimely demise and *Alice in Wonderland* was published. I could relate to Alice at that moment. I had definitely gone down a rabbit hole and I knew very little about the world that awaited me on the other side.

Mr Roberts, the captain and second-in-command, took the parade and let the company know that we would begin training in earnest, from tomorrow.

'You are in your own time now. Breakfast at 0600, PT at 0700', concluded the CSM.

There was talk of a bar that the Company Quartermaster Sergeant (CQMS) had set up. The headquarters part of the company had set off before the rest of us. Bons, Pat and Mark had arrived a few hours earlier with the rest of the signals and stores and got everything ready for the main body of troops. They had checked the billets, secured the equipment and put together a conference room for the officers. Upon being dismissed I noticed that the senior NCOs joined the officers and disappeared into one of the few buildings that could be considered modern. The rest of us got out of the cold and returned to the accommodation block.

Normally, reservists are required to attend a two-week annual camp. I had done my first and only camp so far with Broz at the Infantry Training Centre. Others did theirs as part of ongoing training or full battalion exercises. With so many from the south-west needing training, undeployed reservists could support Salamanca Company instead of attending camp. That seemed sensible. Following the efficient lance corporal in the food queue, I scanned the assisting staff. I saw a few RGBW badges on T-shirts and headwear, but didn't recognize anyone. They likely came from our sister battalion, the Royal Rifle Volunteers, also known as the M4 Rifles, due to their recruitment area along the M4

CHAPTER SIX

corridor from Swindon to Reading. At the servery I discreetly asked if there was a vegetarian option. Having learned to avoid openly declaring my vegetarianism in the infantry, I was relieved to find there was an option, handed to me on a plate too hot to hold. Managing to set it on my tray without showing discomfort, I continued down the line.

'Chef's special?' the lance corporal in front asked.

'Veggie option,' I replied, focusing on my food.

'Fair enough,' he accepted.

It was probably the first time ever that a member of HM Forces did not take the piss out of my dietary preferences. I had grown used to being told there was a fresh portion of grass just outside the cookhouse or making do with a double portion of chips. We sat down and began to eat our only hot meal for the day.

'You're 3 Platoon as well, aren't you?', the lance corporal said more than asked.

'Yeah.'

We started eating, along with everyone else at the long table.

'Cheer up, mate' he added. 'No need to look so worried.'

I didn't realize that I looked worried. It wasn't the first time that I had heard that, though. It seemed that, throughout my life, my emotions had showed up very easily on my face.

'Still thinking about being last on parade, are you?'

I had forgotten about that – being more preoccupied with trying to adjust into this new environment.

'Forget it. Nobody cares. Look.' He pointed left, right and behind. 'They're more interested in their pies than that.'

Seeing that the subject had now been brought up, I thought I might try to justify how and why I was late – shifting the responsibility onto the nameless NCO who had called me across to load equipment. But I thought better of it, and introduced myself instead.

'Tim', he replied. 'Ford. Fordy. Barely been in any time at all, haven't you?'

He was right.

'Just a few months.'

I didn't ask about his service, assuming that as a lance corporal he must at least have a few years under his belt. Then the standard TA question followed.

'What do you normally do?'

I told him, and mentioned for good measure a little about school as well.

He took it all in and replied, 'Painter and decorator. Cleanest ladder in Somerset.'

Everyone in the company had put their regular employment on hold; all except two who had not been accepted into the company as a result of issues identified at the mobilization centre. One, from the RGBW, had not joined us, and another, from the LI, was out as well. We were expecting short-notice replacements in a couple of days' time, and the OC's driver had been reassigned to assist the quartermaster sergeant and Mark in the stores. As I was to discover, the best place to find out what was going on was the cookhouse. A conversation started at one end of the table could easily end up at the other – either by design or through eavesdropping. Chinese whispers often distorted the 'whole truth' of the rumour, but generally speaking it was a great source of intelligence.

Back at our room, the platoon's sole corporal introduced himself. Corporal Parsons had been in the TA for quite a few years at this point, and most people already knew him.

'I was on the parade ground whilst you were on the playground', he told me at one point.

Seeing that he introduced himself using his full name, I adopted a false sense of formality and spoke to him as if he was a client of the bank.

'So should I call you Brian, or . . . ?'

'Well you can fucking start with "Corporal"', he replied, albeit with a touch of humour.

He was a brute of a man, looking like a low-division rugby player, minus the cauliflower ears. But he was razor-sharp and a solicitor in his regular line of work. As the Army had to match the salaries of called-up reservists, he was taking home more than most of the officers were. He spoke to the rest of us in the billet.

'Mr Sherwood wants me to run a knowledge check with you, before you go to the bar or turn in for the night.'

They were both from the same company in Dorchester. Given the number of D&Ds called up, I wondered if there were any reservists left down there.

CHAPTER SIX

'And we have a new guy coming tomorrow from the LI. He'll be joining our platoon.'

The whole week at Tregantle was aimed at weapon-handling, fitness and a little bit of comms training, so the knowledge check he conducted revolved around the individual weapons and radios we were going to be carrying – how to adjust for wind conditions, a talk over some simple battle drills that we might be expected to employ in the near future, and similar issues. It was an easy introduction to full-time service. I suspected that the more important aim was for all the blokes to get to know one another. Satisfied with our performance, he repeated what the CSM had said about the timings for the morning, and with that, my first full day as a regular soldier had come to an end. I noticed my eyes were feeling heavy. Nobody else seemed to be tired, though. With my habit of over-thinking and asking myself too many questions I had really exhausted myself mentally and was looking forward to the morning run. Disengage brain, engage legs – go. I wanted to get into my maggot, but not wanting to seem antisocial I joined the rest of the RGBW guys in the bar. There was an honesty system in place, along with some open boxes of drinks and snacks on a table. There wasn't anywhere for me to sit, so after quickly finishing a can and catching up on the day's events, I went outside and walked around the fort, thinking about the day so far and the upcoming training.

Chapter Seven

Tregantle Fort backed onto several shooting ranges and had plenty of nearby space for physical training. After the light had faded the company had lectures and briefings about the nature of the deployment and what the situation in theatre was like. Our first briefing, the day after we arrived, was about the composition of Salamanca Company. With eighty-five men, the unit was split into three platoons, and a headquarters platoon. 1 Platoon and 2 Platoon were further split down into half platoons, or multiples. Including 3 Platoon, which was already half-sized, that meant there were five sub-units available for tasking. The headquarters platoon, on the other hand, held the command, comms and stores and was not expected to deploy regularly.

3 Platoon were joined by a new arrival, Uzi. A well-established figure in the Rifle Volunteers, he had been called up with only a few days' notice. At first I thought his nickname, Uzi, must have been in relation to a killer instinct or diehard attitude; but I was wrong. He had a mild case of strabismus, or misaligned eyes, and someone had once asked in a thick Cornish accent, 'Who's he looking at', which came out as 'Uzi lookin' at' – and the name stuck. Uzi had brought what he could think of at such short notice, been processed through the mobilization centre and had driven down to Tregantle in double-quick time. He was unpacking his kit on the bunk next to mine and let out an annoyed sigh.

'You got any spare PT kit?' he asked, looking at me – at least I thought he was looking at me.

Being around the same height as him, I chucked a pair of Adidas running shorts that were more suited to training in the summer, not a cold February morning. I opted for my Forest Green Rovers training pants in order to keep the cold wind off.

CHAPTER SEVEN

'Thanks', he said, whilst kitting up for company PT along with the rest of us.

The OC was going to lead the entire company on a run, something that the major seemed to enjoy. Uzi fell in beside me and we started talking. He explained how he had initially been disappointed at not being called up, whilst so many others from the LI had been. But his short-notice orders to join Salamanca Company had turned his disappointment into frustration, as he only had a few days to sort himself out before reporting for mobilization. As we ran, the pace was easy, with most of the company making idle chatter. Uzi seemed to know a lot of the soldiers in the company as well as the officers. At the head of our platoon was Mr Sherwood. An officer in his mid-twenties, he had been through the UOTC – University Officer Training Corps – at Exeter before taking on a reserve commission. Out of the three platoon commanders, he definitely seemed like the 'cool one', with an easygoing but determined attitude.

2 Platoon was led by Lieutenant Thynn, a cousin of the Marquess of Bath. He always seemed angry, and I was glad I wasn't in his platoon. His second-in-command was the irate sergeant who came to round me up for parade a couple of days earlier. It seemed as if the sarge, rather than the officer, was more or less the platoon commander. I decided to steer clear of 2 Platoon until I was sure they had forgotten who I was.

Finally, 1 Platoon was headed up by a horse-riding, brightly smiling and handsome young officer who seemed to excel at everything.

'I bet his knob's bigger than mine as well', said Uzi in disgust.

Lieutenant Sparks and Lieutenant Sherwood were both from the D&Ds, along with most of the sergeants. The LI had the second biggest component, and the RGBW were in the minority.

With a busy training schedule, the first week flew by, and before long we headed to a camp in the middle of Dartmoor in order to start training in the skills that we would need to employ whilst on operations. As a force protection company, one of our roles was guard duty – at both access gates and towers, known as *sangars*. A fellow RGBW soldier in 3 Platoon called Mark, or Elvis owing to his luxurious and natural coiffure, expressed his disappointment at that assignment. A Bristol lad from a satellite unit of 'A' Company, his mood changed during one briefing when the major explained that Salamanca Company would also be responsible for an area of operations around Basra Palace – meaning that we would be out on patrol a lot.

Our move to Willsworthy Camp was intended for us to get used to live firing and to ease us into the patrol skills that we would be expected to employ whilst in the city.

A seasoned complainer, Elvis accurately pointed out that 'It's fuckin' snowin', right? And Dartmoor has about as much habitation as it does vegetation. We should be sunning it up in Cyprus and training over there – not freezing our bollocks off here.'

As he spoke, the cigarette between his lips seemed to wag like a finger, further emphasising his words. He had previously been to Cyprus on exercise with the 1st Battalion of the RGBW, along with several other reservists. Uzi agreed with him. They had become smoking buddies and could often be seen 'having a tab' whenever there was a lull in activity. Between the two of them they were able to sort out most military hardships with their cutting and insightful criticisms. The rest of the platoon loved their accidental double act and would even join them for a smoke, even if they weren't smokers themselves, just to hear the latest opinion piece.

Lying on my camp bed one evening listening to my minidisc player, my reverie was interrupted by a shake of my leg. I usually lay face down to rest or sleep, so rolling over I looked up to see who it was: Mr Sherwood.

'Private Okuhara', he said, in a way that gave the impression he had already had several attempts at securing my attention.

'Sir?' I said in a barely coherent way, before coming to my senses. 'Yes, sir? Can I help with something?'

He didn't need my assistance but was just working his way around the platoon, conducting a mini interview with all those he didn't already know. We went to a small room and had a one-on-one chat – or rather a question-and-answer session. With the officer asking all the questions: 'What do you do for a career, what music do you like, what hobbies', and so on. I couldn't see Mr Thynn being as personable. He also asked if I could drive.

'I have a driving licence', I replied.

'I asked if you *can* drive', he reiterated.

In truth I had not driven in over a year since passing my test.

CHAPTER SEVEN

'Thought as much. Come with me.'

He took me to a room where several of the company were booking themselves for an initial or refresher driving course with an MT (motor transport) NCO on attachment from the battalion.

'Book yourself some initial training and tell Corporal Parsons when you're squared away.'

Chapter Eight

Cross-country driving was quite easy, I found, mostly due to the lack of other cars, people or road furniture to hit. Operating a long-wheelbase Land Rover Defender, or Wolf as it was known, was also straightforward. The instructor explained that the vehicles were 'squaddie-proof' and 'robust enough for most conditions'. However, driving on the road was not as simple, my roadcraft being barely better than that of a learner.

'Well,' concluded the instructor after a day of driving, 'you struggled on the road a bit, but that's good enough for Iraq . . . I don't think they have any traffic laws you need to follow.'

He completed some paperwork and handed me a pink FMT600 that permitted me to drive Wolf-type vehicles in any configuration. Before I managed to take it from him, he added, 'You'd better get some practice in, PDQ.'

I went to see Corporal Parsons and showed him my shiny new pink driving licence. I hadn't missed any vital training whilst I had been away. While a handful at a time were rotating through some basic driving skills, the rest of the company were going over the General Purpose Machine Gun (GPMG), or 'gimpie', for a few days. As we only had four of these belt-fed machine guns for the whole company, it was quite a slow process to get everyone through and was due to take the rest of the week. Concurrently, others were training on the 51mm mortar and the brand-new UGL (underslung grenade launcher) for the L85A2 rifles we were equipped with.

'You can drive tomorrow then,' said the corporal.

We were due to head up to a gunnery range and conduct some sustained firing drills with the gimpie. A news crew from ITV was also expected to be there to document our progress and to interview the OC about the upcoming deployment.

CHAPTER EIGHT

'The MT bloke said you can barely drive,' the corporal continued.

I didn't think I was that bad. I hadn't stalled or crashed. I supposed it had been a close-run thing, though. My previous driving experience was in a Ford Fiesta, and that was well over a year ago. 'Perhaps some practice would be a good thing,' I thought, although I did feel a bit embarrassed. On the positive side, there were heaters in the front of the vehicle which would provide a moderate amount of comfort, while those in the back of the Wolf would be freezing their nuts off.

After breakfast the following day, Planty, Stick and I 'first paraded' the vehicles our platoon was going to use to get to the range. Planty was an LI soldier from Taunton. He had a disproportionately large chest from all his weight training but the legs of a marathon runner. It made him look a bit like a greyhound standing on its hind legs. He enjoyed reading in his downtime and had a habit of muttering the words he read, much to the annoyance of those who were trying to get some sleep. Without a doubt, he was the fittest guy in the company, and he never seemed to get tired. Stick, on the other hand, was not underweight or skinny, as his name might suggest. In fact, he was distinctly average. He was, however, as agile as a stick, pretty much inanimate at times. Unless he had had a cup of tea first, getting Stick out of first gear was not always possible – especially on cold February mornings.

A 'first parade' is when the soldiers designated to operate a vehicle go through a checklist and establish its serviceability. Do the lights work? Is there oil? Simple tasks that did not require the assistance of REME (Royal Electrical and Mechanical Engineers) craftsmen. At the end of the day, the same process was repeated, now called a 'last parade'. We completed our checks and squeezed the platoon aboard the vehicles. Mr Sherwood and Stick led the small convoy, with Sergeant Derrick and Planty following them. The new driver, Corporal Parsons and I brought up the rear. The range was not nearby, and we were expecting to be gone all day, so along with weapons and ammunition we had also brought a couple of Norwegian containers (basically super-sized thermos flasks) full of tea, and for lunch some 'horror bags'. These were brown paper bags that usually contained some less-than-desirable food. If you were lucky, there would be fresh fruit, a pasty and a bottle of Panda Pop. At other times you might find a tin of European bulk-purchased items such as *guflungen* paste – to this day I have no idea what it was – or a packet of crisps that was 90 per cent air and 10 per cent crumbs.

After being mercilessly harassed by the occupants of the vehicle in front the whole way to the range, I eventually parked up, and we set the guns up for SF (sustained fire) shooting. We were on the side of a tor (mountain in the local dialect), and the wind cut through every piece of clothing I was wearing. With such a strong wind, we would need to lay the guns correctly, taking into account the its strength and direction to effectively hit our 'target'. Our target, however, was not a cardboard soldier, often called a 'Figure 11' or 'Hun's head'. Instead, we were looking to create a 'beaten zone' that our SF fire would drop into, thereby eliminating a whole area as opposed to individual targets. It was still early, and there was no news crew, so we went about setting up our positions and check-firing the gimpies.

After the news people had conducted their interview with the OC, and after our impressive display of firepower, we began to dismantle the guns, ready to head back to Willsworthy. We would need to clean the weapons thoroughly and last parade the Land Rovers before getting some scoff. We had been taught and regularly reminded of the mantra 'My weapon, my kit, myself'. This short list indicates the priorities of a soldier and the order in which they should be dealt with. Before we could bring in the final gimpie, however, one of the producers suggested that maybe the attractive blonde news reporter would like to have a quick go with one of the machine guns. She agreed, and the cameraman got himself in position to film the action.

An NCO from the Small Arms School Corps (SASC) who had been accompanying us helped get her settled behind the gun. He loaded a belt of twenty rounds of 7.62mm ammunition and told her what she should do.

'A quick squeeze of the trigger, and release.'

That would deliver a burst of three to five rounds. She didn't have to cock the weapon or set it up – that was all taken care of. It was pointing into the beaten zone we had been using. All that was required was a press on the safety catch and a squeeze of the trigger. Nothing to it. Looking at the determination on the novice gunner's face, it was obvious that she was having trouble with the safety catch. It was cold, though. Very cold, and wearing fashionable but thin gloves probably gave the reporter very numb fingers. Then all of a sudden,

CHAPTER EIGHT

'Click . . . dadadadadadadadada . . . clunk!' Rather than a quick squeeze, the reporter had chewed up the entire belt in one go. Staring at the empty cases smoking by the side of the gimpie, she looked shocked. The SASC NCO was staring at her, distinctly unimpressed. The rest of us looked at each other. Thewy was shaking his head while staring at the floor, and Planty's shoulders bounced up and down while he tried not to laugh. He just grinned and continued carrying ammo cans back to the vehicles.

Over the next few days, we practised manoeuvring as a platoon. This was an important part of training for the platoon commander, as he needed to demonstrate not only his authority but also his ability. It was straightforward for the grunts in the unit – we just did what we were told: 'Go there, carry that, do this . . .' The officers, however, had to show that they knew what they were doing and could lead their men into battle or at least get them organized so that a senior NCO could take control of the situation. To assist with this, Salamanca Company had been assigned two sergeant majors: one was the CSM, and the other was a full-time soldier from the Light Infantry, who would fulfil a training role during the build-up and an advisory role on deployment.

To me, both the sergeant majors seemed like pretty fearsome guys. Most men with that rank did. The only time people like them had spoken to me was to remind me, in no uncertain terms, of what I had done wrong and that I was in for some trouble if I didn't sort myself out. Whilst on my infantryman's course I had had a run-in with a sergeant major twice. The first time was for having hair that wasn't to his liking. I had been in the cookhouse, without my beret on (as I was indoors), when the nameless warrant officer came up to me, demanding to know, 'Does your CSM know you have your hair like that?'

Not realizing it was a rhetorical question, I answered, correctly, 'I can have my hair however I like under my beret.'

That was like a red rag to a bull, regardless of whether I was correct or not. Thereafter, I had to wear my beret both indoors and outdoors, generating further advice and guidance from lower-ranking NCOs about the correct and proper wearing of headdress.

The second time was when Broz and I were sharing a shell scrape in the middle of a forest during a four-day-long exercise. This final exercise had been designed to test all our skills as infantry soldiers, and we were part of a 'multinational effort' to reclaim Norfolk from the Russians or one of their breakaway republics. We had returned from a deliberate attack on an enemy position and had finished sorting our weapons and equipment, just in case we needed to get stuck in again. With apparently some time in hand, I had lit a stove and started to cook some boil-in-the-bag food, chocolate pudding as it happened, when the same sergeant major came along and offered feedback on my performance during the attack. He indicated that I was not infantry material and that unless I performed more aggressively it was very unlikely he would allow me to pass the course. By now it was quite clear that my soldiering style was more laid back than, say, a para's or a marine's, but to my mind it seemed to work. I didn't get stressed under fire, I was fit and I shot very accurately. I just wasn't overly noisy when it came to bayonet work. I felt the criticism was unfair, and when he left, Broz and I thoroughly debriefed the feedback and concluded that, despite the sergeant major's superior experience, rank and knowledge, we two wax-jacketed privates from Gloucester knew better.

Salamanca Company's training sergeant major joined us for an exercise to run the lieutenant through a scenario commonly encountered during the Troubles in Northern Ireland. The situation in the theatre was being compared to that of the province, and several of the blokes had experience there. Willsworthy, with its abundance of rural roads, was ideal for practising Vehicle Check Points (VCPs). Mr Sherwood had arranged for his platoon to conduct some 'vehicle stops' on the sergeant major, who acted as several different drivers: a non-compliant one, an overly chatty and friendly one, and, of course, one who would run the blockade. With such a wide range of characters to handle, the officer certainly had his work cut out managing his deployment.

Eventually, the time came for the vehicle to run straight through the VCP. Cut-offs had been positioned and would have been able to stop the runner, but we were all ordered into cover and told to put our helmets on before conducting a foot chase. It could have turned into a Benny Hill moment, but the sergeant major called 'End-ex!' and brought the platoon in for a debrief.

Mr Sherwood gave a fair account of himself, but when he was out of earshot, a few others in the platoon discussed their own solutions. Letting Planty off the leash was probably the best solution, and we had

CHAPTER EIGHT

no doubt that with his lurcher-like ability he would have caught up with the quarry in no time. However, it was the lack of 'action and reaction' that seemed to grate on a few of the NCOs. Over the course of an hour, we had successfully dealt with a security scenario, only to mess it up at the end by getting into cover from a non-existent threat. We concluded the training and made our way back to camp for the start of a march-and-shoot serial.

I enjoyed 'march-and-shoot'. All we had to do was run from A to B, a distance of 2,400m. B was invariably a shooting range. Then we had to shoot the steel targets at the end of the range and collect our scores. Being quite fit, I found the exercise almost fun, as it required very little effort to do well. The company major, Mr Evans, had done the serial four times already that day, once with each multiple. We were the last.

As he ran alongside us, I found myself at the front of the platoon, overtaking the officers and NCOs.

'Keep up, sir!' I said, for no good reason other than that I was enjoying myself.

The major didn't see it that way, though. I had to be reminded by the CSM that a private soldier does not speak impertinently to the OC, regardless of the situation, and that I should 'keep my fucking mouth closed, you chatty fucker' or suffer the violent and unpleasant consequences that the CSM would surely come up with. So I did just that. For now.

Chapter Nine

We had worked solidly for the first three weeks and had finally enjoyed a full day off. Travelling home late on a Friday we had the luxury of a Saturday with friends and family before the company regrouped at Okehampton Camp, a little way north of Willsworthy. This large base at the edge of Dartmoor had plenty of space for the build-up training to continue. With only Salamanca Company in residence, the camp felt deserted. Many of the troops had a lot of experience with this venue owing to its proximity to Exeter and Plymouth, where the largest presence in the unit was drawn from, but I had never been here before.

I liked the camp. Most people didn't. I liked that it had a 'Great War' feel to it. The long accommodation blocks had probably served as the inspiration for more than one military movie. I knew that some of the 1969 film *The Virgin Soldiers* had been shot there, before the production moved to Malaya. Basically a 'Carry On' movie, it occasionally turned up on Channel 5 to keep the 'greatest generation' entertained in their retirement. After our stay we would also be moving on to warmer environs too, I thought to myself as I unpacked my kit into a paper-thin wooden locker. The camp was originally built in the 1890s but really came into its own as a training establishment during the two world wars. With enough space to hold more than one regiment, the camp had services – a laundry, decent showers, decent food and a bar complete with dartboard and pool table.

Another reason to like the camp was that I was starting to get to know everyone in the platoon, and they were getting to know me. We had been living in close proximity for nearly a month and were coming together quite well as a unit – probably better than the rest of the company. As in any large organization, there were often personality clashes and differences of opinion. Certainly 1 and 2 Platoon had a few squaddies

CHAPTER NINE

who didn't see eye-to-eye with each other. But 3 Platoon didn't have that problem. My biggest gripe was that the wind-up radio that one of our lance jacks carried was tuned to BBC Radio One, and at that time I could not stand the morning DJ who seemed to talk nonstop and never play any music. Rob, from the D&Ds, who provided the morning reveille just as this insufferable chatterbox came on air, also had an interesting job outside of the TA. He was a bouncer at a strip club. Being a generous and kind-hearted sort of guy, he assured me that should I ever feel a desire to visit his club, then he would make all the necessary arrangements and introduce me to some of the more popular staff members. It was a kind offer, and I was keen to take him up on it, if only to become a more rounded and worldly individual.

We were lucky to have Rob in our platoon because he was as hard as nails. Along with Mick and Fordy, we had some real monsters going on Op TELIC. At least they seemed like monsters to me. None were veterans of the regular military, and only time would tell how they would react – but they had proved utterly dependable so far, both to the higher-ups and to those they were in charge of. Rob was also pretty switched on. This came in handy after Sergeant Derrick was reassigned to HQ in order to run the operations room. We no longer had a platoon sergeant, which meant the corporal had to take on that role. Rob took on Corporal Parsons' position with regard to personnel matters. Most issues were dismissed or resolved with his 'take a chill pill' catchphrase. The 'chill pill' was not a suggestion either. The prescription was mandatory.

Rob's sidekick from the D&Ds was L2. 'L2' – as the M26 grenade was designated by the British Army – was the nickname of Matt (another one, but luckily the nickname helped with identification) La Grenade, a builder from Plymouth and a friend of some of the Rifle Volunteers' casualties from Afghanistan. He had needed some time away in order to help form a burial party but had rejoined the platoon just after we arrived at Willsworthy. L2 always seemed cheerful, even though he was probably the most reluctant of us to be deployed, followed closely by Drewy.

Most of the training happened at a platoon level – replicating what the deployment would look like. Each multiple would be assigned tasks and be expected to carry them out, whilst the operations room would direct the multiples. Mr Evans explained what tasks we would be assigned: guard duty and sentry tasks. Gate duty for 24 hours. QRF (Quick Reaction Force). Day or night patrols.

The OC went on to explain, 'Guard duty is not just about protection for Salamanca Company – but the entire garrison at Basra Palace, including multinational units, local security forces and the Coalition Provisional Authority.'

That sounded grand, but in reality we all knew it meant stagging on (guarding) in a *sangar* and keeping a decent lookout. We would also need to become familiar with the Clansman 351 radio sets that Bons and Pat were issuing; these would be vital for staying in touch with the ops room. To that end, the signallers were due to run some refresher sessions on the communications equipment during the evenings.

The guard towers would only have one soldier each. The officers and senior NCOs would manage the multiple by rotating the guards every hour, in an effort to allow some rest and prevent fatigue from setting in. Gate duty, however, was slightly different. At any one time, most of the multiple would be on duty.

The major explained, 'There will be two fortified positions on the gate; both equipped with a GPMG. There will also be men needed for radio stag and keeping the comms smooth, access control and the search of individuals and vehicles arriving at the Palace. For the latter role you will be assigned an interpreter to assist you.'

Again, that sounded reasonably straightforward. It was not a task that could effectively be practised whilst on build-up training, although some of the skills, such as comms, giving a sitrep or searching a person or vehicle could be looked at.

'The main direction of the next three weeks', concluded the major as he outlined the plan for our stay at Okehampton, 'is to review and enhance your abilities to patrol as a multiple and to be able to respond' – he paused and made a chopping motion as he completed his briefing – 'to be able to respond effectively to any threats or situations we may encounter.'

Elvis and Uzi nodded stoically. This is what they had wanted to do – not guard duty but patrols and QRF. As I looked around I could see some of the NCOs and soldiers writing down a few notes. I wondered if I should write something too; just to look busy or keen. But without any serious revelations during the briefing I decided that I would save

CHAPTER NINE

my notepad for Bons' and Pat's 'comms workshop', where I was due to head to next.

L2 joined me as we left the lecture room and made our way to the building where the signallers were going to refresh us on the Clansman radios, sitreps and OBAF – 'Off, Battery, Antenna, Frequency', commented L2 as we talked, running over some of what we had already learnt about signals. We talked about situation reports, casualty reports and weather reports.

'Nothing to it. Easy evening then a drink in the NAAFI', I agreed.

We knew that some larger exercises and more complex training were only just around the corner.

'How many of these workshops do you think we will have to do?' I added.

They were necessary but also hard to sit through after a full day of hard physical training on the cold tors of Dartmoor. More than once a well aimed broom handle had been used to bring someone out of their spontaneous slumber. L2 didn't answer the question directly. We knew that things were about to get a lot tougher now that we were looking to join up with the Cheshire Battlegroup after Okehampton.

'To be honest', he replied, 'I'm always sceptical of a "workshop" that doesn't at least involve light engineering. Let's get on with it then watch Katie Price in *I'm a Celeb* in the bar.'

Chapter Ten

'Contact front! Charlie, prepare to move . . . MOVE!'

Fordy directed the section forward. While the three soldiers making up the Charlie fire team charged towards an enemy position, the two in the Delta fire team provided covering fire.

A section is typically made up of eight soldiers, divided into two fire teams of four known as Charlie and Delta. However, as we were a small multiple of only fourteen, Mr Sherwood had organized us into two teams of five and one team, his one, of four. All the multiples in the company were employing a similar model. This setup offered the same flexibility as a platoon – three sections – but it diluted the fighting strength over a wider area. If any one section came into contact with the enemy, at most only five men would be able to engage before the rest of the unit could join them. This was as opposed to the full weight of firepower a section of eight could normally deliver.

We were practising contact drills against an imaginary enemy. Mr Sherwood and the other officers had devised training scenarios based on the latest contact reports from the theatre. Fordy moved his Delta fire team up while we delivered consistent and deliberate fire – one round every six seconds or so. When he saw they were in position, it was our turn to move again.

'Charlie, prepare to move!'

I checked my pouches and pockets, then shifted my position in cover so I did not emerge in exactly the same place as I had entered. If someone was watching that area, I would be an easy target.

'MOVE!'

I was up. A few fast, powerful steps to the next piece of cover. Staying up too long would make me an obvious target. Running in a straight line would make me an easy target. Ideally, I needed some cover that could

CHAPTER TEN

disrupt the energy of incoming fire, but failing that, anything that made me harder to hit.

I crashed behind a low brick wall that probably used to be a barricade for a fuel depot. It was only a metre tall but wide enough for me to crawl along the base before popping up and opening fire. In all, it took seconds. I could hear Fordy and Broz beginning to shoot, indicating that they were in position too. I adopted a fire position, steadying my aim using the low wall. Bang! Bang! The fire team was suppressing the enemy as Delta prepared to move. The section was close now. Charlie's next move would probably be to finish the contact and do for the 'enemy'.

Delta was in position again.

'Delta! Rapid! Fire!'

Uzi and Elvis let rip. With only two people firing, it would not be long before they ran out of ammunition and needed to change magazines. Fordy took a blue training grenade and tossed it at the target. A small pop.

'Switch! Fire!'

Uzi and Elvis continued shooting, but near the target, not at it. This was our fire team's opportunity to get in there and finish the job. No word was given. Fordy, Broz and I were up and in. Broz had changed to automatic fire and used the rest of his magazine, hosing down the contact. It was over.

The rest of the platoon had been watching us. Our target was a disused trailer at the far end of a car park in Okehampton Camp. Now that the contact had been won, it would soon be Rob's turn to try a different scenario. Mr Sherwood debriefed us, highlighting good and bad points, best practice and things to avoid. It was better than classroom exercises or TEWTs (Tactical Exercises Without Troops).

I was out of breath. We had probably covered less than a hundred metres. I guessed it was closer to eighty. However, the speed and need to constantly shift position while carrying a full fighting load made it hard work for most people. I don't think Fordy had even broken sweat. Broz unclipped his helmet and hung it off his webbing. He ran his hand through his hair, dispensing with excess perspiration, while the officer continued his debrief.

'Once you are in position, don't forget to carry out your five and twenty checks. A thorough check of the five metres around you and a cursory search of the twenty as well.'

It was important new knowledge for most of us. This kind of tactic was not covered at ITC (Infantry Training Centre).

'Check obvious receptacles such as bins, oil drums, tyres . . . don't discount the idea of a come-on. The contact could have been designed to lure us within range of an IED or a follow-up ambush.'

Next, it was Q and A. As we were not technically at war, the Royal Military Police would be required to take statements from us and investigate any use of force that had taken place.

Elvis and Uzi sparked up a couple of ciggies. I saw Elvis take a long drag on his Marlboro, letting the smoke out slowly as he settled himself to watch Rob's section fight their way back in the opposite direction to the one we had come in.

'Fuckin' monkeys,' Uzi muttered.

He clearly didn't see the need to justify his use of force to the RMP and made his opinion known.

'This is my statement.'

He held up his hands as if describing a billboard. 'They be shooting, I be shooting back.'

Elvis agreed. 'Big boys' games, innit? Big boys' games mean big boys' rules.'

Mr Sherwood was pretending not to listen. He knew better than to interrupt the 3 Platoon High Council. Besides, Uzi and Elvis had followed their instructions to the letter. They knew what they were doing.

I joined the rest of the company in the NAAFI on the camp. The training for the day had come to an end. We were also nearing the end of this part of pre-deployment. Next, we would be linking up with the Cheshire Battlegroup at a massive training complex in Kent known as the Cinque Ports Training Area, or CPTA for short. As we were only a company, we were due to be subordinated to a battalion of the PWRR (Princess of Wales's Royal Regiment), who would be deploying on the same operation. For now, though, the company 2i/c had arranged an evening off and booked out an entire local pub for the company. Although everyone was in their civvies, everyone also had their desert boots on, taking the opportunity to wear them in while throwing a few shapes or downing some drinks. Anyone who had a hangover, it was noted, could sleep it off on the journey from Devon to Kent.

CHAPTER TEN

We boarded the coaches and were driven to a pub called The Fox and Hounds that was, to all intents and purposes, in the middle of nowhere and thus somewhere a company of intoxicated infantry were not likely to cause too much trouble. Some of the company had been pre-loading at the NAAFI bar and were well on their way to an enjoyable night. I had never been out in such a large group before and, as the youngest, barely old enough to drink, I felt a little out of place while the rest of the company formed small groups and settled into some well-deserved beer and pork scratchings.

I saw Rob sitting with two other D&Ds and went to join them. They were from 1 Platoon but had been in Rob's section prior to the pre-deployment training.

'Matty, this is Carlos and Ash.'

I nodded as I set down my drink and took a seat. Carlos noticed that I was not in possession of the standard libation of the infantry at that time – a beer. I had a Coke.

'Get yourself a beer, boy, it'll put some hair on your chest,' he suggested. 'Get one for me while you're up there.'

I did as instructed, although I opted for a half pint, which again did not go unnoticed, this time, however, without comment. Rob continued the conversation. 'Army' talk was not allowed at this table, so instead, Rob explained how Carlos worked at an abattoir, something which in his lubricated state he took great pleasure in telling me about. After some vivid descriptions of that line of work, I got to hear about Ash and his job as a bingo hall announcer. A few impressions of number-calling went down a treat. I went to the bar to get another round – payment for their vivid storytelling. Waiting to be served, it struck me that the three D&Ds at the table were the butcher, the announcer, and the titty bar bouncer. I decided not to share that with them. Instead, I joined them for a rendition of 'Come on Eileen' now that the karaoke machine had been fired up.

Chapter Eleven

CPTA was the first time we applied in realistic training scenarios the skills we had been practising. There were no stop/starts, no pauses and no hints – just a review of the exercise after it had concluded, one way or another. These skills were designed for 'low-intensity conflict' – a misleading term suggesting minimal risk to the troops. We had been told that the integration of the TA with the regular Army was a key focus. This number of reserves had not deployed alongside the regulars for a generation. We began a programme of these skills almost as soon as we got off the coaches. The training area allowed the troops responsible for the 'soldiering' to run through exercises and provided an opportunity for the higher-ups – the OC and his team – to work alongside other senior officers who would be in theatre.

The CPTA area was massive, so big that parts of it used a rail network to shift the vast amounts of ammunition required for constant training. There was even a mock town built with Northern Ireland operations in mind, featuring rows of terraced housing similar to those on Belfast estates. Arabic-style posters and graffiti were now liberally applied to create a more Mesopotamian setting. The area also included simulated explosive devices that could be set off by the directing staff (DS), who oversaw the training both on the ground and via a large CCTV network covering the site.

Now subordinated to the PWRR, Salamanca Company deployed to a patrol base in the centre of the mock town. A lieutenant colonel ran the show, with various company commanders and majors under him assigned tasks replicating expected scenarios in theatre, such as civil disorder, IEDs and ambushes. However, we were only tasked with force protection duties while at CPTA. Mr Evans decided to focus our limited time on worst-case scenarios – the kind that could easily lead to a BBC bulletin starting with, 'Yesterday, a British soldier was . . .'

CHAPTER ELEVEN

The five multiples of Salamanca Company were set to take part in five one-day scenarios. It was going to be busy and tiring, but we were eager to apply what we had been training for in a more complex setting. Whilst the other platoons were assigned tasks outside of the patrol base, 3 Platoon got to grips with the very boring and routine matter of guard duty. With only one 'Northern Ireland'-style guard tower and a small control room with CCTV, there was only enough activity for a section at a time, giving the rest of us a lot of downtime, even though we were supposed to be 'on duty'. It was 'Hurry up and wait', as Uzi commented. After a brief experience of opening and shutting the solid steel gate to the compound, we found ourselves at a loose end with nothing to do. After last light, the opposing forces would be stood down, so we basically had nothing to do for the next however many hours.

'Let's go to the NAAFI,' Uzi suggested. 'I've been here a few times before. It's not far.'

I felt a bit uneasy about it at first but was easily persuaded. We were supposed to be 'on duty'. But it was starting to get dark, and the idea of some decent food was appealing. Broz agreed to look after our kit whilst we were gone. He had secured himself a bed and was not going to give it up easily – defending his position. There were more blokes than beds, so I could see his logic.

'Bring us back a pack of Mars bars', he added.

Uzi and I snuck out through a loose piece of fencing on the patrol base and sprinted a few metres to get into 'the village' that made up the operational patrol area for the week. Trying not to draw attention to ourselves, as other units were still training, we eventually reached another fence, climbed over and were safely in the accommodation area of CPTA.

'There. Told you I knew the way. Got any money?'

I did have a few quid on me.

'Let's go and get a pint.'

The NAAFI was not completely empty, so two extra squaddies walking in did not draw any attention. It seemed that everyone in the bar was from The Signals or other support units. But nobody batted an eyelid. We sat down to some greasy food and watched MTV.

'This is better, isn't it?' Uzi said.

He was right. It was a good idea. Chip butties and Britney Spears' latest music video riding a motorbike on the big bar television. What could be better? We would need to get back after a couple of hours, though, so that we could take over 'the night shift', which was the directing staff's way of saying we were supposed to be the fire picket. That was something I was not looking forward to.

When morning came, 1 Platoon returned to take over guard duty, and 3 Platoon was immediately sent out of the patrol base to an adjoining range complex for live firing training. At least we would be active now. The range package started as they often do – with a check zero group, five rounds shot at a target to confirm our optics were correctly configured for accurate shooting. We then moved on to pair fire and manoeuvre. I was paired with Broz, with whom I had worked regularly since our recruit training. We had developed an effective system of delivering fire as a pair, barely needing to speak. Advancing towards a pair of steel targets that fell when hit, we easily achieved our aim. Withdrawing was just as straightforward. Tucking into a horror bag, we reviewed our performance.

'Good shooting, Broz,' I said.

'I know,' he replied, through a mouthful of Cornish pasty, something which he knew I hated.

Occasionally, he liked to needle me with his proclivity for public mastication.

'Hard work on those stones, though. Like something out of Scooby-Doo!' he added, before swallowing and taking another bite.

He was right. The stones on the range surface made it very hard to move; the first few steps would dig a hole before you gained enough momentum to progress. Watching Stick and Drewy running through the same scenario, I could almost hear that Hanna-Barbera sound effect used whenever Shaggy and Scoob begin to run away from a terrifying ghost. I couldn't help but laugh out loud – and for once it was infectious, causing Broz to chuckle too.

The day continued with different serials on the range: pairs, teams of four, the full multiple and training with other units from different parts of the Army. We chewed through tons of ammunition, which I thought was great. We were also getting to grips with our new Personal Role Radios (PRRs). These small transceivers were designed for short-range communication within a unit, using UHF waves to penetrate walls, cover and vehicle armour. They would come in handy for our last shoot – the 'police station' shoot, scheduled after sunset.

CHAPTER ELEVEN

Occupying a square, two-storey building in the training area, we loaded our magazines and conducted radio checks. The building, known as 'the police station', was surrounded by dozens of metal targets that would fall when hit. Mr Sherwood had to manage his deployment to ensure 360° coverage and a constant stream of ammunition so that those firing would not run dry.

Stick and Planty were 'voluntold' to distribute extra magazines as needed. It was a tedious task involving constantly opening ammo crates, refilling magazines and delivering them to the rest of us shooting from the roof and windows. They would have been better off wearing their Silver Shadow trainers instead of boots. But there was a benefit: their weapons, cleaned during a lull in activity, would stay clean, meaning less admin to take care of once we got back to the patrol base –probably about twenty extra minutes. Valuable sleeping time.

It was cold and dark. Only the ambient light from adjoining parts of CPTA provided any illumination, but it was enough make the silhouettes of the targets visible as they rose and fell. I was in a window on the second floor, using the tritium needle of my SUSAT optics to nail the 'enemy' surrounding our police station. When the working parts locked to the rear of my weapon, I tilted it to see no rounds in my magazine. I took cover. 'STOPPAGE!' I needed to let my fire team know I was unable to shoot while I reloaded. Magazine off. I dropped it down the front of my smock, opened a pouch in my webbing and pulled out a fresh magazine. I inserted it firmly into the weapon, released the working parts and resumed fire from a different window covering the same area. I looked out at the dozens of metal targets rising and falling in sync with the shooting from our fortress.

We shot nonstop for ten minutes, then twenty, then thirty. 'ENDEX!' came the order finally, along with PRR transmissions instructing us to cease fire. Each of us had fired hundreds of rounds. The weapons were red-hot, and the air hung heavy with the smell of cordite. The floor was covered with ejected bullet cases. Satisfied with the platoon's performance, the lieutenant helped us clear the police station, and we made our way back to the patrol base. We had been going nonstop since early morning and were all feeling tired. After weapon-cleaning it was simply a matter of finding somewhere to sleep before our next tasking in the morning.

It was close to midnight by the time I finished my admin. I went to the block assigned to 3 Platoon as a billet, only to find all the beds occupied. The low glow of emergency lighting barely illuminated the room, but I could see every bed had someone in it. I saw Fordy asleep in a bunk bed – his pale complexion making him easy to identify in a sea of slumberers. I propped myself against the wall beside him and sank to the ground. I let my head fall forward onto my chest, crossing my arms to retain some warmth. It wasn't comfortable, but it was good enough.

Chapter Twelve

After a night of constantly waking up to shift from one arse cheek to the other, Fordy kicked my boots to get my attention.

'Matty. Scoff.'

He extended his hand and pulled me up. My hips and legs were stiff from the cold, hard floor; it felt like my hips had restructured themselves, leaving me with temporary arthritis. Eventually, it felt good to be moving again, even if I was lethargic. We walked to the cookhouse in the patrol base, where the resident RLC unit was preparing breakfast. All the usual fare was there – bacon, sausages, eggs, fried bread. With all the physical training we were doing, filling up on calories at the start of the day was not merely a recommendation but a rule. I went straight for the Weetabix, fitting as many biscuits as I could into a paper bowl, covering them in a hyperglycemia-inducing amount of sugar and grabbing two cups of hot, sweet coffee for good measure. That seemed to do the trick. My fatigue was all but gone as we headed to the base for our next task: patrols.

The directing staff briefed us on the day's outline: we would take part in four patrols over the next 24 hours, all challenging and designed to test our soldiering skills and our commanders' ability to manage resources on the ground. With us were several multiples from the PWRR, running concurrent patrols in the same area.

'Sir . . .' began the DS, addressing Mr Sherwood.

I didn't recognize his beret badge but guessed he was from a small county regiment like I was.

'You will be conducting patrols in this area.'

He pointed to a map and circled an area using the tip of a multi-tool screwdriver. Mr Sherwood confirmed with his map, a poor-quality photocopy wrapped in see-through plastic.

'Your objective is to patrol the area and maintain a presence until 0900, at which time you will be relieved by another multiple.'

We all listened, even though the lieutenant would repeat the information after confirming his brief. It sounded straightforward. All of 3 Platoon were infantrymen, so we were used to conducting patrols to 'deny the enemy freedom to operate'.

'You will be required to prevent crime and deter terrorism.'

This part was less familiar. The officer paraphrased the brief to us, repeating, 'prevent crime and deter terrorism'. I guessed that being a highly visible, well-armed patrol could achieve these aims, but I also figured it could be like a red rag to a bull – 'Here we are, come and get us.'

The Coalition forces had been in Iraq for almost a year. While armed opposition from the conventional Iraqi military and security forces had quickly folded under the weight of the well-equipped and well-trained alliance of Western militaries, this led to a problem where infrastructure – both physical and in terms of public services – had been almost entirely wiped out. The task of 'preventing crime and deterring terrorism' became necessary due to the absence of local security forces, who were still in the process of being recruited, equipped and trained. The British Army had considerable experience in this type of task, especially from operations in the Balkans and Northern Ireland.

Patrolling down parallel streets, our call sign, Sierra Three Zero, started our patrol routine. We had 'bomb-bursted' from the base, running out and into cover as quickly as possible to avoid becoming easy targets for any snipers or nearby armed insurgents watching the gate. Sierra Three Zero Charlie, under Corporal Parsons, took the far street; Zero Delta, under Rob, took the near street; and Zero Alpha, with Mr Sherwood and Fordy, took the middle. Mr Sherwood decided that three small teams capable of repositioning if they came into contact would be best, covering more ground. We patrolled the streets, with occasional bursts of radio traffic coming over the PRR. We went firm in covered locations to provide overwatch and repositioned to create an unpredictable direction of travel. Overwatch, a desirable security feature where possible, meant some of the unit providing cover from an elevated position to the balance of the patrol. Every time we stopped we carried out our five and twenty checks – looking for signs of disturbed ground and examining cavities that might conceal a weapons cache or worse.

CHAPTER TWELVE

Suddenly, Sierra Three Zero came under fire. The patrol I was in had gunfire going off all around. In reality, it was the facility's pyrotechnics, but there were also a handful of OPFOR (opposition forces) role-playing as insurgents. We took cover, and Corporal Parsons gave a contact report. 'SIERRA THREE ZERO CHARLIE. CONTACT. WAIT. OUT.' He needed to make a rapid appraisal of the situation before directing any follow-up support. While he scanned the area in front of and around us, we identified targets and pulled the trigger when possible. Seeing armed personnel darting between cover, the four of us returned fire as the pyrotechnics continued to add to the scenario. I switched position by a few metres, moving from a narrow doorway offering little protection to a more substantial concrete traffic barrier. BOOOOOM! A device went off behind the cover just as I put my head up to look around.

The DS behind me indicated with a chop of his hand: 'You're down! Make your weapon safe, then act like you are wounded.'

I did as instructed, going through an unload and making the weapon safe. Then it was time to act. I had never been a casualty before, either in real life or in a military exercise. Somewhat self-consciously, I began to shout and scream, trying to act like an injured person and attract the team leader's attention.

I could hear on the PRR that my section, Zero Charlie, was going to withdraw. Zero Alpha and Zero Delta were moving in from the opposite direction to outflank the enemy. Broz and Uzi grabbed my shoulder straps and began dragging me back to the corner of a row of terraced houses. Corporal Parsons and Elvis withdrew, taking turns to move and fire, just like on the range the day before. Once around the corner, Uzi tried to pick me up in a fireman's carry but was stopped by the DS.

'OK, that's good. You can come back to life now.'

I got up. Our patrol had reassembled but was out of the game, having withdrawn from the contact. A few metres away, we could hear Mr Sherwood's and Rob's patrols doing battle. The snippets of information coming through the PRR suggested they were advancing quickly and would soon have the situation under control. As for Zero Charlie, we had to give a CASREP, or casualty report. Along with the PRR, our multiple's NCOs also carried 349 radios, which were more powerful and could send messages on a different frequency back to our ops room, run by Sergeant Derrick.

The CASREP is supposed to be short and to the point so that medical staff can prepare for the casualty's arrival. It also needs to be simple and easy to remember during the stress of battle, to avoid undue complications for the troops dealing with the contact. The first two letters of the surname are given, along with the last four numbers of the soldier's regimental number: 'OK3850'. This identifies the soldier, providing necessary info such as blood group, known allergies and other relevant medical information. Then comes the type of injury: 'explosion' – simple, but 'blast,' 'IED' or 'bomb' would also suffice. Next, the injuries: 'soldier is unconscious, no visible injuries.' It could just as easily be 'traumatic amputation' or 'head injury', and so on. Then the symptoms of the wounded person: their heart rate, breathing rate, whether they seem confused, and so on. Finally, the treatment given: morphine, bandages, tourniquet, and if so, what time. Fortunately, this was just a training exercise, a chance to practise some of the life-saving skills that might be required in Iraq. At this point in the UK campaign, sixty-one British soldiers had been killed, along with two British diplomats. The odds were that we would need to apply these skills for real.

'Thank fuck Matty was the casualty and not you, Broz,' said Elvis. 'There's no way we could've dragged your fat arse outta there.'

Uzi agreed, of course: 'We probably would have had to do the merciful thing, I reckon. Like a wounded dog.'

Broz took it in good humour, replying, 'We should have carried "veggie boy" like an old rolled-up carpet and thrown him in the nearest ditch.'

We weren't expecting a debrief until the end of the day and had to wait around until the DS reinserted us into the patrol exercise.

'Time for a gasper, yeah?'

Elvis produced a pack of smokes and got a couple out for himself and Uzi. To be fair, he always offered one to everyone, despite nobody else being a smoker. He opened his Zippo with a satisfying metallic 'click' and rolled the mechanism over his thigh, bringing the flame to life. It always looked cool when he did that. It was his normal way to spark up for some reason.

'You'll have to show me how you do that,' I said as he put his paraphernalia back into his smock.

'How I do what?'

CHAPTER TWELVE

I mimicked the action of him lighting his smoke.

'Oh, right. Yeah. I'll show you when you start smoking,' he said.

It was odd how none of us, including me, were overly concerned about becoming casualties. The odds weren't in our favour. The exercise was designed to replicate breaking contact with a wounded colleague, and we had done just that. But there was a sense of unreality to it. If one of us was actually to take a round or be caught in an explosion, I doubted we would react with the same calm and detached demeanour.

3 Platoon continued the patrol exercises, culminating in a mounted night patrol – conducted from vehicles. We were assigned three old Wolf Land Rovers, probably around my age and with countless miles on the clock. Drewey, Stick and I were designated as drivers and went out to conduct a first parade. After finally getting mine started, I decided to test-drive the bloody thing, as I had been told there was no power steering. I had never driven without this luxury. To me, the vehicle felt heavy and agricultural, but I could just about manage it.

This patrol was going to be a lot easier for the drivers, we hoped. Mr Sherwood decided that when the multiple dismounted, the drivers, along with Fordy as a commander, would remain with the vehicles, while the rest of the multiple formed two sections of five. Parking in our RV (rendezvous), we went into an all-round defence, providing 360° coverage around the Land Rovers while the dismounted patrol headed into a housing estate. There were no DS watching over us, so we took that as a sign we would be left alone. There was a chance we could be called forward as a team of four, but Fordy discounted it as unlikely. He was right. Positioning ourselves out of the biting cold wind, we waited for the rest of 3 Platoon to rejoin us. There was distorted traffic on the PRR, indicating some kind of civil disorder up ahead, but nothing unmanageable. Bringing vehicles into that would be dangerous anyway, as the roads would be congested with foot traffic and almost impossible to navigate.

Feeling quite relaxed as I kept lookout, I reached into my smock and pulled out a choccy bar. It had gone rock solid from the time spent outside. I was feeling rather cold and wished I was wearing my wax jacket instead of the DPM smock. Even though it was supposedly windproof and had elasticated cuffs to keep out the worst of the wind chill, being inactive for so long made me start to shiver. I tried my best to fight it, not wanting to show that the cold was getting the better of me. I convinced myself the rest of the section was probably tougher and showing no signs of discomfort. The end of the exercise couldn't come soon enough. Eventually, we retired to the patrol base and got our heads down. The next day would bring a briefing from the RMP on the use of force, search techniques and methods of detaining people. This would be in addition to a live firing indoor patrol range, where we would be equipped with a .22 calibre version of the L85.

Chapter Thirteen

After every multiple had been through the CPTA training regime, we moved to another training area called Longmoor to complete a 'confirmatory exercise'. This one was more useful for the HQ unit than for the platoons, offering Major Evans and Captain Roberts an opportunity to stretch their strategic thinking and respond to changing situations using the resources in Salamanca Company. For those of us on the ground it felt similar to the previous week, perhaps even less demanding. I don't recall doing anything of significant value or remarkably different while there. But that isn't a criticism; it gave us the chance to go over the same skills and drills repeatedly. If these techniques were to be used operationally, I wanted to leave as little room for error as possible.

I found myself in the middle of some woodland in the Longmoor training area with Elvis. Longmoor, in Hampshire, was a comfortable base adjacent to a large training area. Although it wasn't as large as CPTA, it had an integrated road network, allowing us to set up VCPs for traffic checks. The area also had plenty of real estate for scenario-based training, meaning we spent a lot of time mounting and dismounting from four-ton trucks, which were supposed to represent Chinooks. For days and nights we were ferried around the area, conducting both security and military scenarios, while the higher-ups controlled everything from the ops room back at the Longmoor camp.

In one scenario, Elvis and I were part of a ring of defences around a crossroads. Elvis broke out his brew kit and started making a big mug of tea. He flicked his lighter open and lit a hexamine block.

'Go on then,' I said as we waited for the water to boil. 'Show me how you do that lighter trick.'

We should have been taking turns to stag on, but we were far from any roads or tracks. Essentially, we were just a comms relay for any short-range transmissions.

'All right,' he replied.

He put a cigarette between his lips and produced his Zippo lighter. He showed me a few times, flicking the cover open and striking the mechanism across his thigh, creating a lazy yellow flame each time. On the final go, he lit his smoke and passed me the lighter, along with his mostly empty pack of Marlboros.

'When in Rome, Matty, when in Rome.'

I placed a cigarette between my lips and followed his demonstration. To my surprise, the lighter ignited on the first attempt. I lit the ciggie and took a drag. I couldn't see the appeal. It tasted okay, I guessed. It didn't seem as filthy a habit as social education at school had made it out to be. But it did make me feel like a cowboy who had just struck a match across a coarse five o'clock shadow, now smoking a well-earned stogie after a hard day on the range. I decided I would buy a lighter next time I had a day off, not for smoking but to practise that trick and light up my brew kit.

Elvis and I were both from the same regiment, but his unit was a satellite of the one based in Gloucester. I had never met him or many of the platoon before arriving at Chilwell almost two months before. By now, however, I knew everyone quite well – an added benefit of the training scheme we were part of. A few faces in the other platoons were still unfamiliar to me, but they probably knew me as the highly-strung veggie. I had also noticed that a few people did not show much patience with me and my chatty nature when not soldiering. No doubt the upcoming tour would give me the opportunity to get to know those I hadn't spoken to yet.

We were nearing the end of the pre-deployment training and had returned to Okehampton for the last three weeks. This time, we weren't alone. The Marines were in camp, too, training to earn the coveted green beret. Standing in line for scoff, a young lad – younger than me – walked up from somewhere down the queue and approached me. He was wearing his 'cap comforter' and had his sleeves rolled up, indicating he was a marine recruit.

CHAPTER THIRTEEN

'Excuse me, mate, is your name Matt?'

I looked at him, trying to decide if I had crossed paths with him before. A bank customer, maybe?

'Yes,' I replied simply, still going through my mental archive of familiar faces and names.

He stuck out his hand to shake mine, so I obliged.

'Craig,' he said. 'Craig Jones? Remember we were on the 200m team? I was in the year below you?'

I did recall him, now that I had been prompted.

'Bloody hell, mate, that's some memory . . . I only ran for one season!'

It was good to catch up and talk about school days.

Craig was training on Dartmoor for the final part of their commando course. He was within sight of his ultimate goal of becoming a Royal Marines Commando.

'Why are you here, Matty? I didn't realize you'd joined the Army.'

I corrected him: 'We're a TA unit, mate. We're gearing up for TELIC.'

I told him about the past weeks' training. Compared to his thirty-two weeks, it seemed inadequate. But there we were, confident and all but ready to deploy.

At Craig's invitation I joined his fellow trainee Royal Marines. The bootnecks had stacked food high on their plates. I had heard that by the end of their course marines were as fit as professional athletes. I guessed their fitness would probably surpass that of most athletes, depending on the sport. I asked them about their training over the many, many months. It sounded very similar to the infantry training I had carried out, although a lot more intense and, of course, with the added water that is the essence of amphibious warfare. Unlike us, nothing they were doing in training reflected the current activities of the British forces' two major deployments. When I asked about it I was reminded that their elite status would surely preclude them undertaking any ground-holding roles. Instead, as with the invasion of Iraq, they would lead the way, and the PBI (poor bloody infantry) like The Rifle Volunteers would follow.

I really admired those who had the determination to earn the status of a commando or a para. They really had to want it. Sometimes I felt I was in the Army by accident. But we still had a few things in common. First, we were all volunteers and had not been forced or conscripted. Second, while the Royal Marines were proud of their uniform distinctions and history, I was equally proud of mine.

'Good luck with your endurance run,' I told him as we finished up our food.

'Yeah, cheers, Matty. Good luck over in Iraq.'

Chapter Fourteen

I have always hated being sick or injured; partly due to the discomfort, but also because of my insecure nature. I never enjoyed telling someone I was unwell, or the attention that followed. Moreover, I disliked the feeling of not contributing when I normally would. This likely stemmed from my childhood, when my parents never believed I was genuinely ill. A serious leg injury? 'Go play rugby.' Covered in an itchy rash? 'Go to school.' Shingles? 'You'll get over it.' Even when I caught scrub typhus I didn't receive so much as a sympathy card. I wasn't expecting any sympathy from the military either if I got sick or injured, so decided early on just to 'get through it'.

During the exercises at CPTA and at Longmoor I injured my knee. However, because I was so busy and generally active, the tendon that ran down the outside of my left leg had remained reasonably supple. After a morning run over the cold tors of Okehampton, however, I suddenly, and painfully, found my knee locking up like a stalled engine component.

I had had a weakness in my knee since my teens. However, the TA didn't give me any kind of physical examination before I joined, aside from a standard piss test. As long as I could pass the strength and fitness requirements, had all my limbs and a strong pulse, I was considered infantry material.

On reporting to Mr Sherwood, he allowed me to take it easy for a few days to see how I fared. Whilst the rest of the platoon went for a run, I remained in the billet, kept company by Rob's wind-up transistor and the insufferable morning DJ. To make myself useful I carried out some block jobs – sweeping out the room, taking out the rubbish and cleaning the ablutions. It was all I could think to do, and it saved the rest of the unit from thinking I was skiving. Seeing that my knee was not improving, I was taken to HMS *Raleigh* to see one of the doctors to ascertain the seriousness of the condition. Sergeant Derrick, who had also suffered a knee injury, was recovering well and drove with me and Foz down to the med centre. Foz had been ordered to report for a check-up, much to his surprise and annoyance. Assigned to 2 Platoon, things were going great for him. His multiple had most of the other Glosters assigned to it, and they were excelling under his leadership.

I remembered HMS *Raleigh* from my phase one training. We had used the ranges there to begin learning our craft of weapons-handling. It was a nice base. It may as well have been, as it was also the recruit training depot for Royal Navy ratings. Driving through the gates, past the MoD guards, we saw some brand-new matelots going through their drill movements whilst holding balsa wood cut-outs of the L85. The sarge was staring hard at them, trying to distract them from the petty officer taking them through their movements. A few eyes tracked us as we drove slowly past.

'I guess the Navy don't trust their lot with gats,' noted the sarge.

I had been issued my weapon on weekend one, day one. Although that was just to get used to the weight and always having it in my possession. I had to wait three whole days before I was allowed to shoot the thing.

The diagnosis was promising. After some RICE – Rest, Ice, Compression and Elevation – I was advised that the swelling would subside quickly and I could resume physical training within a week. I was given a bag of ibuprofen, the Army cure-all, and sent on my way. I left the med centre and sat in the wagon behind Foz, who had already returned to the vehicle and started the motor to keep warm.

'All sorted?' he asked.

'Yeah, no problems. Just a subacute injury to the lateral collateral ligament.'

He turned around.

'What?'

'Sore knee,' I replied. 'How about you?'

He turned back but continued the conversation using the rear-view mirror to look at me.

'Nothing. I just missed my smear test.' He laughed. 'I told them I had never missed one before and that maybe they wanted a different Corporal Foster.'

We returned to camp. Having been out all morning, before arriving back at Okehampton we stopped for a pub lunch. We weren't expected

CHAPTER FOURTEEN

back until the afternoon anyway, and it was good to have something from the menu instead of the steam trays. The NCOs returned straight to their work, but I could not join the rest of the company, who were training for vehicle checkpoints. However, I was in luck. It gave me the opportunity to take part in an OPTAG medic course. The training was being run at our camp for the entire battlegroup, and every platoon had to nominate two privates to attend. The Operational Training and Advisory Group was made up of recent returnee instructors from either Iraq or Afghan. The course, which lasted five days, only had one exercise at the very end but was designed to upskill the medical training that we already had. Mr Sherwood decided that Uzi and I should be nominated as the medics for his platoon, and we were promptly told to report to the OPTAG buildings at the other end of the camp. The course would give me time to recover and also let me do something useful in the interim. Even if I had not been limping around, I would have been keen to attend the course, figuring I was more compassionate than violent. 'Strange kind of infantryman you are, Matt,' I thought to myself as I packed my daysack with the required kit.

The course structure was as simple as it could be. Run by some medical NCOs from the Royal Army Medical Corps, still in their desert fatigues, the training was split into five sections with a confirmatory exercise on day five. Day one was breathing. Day two – bleeding. Day three – breaks. Day four – burns. Breathing, bleeding, breaks and burns. These were the priorities for dealing with a casualty. We were also taught how to triage casualties if involved in a mass casualty event, and were taught how to administer the types of equipment that we carried for medical emergencies. To be honest, we didn't carry much. But we were primarily infantry, so anything else we carried was in addition to our fighting equipment and was thus extra weight. The idea, the RAMC staff sergeant explained to us, was that we should keep equipment to a minimum out of necessity.

'Your main purpose is to keep the casualty alive until they can receive definitive care', he concluded. 'If they can breathe and you stop them from leaking blood, then there's a good chance that they will survive until they can get to an aid station or even a well-equipped ambulance.'

Some helicopters flew over the classroom we were using for training. We were going over some of the basics, such as how to insert an endotracheal tube in casualties who were having trouble getting air down their throat.

'I might nick some of this lube for our two weeks off', said Uzi, who had a decent sized dollop on his first and second fingers as he prepared to lubricate the breathing tube.

I hoped he was talking about time off that didn't involve me. My plans involved copious amounts of chocolate and watching Forest Green play Doncaster Rovers. Other than that, I hoped to pick up where I had left off several months ago, when my relaxation was interrupted by some mobilization papers.

We went outside to watch the rookie marines fast rope from the back of their Merlin helicopters. They looked very good.

'I wish I could do that', I said, turning to Uzi as he produced his obligatory cigarette. 'I'll light that for you', I said, producing my brand new Zippo, intent on copying Elvis's lighter trick. Click . . . Zip . . . there was a flame. Perfect.

'Ta', Uzi said as he leaned his head towards the source of ignition.

I didn't realize he was going to move towards the flame, so as my hand went towards him, I initiated combustion well over halfway down, close to the filter.

'You dickhead!' said Uzi, taking a single drag before extinguishing the butt underfoot.

He took out another smoke and his own lighter, then pinched his nostrils to ensure that he still had nasal hair.

'Breathing, bleeding, breaks and burns? We ain't on that part of the course yet, you twat. If you are going to set fire to my snout, wait until day four, yeah?'

The course was a good week for me. It gave me time to rest my knee and it allowed me to stretch my mental agility a bit further. During the final exercise, Mr Wood from 'A' Company came to see how his Glosters were getting on. He had travelled down with the local media – *The Citizen* newspaper – in order for them to get a scoop on the training we were just about to complete. Seeing that I was otherwise unoccupied whilst some of the other OPTAG medics did their casualty exercise, he called me over to where he was standing on a high bank, surveying Okehampton in all its glory.

'How are you getting on, Okuhara?', he enquired. 'You're not training with the others?'

CHAPTER FOURTEEN

I explained about my knee but added that I was feeling a lot less discomfort now.

'Well, you're young and fix up easily, no doubt . . . Now look, I've got a couple of people from *The Citizen* here. Would you mind having a chat?'

I didn't mind. The Media Operations Group had given us all a briefing whilst we trained on the grenade range at CPTA. Seeing as only a handful of us could train at any one time with the grenades, it made sense for the volunteer soldiers of the MOG to give us a heads-up about the press whilst we waited. In this interview, though, I was sure that the major would jump in if I started to talk about things that I shouldn't or came across as overly negative.

After a few words with the journalist and a couple of snaps with the photographer, I went to join Uzi so that we could do our final exercise. We weren't expected to be overly tactical. We had no weapons and were being assessed on the week's learning as opposed to infantry skills. Coming across the scene of an IED explosion that was now secure, Uzi and I, along with a half dozen PWRR squaddies, set about triaging and treating the vehicle crews. As there were no role-players, the casualties were mechanic's coveralls with a resuscitation doll inserted into them. I felt a bit stupid giving reassurance to 'Bob' whilst his rubber face stared back at me, utterly devoid of emotion. But with an RAMC instructor looking over my shoulder, I made my best effort to keep his mind off the fact that his limbs had apparently been reduced to bales of straw and rolled-up newspaper by the strength of the explosion.

Unbeknownst to me, a TV crew was also filming the exercise for that evening's south-west news bulletin. In the NAAFI that evening, my reassurances to 'Bob' were broadcast along with other aspects of the training. Much to my surprise, a piss-take did not immediately follow. Just a few 'good jobs' and quiet but encouraging words. As far as I could tell, this was the highest form of praise I could expect from Salamanca Company. I stepped away from the bar and joined a 1 Platoon lad so that I could be beaten at a game of pool. After three months of build-up training, the company was going to disperse for two weeks' leave, before deploying.

Part III
THE WAIT

Chapter Fifteen

When I was younger I used to look forward to Christmas. In the two weeks leading up to the big day I would eagerly review the list I had left for Santa, in eager anticipation. During the summer holidays, the opposite was true. I dreaded going back to school. The two weeks before returning to school were spent procrastinating on assignments and coursework, feeling quite blue and depressed about it. These two weeks before deployment were a mix of those opposites. With little life experience to draw on, this was the closest I could come to assessing my feelings.

I wanted to be back with 3 Platoon and Salamanca Company. The pre-deployment training had been a great experience for the most part. Of course, I had made mistakes and had the piss taken out of me nonstop, but it never felt out of place or unwarranted. I felt I had done okay – better than okay, actually. I had surprised myself. On the other hand, the reality of Iraq – Basra – was beginning to settle in my mind. We had a briefing at CPTA about what to expect in the country and city. Some English-speaking Iraqis had been brought in to teach us about cultural differences and give us some basic language skills. I enjoyed this, and during my leave I flicked through the OPTAG language pamphlet they had put together.

Lying on a long sofa at home, eating pieces of an Easter egg and looking at Iraqi phrases like 'Stop, Army' and 'Open the trunk', I flicked back to some of the pleasantries and greetings. It seemed surreal. I wasn't even twenty years old, still trying to outgrow my teenage habits. Everyone I had gone to school with was either at university or working in safe occupations around the county. I started to think about how different my life would have been if I had made different choices.

CHAPTER FIFTEEN

If I had gone to university I wouldn't have been called up. Members of the UOTC (University Officers' Training Corps) are not liable for deployments. I would probably be lying on the same sofa, eating the same Easter egg, enjoying a spring break from academic studies. Maybe I would have had coursework, maybe not. If I hadn't been called up I might be away training, unless it wasn't a 'green weekend'. In that case, I would still be lying on the sofa eating chocolate eggs. Finally, if I hadn't joined the TA at all I would be at work – and I really hated work. The TA didn't feel like work to me. It didn't feel like duty either. It felt like the right thing to do at that time.

No doubt the other members of Salamanca Company were making the most of their two weeks' leave, enjoying time with their wives, kids and friends. I had nothing significant planned. My own family was very busy and hadn't arranged any time off. If I wanted to do something with them, it would have to be on the weekend. But since my parents were separated, choosing who to spend time with would likely cause some upset. My father had left home five years earlier and was living in Gloucester city. He had a room set aside for me in the large house he shared with his new wife. Conveniently, it was close to the TA centre. If I stayed there, it would make moving my kit and personal effects easier. I could also stretch my legs and enjoy the Gloucestershire air one more time. If there were any emotional goodbyes, my father could quickly retreat to his home, hiding his emotions – something of a family tradition. I concluded that I liked this part of the world and should make every effort to return to it safely and in one piece.

The Gloucestershire countryside where I lived was a decent place to take some time off. This was a nice house, with two rooms for me to live in, and a large lawn. It was hard to believe I would be trading it for a camp bed or bunk bed in the Middle East. At home, it was easy for me to leave the front door, turn either left or right, and enjoy the Cotswold Way and the hills surrounding the Severn Vale. That would be replaced by desert. I was never bored at home. I could go to Cheltenham or Bristol, watch a football match, or a game of cricket in the summer. In Iraq, I guessed there would be very little time for anything other than army stuff. I only had one full weekend off before I had to go to the TA centre on Eastern Avenue, board the coach bound for Brize Norton and then fly on to Iraq.

Chapter Sixteen

Forest Green Rovers 1 – Doncaster Rovers 2. That was the last game I would be watching for quite some time, and it was a defeat. At this rate, FGR would be doing well to stay in the league. Any news about the rest of the season would have to be sent to me on a 'bluey' – a BFPO (British Forces Post Office) aerogramme sent free of charge to deployed personnel. That evening, I was going to meet some of my school friends who, like me, had avoided university. Out of the whole VIth Form, only three of us had not gone. My closest friend, Adam, had become a landscape gardener – not because of his love of gardens and the outdoors, but because it gave him time to pursue his interest in amateur dramatics. He enjoyed the outdoors as much as I did, probably more. However, it was the flexibility of his friend and boss that sealed the deal for him. When he needed time to study scripts or help with set-building, all he had to do was ask. Usually, it worked well. I had seen his performances on a few occasions, and as far as I could tell, he was very good. I preferred music, where I could blame my guitar if something went wrong.

My other friend, Gareth, was into technology and, like me, had decided that the best way to gain experience was to find employment. He reasoned that 'A lot of graduates will be leaving with a similar skill set' and decided it would be a better use of his time to apply himself to real-world situations instead of classroom problems. He was right. Within a year he was earning more than Adam and I combined.

'I should have studied harder,' I told him after he let me know about his latest project at work.

We were at a local pub near Cheltenham, somewhere we had enjoyed ever since we were old enough to spend our own money and drive our own cars. They had arranged a surprise for me and invited quite a few

CHAPTER SIXTEEN

friends from our recent school days. A surprise farewell. I was due to leave in less than a week. Along with my friends, my twin brother was there. He had gone to a different school, owing to his being a lot smarter. He was now studying History at university – a testament to his desire to consume and analyse information, something I did not particularly enjoy. He did not live at home but in university accommodation. He enjoyed the independence and was making his own way in the world, although on a different path to mine. We also had an older brother who, like me, worked in retail banking, but for a rival outfit. We did not see him very often. At school he had been the captain of the rugby and cricket teams and achieved excellent results – a boffin, like my twin, but skilful on the rugby field as well. By now, he was playing high-level amateur games in Gloucester. If he wasn't so focused on his banking career he would probably have been making money out of the sport.

I was driving, so I did not want to drink. I very rarely did at that time. A few of the names around the table had a pint, now being legally able to do so. The barman, of course, had needed to check a few IDs as, like me, some of us looked barely legally old enough to consume such libations. We spoke briefly about what the pre-deployment training had involved. The anecdotes I found funny went over most of their heads – squaddie humour being notably abstract and dark. So instead, the subject turned to the things we had done together and what plans people had for the future. I was sitting between Adam and Gareth, with my twin brother opposite. Gareth had brought his girlfriend, someone he had had a crush on for years. I did not know her well, but Becky seemed like a nice girl, and they suited each other. They had very similar tastes. In between conversations with the lads, Gareth would take the time to talk to her, as it was clear she wasn't overly familiar with many of the people around the table.

I spoke to Adam about our first years at school together. He lived close to the school, so I would often go home with him after class – or just skip class entirely to do something more interesting. To his parents' eternal credit, they knew full well that we weren't at school but never once complained and only ever showed me kindness and hospitality. They were interested in the theatre, too, and had encouraged and supported Adam in developing his thespian skills outside of his regular job. It was a good time to reminisce. Up to that point, I felt I had not lived much of a life. In truth, I hadn't. But the time had come.

It did not feel like long before I was lacing up my desert boots and dropping my bergen into the boot of my father's car. It was a Saturday morning and had been raining all night. Now the skies were grey, but it was drying up.

'Just drop me off at the gate,' I told him. I did not want any goodbyes. 'I'll see you when I get back in a few months.'

I knew the rest of the Glosters would be there, and some well-wishers who would not be deploying, such as Mr Wood, Captain Fry and a handful of the lads. I did not want a fuss. My plan was to throw my kit into the luggage hold of the coach, get on board and listen to some music. I had bought myself a minidisc player especially for that purpose and put together a dozen compilation discs to take with me.

'Okay, son,' my father said, as we made the short drive to the gates of the small Army base.

It took less than five minutes, and I spent the entire time trying to think of something to say. But nothing came to mind. If they were going to be my last words to my father, what would they be? There wasn't really a lot to say. I had written a simple last will and testament, detailing what to do with the few things I owned. But that was more a list of instructions than a meaningful testament of my life. There was nothing poignant or remarkable in the document. So I said nothing out loud, even though inside I was urging myself to find what could very well be my last words to my father. We parked, and I took my kit out of the car. I tapped on the window and waved as he remained in the driver's seat, engine idling. I put my bergen over one shoulder, picked my kit bag up with one hand and made my way to the waiting transport.

The TA centre was a hive of activity. I had not seen it so busy before, but I could understand why. Most of the Glosters had brought their entire families. Pat, the signaller, was surrounded by his wife and kids, kneeling down so that he was at the same eye level as his daughters. Foz was standing close to his family, telling them something meant only for them to hear. I boarded the coach and looked for Fordy. Gloucester was the last stop before Brize Norton, and most of Salamanca Company were aboard the convoy. I took a pair of seats in front of him and turned to ask him about his time off. He had enjoyed it but was pretty tight-lipped, so I left him to his thoughts. Instead, I looked out of the window and continued watching the exchange of emotions happening in the TA

CHAPTER SIXTEEN

centre car park. I could see my father's car still there, although now parked somewhat out of view. That was fair enough. The Company Sergeant Major (CSM) started to gently usher everyone along, bringing the farewells to an end. Usually, the CSM was a figure of authority and, to me, quite fearsome. But as I watched him out of the window I saw him slowly walking between the families and gently bringing their conversations to an end. With everyone eventually aboard, I put my earphones in and pressed play. Nobody was in the mood for talking, it seemed. I think everyone had more important things to think about.

Chapter Seventeen

The entire company stayed overnight in a logistics base close to Brize Norton, the Duke of Gloucester Barracks in South Cerney. I actually knew the neighbourhood quite well as it was not too far from where I lived. With an entire battlegroup to deploy, the RAF had their work cut out – so the units were being taken from South Cerney to Brize in smaller groups. Whilst we waited, in the basic accommodation, units were gradually called for and driven to the airbase, where they were embarked onto transport aircraft and then flown out to Iraq.

There was nothing to do whilst we waited at South Cerney. People just talked amongst themselves, made the odd phone call or had a cigarette. Mr Sherwood and all the officers were already in theatre, so command of our multiple reverted again to Sergeant Derrick, who was seconded to us from the ops room. His job was to deliver the entire platoon to Mr Sherwood and then rejoin the ops room and assist the officers in forming their strategy. We also had a temporary member from the Staffordshire Regiment join us. Staffs was probably as young as me and had not been with us for the training. He was due to join the HQ multiple, but his role was unclear. Driver, messenger, coffee boy? Even he wasn't sure where he fitted in.

We were eventually given notice to move. Some unnamed NCOs from the logistics corps who were based at the Duke of Gloucester Barracks were cutting about talking to our own hierarchy and getting us onto the transports for the ten-mile journey to Brize. The sarge looked around to make sure everyone in his multiple was present. They weren't.

'Where's Planty?' he asked, expecting an immediate answer.

Nobody knew. We all looked around trying to see if he was anywhere nearby. He wasn't.

CHAPTER SEVENTEEN

'L2, go and see if he's having a dump or something, Stick, go and see if he's taken up smoking all of a sudden.'

They went to have a look. No luck.

'Fucking idiot!' exclaimed the sergeant.

The entire company by now was moving out of the building and were waiting in the coaches that were going to take us to the air base.

Walking back, slowly and without a care in the world, Planty picked up his kit and said. 'Are we off then?'

Sergeant Derrick all but cut him in half with his stare: 'Yeah, WE are off but now we have to wait for L2 and Stick to come back 'cos I sent them to find you. Where were you anyway?'

Planty didn't seem bothered at all.

'Just went to the shop to buy some sweets.'

He reached into his leg pocket and produced a bag of Haribo.

'They won't melt in the desert', he added, opening the pack and offering them around.

Most of the unit took one, and the sound of a platoon of fully grown men eating children's confectionery was at full volume by the time L2 and Stick returned.

'You found Nemo, then?' asked Stick.

'He found his own way back, actually', Rob commented as he slung his bergen over his back. 'Time to go.'

We boarded the coaches and made the short journey to the RAF base on the Gloucestershire and Oxfordshire border. We drove through a picturesque little village called Bibury on the way. With its honey-coloured cottages and crystal-clear river, I was almost certain the driver had taken us this way in order to give us one last glimpse of England's green and pleasant land. It wasn't a long detour, and soon enough we were in the departures area of RAF Brize Norton. To my surprise it was exactly the same as an international departures lounge – with check-in desks and luggage trolleys, and adverts showcasing nearby businesses and taxi services lining the walls. I joined a queue and inspected my surroundings. I guessed it made sense. The civilian air transport business shifted countless people every day – more than the military. They probably knew a lot more about passenger-handling than the RAF. When I got to the front of the queue I had to produce my passport and ID. Then I got a boarding pass. I walked back to the waiting area and found the rest of the platoon. I double-checked my ticket and sat on a spare piece of floor.

'So are we going to Qatar then?' I asked Fordy.

I was looking at the ticket and not at him.

'Does your ticket say Qatar?' he asked.

I showed it to him.

'Fucking hell, mate, looks like you're going to Qatar. All of ours say Iraq!'

That was a shock.

'How come I'm going to Qatar?!'

'Probably because you're a veggie.' Rob said. 'I guess they don't have the correct rations for you in Basra.'

'What? Rations?'

There was a pause. then Uzi chipped in: 'We have to change aircraft in Qatar. Look.'

He put his arm around my shoulder and guided me towards a large window looking out towards the taxiway and runways. Some civilian aircraft had been contracted to take us to Qatar.

'We're gonna change to military transports in Qatar and make the rest of the journey to Iraq from there. Weren't you listening to the loggies?'

There were a few laughs along with Thewie's all too common shake of his head. He couldn't believe I had been so easily fooled by such an obvious wind-up.

We boarded the plane. Fordy and I had three seats between the two of us. He took the window seat and I sat beside him. It was due to be around a seven-hour flight. There was no inflight entertainment and no food. Just the horror bags we had been given just before boarding.

'Long journey, Matty', Fordy said as he made himself comfortable.

He folded his desert jacket a few times to make a pillow and placed it on the wall, resting his head against it.

'Better get some shut-eye.'

I was tired too. The journey from the TA centre to the aircraft had only been a few dozen miles but it had taken nearly thirty hours – and most of that was spent sitting around eating crisps. I was still wearing my smock. The air conditioning on the aircraft seemed to be set to a low temperature. I reclined my seat as far as it would go but couldn't get comfortable, so rested my head on Fordy's shoulder instead and fell

CHAPTER SEVENTEEN

asleep. By the time I woke up, my ears had started popping and we were descending into Qatar. I looked out of the window as the aircraft got lower and lower. The Al Udeid Air Base was covered in military aircraft and military vehicles. As we landed, a couple of F15 fighter jets were taxiing in the opposite direction. I leaned over Fordy to see what else I could see – Hercules, Globemasters and all kinds of transport aircraft. I guessed that they were waiting for us.

The aircraft came to a halt and we disembarked down the stair at the front. We had boarded as multiples, and left the aircraft in the same way. When 3 Platoon assembled at the bottom of the stairs Sergeant Derrick called us all together and shouted over the sound of the engines of the aircraft winding down.

'Follow me.'

We went to a holding area underneath a large tent. There were crates of water and some porta-toilets as well as a couple of picnic benches.

'Wait here. We'll be boarding the C130 soon. Make sure you drink at least two bottles of water. I don't want any of you going down sick on the first day.'

There were plenty of bottles of water around, so I took a couple and went to a table. I sat next to another Gloster from 1 Platoon called Mark, who had decided to get married just weeks before the deployment. I remembered him as one of the TA lads I had seen when I was on my induction weekend the year before. He had brought a mascot from Gloster with him and dubbed it 'Woody' after our erstwhile company commander, Mr Wood. His plan was to take photos of Woody in as many different places as possible and send the photos back to the TA centre for the rest of 'A' Company to look at. It seemed like a good enough hobby. At least he would have something to do if he had a few spare moments between force protection activities and personal admin. I, on the other hand, had not thought that far ahead and only had a minidisc player with some mix discs of music I was enjoying at the time. He passed me his disposable camera and placed 'Woody' on his shoulder like a pirate's parrot.

'Take a picture, Matt.'

With the shitters and Bons in the background, I clicked the shutter and immortalized the lance jack and his mascot onto a 4 x 6 glossy for the rest of time.

BASRA AND BACK

I polished off my second bottle of water and boarded the Hercules transport aircraft. As we entered through a door near the nose of the aircraft, some RAF loadies were inside securing us into bench-type seating that ran along the fuselage. The inside was dull but at least it was cool. The heat of the sun bouncing off the concrete as we waited had been notably uncomfortable, and I had begun to sweat. The flight crew used torches to check that we were all secured properly, then shut the doors. The whole company was aboard. Opposite me was Carols, the butcher. He gave me a nod and put his ear defenders on as the powerful aircraft engines came to life. It was loud onboard. The aircraft had not been designed with comfort in mind, and it was obvious that utility was the only function that this plane had. I looked up and down the seats and could see we were jammed in tight. The loadies were in relative luxury, sitting atop a pallet of equipment – our bergens and weapons – close to the tail ramp. There was no possible way that this was going to be a pleasant flight, but I did feel excited. Unlike the initial part of the journey in ultra-economy class seats, these felt like business class. Not because they were wide, comfortable and came with a pre-flight champagne, but because it felt like the start of something. More than anything I had done so far in life, this was the start of something.

The Hercules seemed to have no trouble at all in reaching its cruising altitude. It gained altitude much faster than our previous transport. I unclipped my lap belt and leaned over to look behind Carlos where there was a small porthole. Below I could see the coast of Qatar as we left the Arabian Peninsula behind. We were heading out to sea, not flying over Saudi Arabia. Basra is at the southern tip of Iraq, and I guessed that the flight crew had been told to make a direct approach from the south. That would reduce the risks of flying close to any other sovereign airspace and limit the time in the air when over Iraq. I trusted that they knew what they were doing. You couldn't become a pilot by accident, after all. Not like me becoming an infantryman. I sat back down and watched as various members of the company took turns looking out of the windows. A few took photos of the view outside. A few took shots of the interior of the Hercules as well.

I watched as several members of the company made their way to the bulkhead that separated the pilots from the cargo area. After a minute or so staring at the bulkhead, they turned around and went back to their seats. Halfway down the bulkhead was a letterbox-type aperture. The toilet – and

CHAPTER SEVENTEEN

not a very private one at that. With the aircraft full to capacity, to the left and right of the slot sat a member of Salamanca Company. I fought the urge to use that particular facility, but Sergeant Derrick's mandatory 'two bottles of water' had worked their way through my system and needed to be evacuated. I unclipped my harness again and, as casually as I could, made my way up the fuselage. Stepping over the feet of the rest of the men, I arrived at my destination and unzipped. I knew stage fright would be a risk, especially with people sitting so close. 'Don't make eye contact. Just relax. Relax and go', I told myself. I had been dying of desperation not twenty seconds ago and now I was standing at the front of the aircraft, humbled and waiting. 'Come on. Come on.' The trickle became a stream, eventually. But it had taken a long time. Repositioning myself, and still avoiding eye contact, I returned to my seat and strapped in. Surely it would not be long before we started our descent, as I could see the outline of a desert coast behind Carlos.

The loadies left their reclining positions on the cargo and made their way up and down the C130, ensuring that cargo and passengers were secure. No sooner had they secured themselves than the aircraft entered a steep and fast dive, bringing us into theatre. I started to feel sick. I had never been airsick before, but this steep dive with the aircraft pulling itself around to line up for a combat landing upset my equilibrium. Unlike civil airline pilots, the RAF fliers were required to take the aircraft out of its vulnerable landing approach as soon as possible. This was to reduce the risk of air defence weapons locking onto and damaging or destroying the plane. Luckily, it did not last long. As soon as we were rolling along the runway I began to feel better. We came to a stop, and the crew opened the doors. We had arrived in Iraq.

I stepped off the Hercules and onto the tarmac at Basra International Airport. A Coalition of American, Danish and British forces had taken over the location in early 2003 after the invasion of Iraq. Along with Baghdad, it now served as the entry and exit point for most Coalition forces in theatre. The heat hit me straight away. It was hot. It was so hot I thought I could taste it on my tongue. A metallic sensation that I had never felt before. The sun started to sting my skin and I began to sweat after walking only a few metres. Nothing had prepared me for this kind of heat. I made my way to a terminal building that was nothing more than an empty shell and joined up with the rest of 3 Platoon. After months of build-up training and a 6,000 km journey, we were only just getting started.

Part IV
THE DEPLOYMENT

Chapter Eighteen

The company was given a week to adjust to the new environment. The advance party, comprising most of the HQ personnel and all the officers, guided us to our accommodation. Living out of tents and sleeping on camp beds, we were now at Shaibah Logistics Base in Southern Iraq. We were issued ammunition, additional patrol equipment and our vehicles. Corporal Hill handed me a Laser Light Module (LLM) and a set of night vision goggles (NVGs).

'You know how to set it up?' he asked.

'I think I can figure it out, thanks,' I replied. 'It's like Lego for grown-ups, right?'

The LLM was a torch and laser attachment designed to fit on the side of my weapon. The powerful beam of light was ideal for illuminating areas we would need to search without taking our hands off our weapons. It also had a red dot laser and an infrared laser to assist aiming or designating targets. The NVGs were attached to a harness that I had to fit onto my helmet. Finally, I was given a basic first aid kit, mainly consisting of field dressings, large bandages sometimes called blood sponges. Everyone carried at least two, and as the team medic I was responsible for replenishing the platoon's supply as needed. I was also given bungee cords to use as tourniquets, large needles, surgical tubing, bags of fluid and rehydration powder to treat heat injuries. The rest of my first aid kit was bought and paid for by me before we deployed. Not ideal, but most of us had supplemented our kit with additional items paid for out of our own pockets.

Mr Sherwood already seemed to be getting a pretty good suntan. Mr Thynn looked unhappier than usual, although there was no reason for it at that moment. If we had to go to war, this was a comfortable way to do it. Shaibah Logistics Base, known among UK forces as 'Shaibiza',

CHAPTER EIGHTEEN

had many welfare facilities: a BFBS radio station, simple shops and even a lorry with a Pizza Hut inside it. The base hosted many units and was far enough from any major settlements to be nearly impervious to surprise attacks. The RAF Regiment conducted security patrols inside and outside the base, and the Royal Navy had set up radar-guided miniguns to take out incoming ordnance. Things would be very different for us in the city, as we were to find out.

I caught up with Metal Mickey from 1 Platoon while walking to the welfare area of the camp after a day of PT and comms training. Seeing him ahead of me, I jogged a few metres to catch up and tapped him on the shoulder. Even though we were both Glosters, I had never really spoken to him.

'Going to get some phone cards,' he replied when I asked what he was up to.

The base was huge, and he didn't mind the company as we walked a kilometre from our tents to the American PX shop, where most essentials were sold. Metal Mickey had promised his wife and son he would call as soon as he could to let them know he had arrived safely. A similar thought had never crossed my mind. My plan was to pick up a pile of blueys for the platoon and then write a few to kill some time in the evening. It struck me that the departure from the UK must have been hard for many of the blokes. It must be even harder for those waiting to hear from loved ones and tuning into the news every night. I put the thought to the back of my mind.

I asked Metal Mickey if it was true about his piercing.

'Yeah,' he told me. 'Wanna look?'

With all the people walking to and from the welfare area, I politely declined and changed the subject to his numerous tattoos. They were all faded and mostly green, which I thought meant the ink had lost some of its original colour.

'These tattoos are older than you, bud,' he said.

I did some quick arithmetic in my head.

'First one of them when I was sixteen.'

The maths checked out. Metal Mickey's tattoos were at least three years older than me.

'What about Prince Albert?' I asked.

'You nineteen?'

'Yeah.'

'He's older than you too.'

My eyes shut involuntarily as I imagined the procedure required to attach the metal loop. I shook my head.

'No way,' I said, more to myself than to Mickey. 'I think I'll stick to the blueys.'

After a few more days of acclimatization and training, we boarded our vehicles for the move to Basra Palace. Formerly one of Saddam Hussein's palaces, it is hard to describe just how big the place is. It was nothing like Buckingham Palace or the Palace of Versailles. The complex was covered in buildings – some erected just after the first Gulf War to subjugate the local dissidents, and some recently built by the Royal Engineers to house the British and Danish forces responsible for Basra's security. It was easily the size of a regional airport – just without any runways. Before the 2003 invasion, the Palace had also acted as a barracks, armoury and security forces location. In a sense, that function was still being carried out by the Coalition Provisional Authority (CPA), who were providing an interim government from the Palace until democratic elections could be held later in the year.

We boarded the vehicles to begin our convoy to the Palace. The Wolf Land Rovers we used were unarmoured and unremarkable, more suited to internal patrol duties around Shaibah or rear echelons than to negotiating a city that was a tinderbox environment. But they were all we had. The Company Quartermaster Sergeant (CQMS) and his stores team had spray-painted 43 Wessex Brigade emblems onto the rear bumpers to identify the vehicles. They had also fitted cage-type armour, bolstered with riot shields. It would not stop bullets or bombs but would protect from hand-thrown projectiles such as bottles and bricks. There was no air conditioning, as the vehicles had been stripped down to allow rapid access or egress. If you wanted to feel the breeze and cool down, the driver had to speed up.

Broz and I were standing in the back of the vehicle, providing top cover. Drewy and Mr Sherwood were sitting in the front, and we also had a passenger from the London Regiment who was to guide us to our lines once we were inside Basra Palace. We had to drive several miles to leave Shaibah, so Broz and I decided to sit on the equipment we were

CHAPTER EIGHTEEN

transporting and find out what we could about what the force protection company had been up to on TELIC III.

'Not a lot, to be honest, mate. Six boring months,' our Cockney companion told us.

'So what did you do?'

He told us as we hung onto the roll bars, while Drewy negotiated the temporary roads that crisscrossed the logistics base.

'Well, there are two riverside *sangars* and a rear gate watch position,' he began. 'Those are good places to stag on because you see a lot of activity, and you have a gimpie if you need it.'

No doubt Mr Evans would touch base with the outgoing company commander and devise his own security arrangements, but we kept listening.

'Then there are the towers.' He counted off on his fingers: 'Tango 16, 13, 10, and Tango 3. Tango 3 looks down into a village. The others look out into the desert.'

Broz queried, 'Tango 3 looks into a village?'

The Londoner nodded.

'Yeah, mate. The legs of the tower are right in the middle of the village. Friendly people, though. If you throw some money down and tell them what shopping you want, they'll buy it for you, and then you can winch it up in a bucket.'

He spoke as though he had long experience of the practice. I thought about whether I had any money on me, and then about whether I would want to buy anything.

I asked, 'What did you buy?'

'Just souvenirs for my mam. A crate of Pepsi or two. Zamzam. Some war trophies. Ripped-off films. Porn. Things like that.'

'What's Zamzam?' Broz asked.

'The local coke . . . cola. Full of illegal ingredients but probably better for you than smoking.'

I wasn't sure I wanted to try it.

We were about to cross the boundary of the base, and Mr Sherwood turned round and ordered us to provide top cover. Broz took the forward-facing position, and I faced the rear. Behind me, I could see Stick and Corporal Parsons' vehicle. I felt Drewy negotiate the last of the blast barriers at the entrance to Shaibah and then pick up speed. We were on our way.

Chapter Nineteen

Our accommodation at the Palace was in the old barracks used by Saddam's Republican Guard. It was a two-storey building with a flat roof, marble floors and reinforced concrete walls. Each multiple was assigned a room and given a few hours to get sorted. After that, the previous force protection company would leave, and we would assume our duties.

1 Platoon's multiples were immediately sent to the main gate and assigned to provide a Quick Reaction Force (QRF), leaving them no time to settle in. The QRF was centrally located to respond to incidents in or near Basra Palace. The platoon would unpack and settle in once off duty. 2 Platoon covered night and day guard shifts, allowing one of their multiples a whole night to rest before starting their shift. 3 Platoon was assigned night patrols. We walked up a wide and luxurious staircase to our room, conveniently next to the TV area and refrigerators.

I put my belt kit and webbing on a top bunk and went down to the vehicles to retrieve the rest of my equipment. I brought my bergen and kit bag up and dropped them on the floor. My kit was ready for patrol, but my medical equipment and night vision goggles were not yet set up. Fordy had taken the bunk beneath mine, but he, along with the other NCOs, had been called away by the platoon commander for an orders group (O Group). It was quite a big responsibility; Salamanca Company's first patrols would be carried out by 3 Platoon, and other than looking at maps and what we had seen on our first, and so far only drive through the city, none of us knew much about the layout of the ground.

Drewy and I were fixing our LLMs and night vision equipment. L2 was relaxing in a camping chair, having already set up his kit and decorated the room with a few posters to give the illusion of female

CHAPTER NINETEEN

companionship. Securing our night vision equipment to our helmets, we used L2 as a point of reference to ensure the devices were in focus and properly positioned over our eyes.

'Hold up a few fingers, L2,' Drewy said, rotating the focus on his NVG.

L2 held up only one finger. 'Cheers, mate.'

Drewy flicked the NVG upright and nodded to himself. 'All set, I reckon.'

I nodded in agreement and looked at my patrol pack. Smaller than a bergen, the pack carried medical equipment, mine-marking tape, rocket flares and extra water. We weren't expecting to be out for long, but a few extra bottles wouldn't hurt. Each of us already carried five litres: three in a water reservoir on our backs and two on the belt.

Everyone tested and adjusted their equipment, ensuring we were ready to go on patrol. Then we waited for the officer and NCOs to return, engaging in some idle chatter. We knew it would be a foot patrol and tried to guess where we would be going.

'Around the perimeter, probably,' said Elvis. 'We're only force protection. There are other units with serious armour to look after the city.'

He was right, but the city was less than half a kilometre from the main gate.

Stick added, 'Probably. But if we're going to be out for a few hours, I don't think the boss will just want to go around in circles. You know what he's like. That's too boring for him.'

Our room had only one window, and the sky looked purple as the sun dipped below the horizon. There were clouds in the distance and the odd flash of lightning. It was the only rain we would experience for the next six months.

After a briefing from our NCOs, we had time for a quick piss before making our way to the rear gate of the Palace. We fixed our magazines and made final checks before deploying. Elvis was wrong. We weren't patrolling the perimeter. The back gate of the Palace led directly into the city. From there, the lieutenant wanted to conduct a 'clearance patrol', to ensure the roads leading to and from the base were clear of obstructions or IEDs.

During our orders he told us, 'The previous force protection company will be leaving tonight. This is well-known local knowledge. With a large amount of traffic, if anyone wanted to cause casualties to British forces, this would be an opportune moment. We will therefore conduct a clearance patrol to ensure the routes out of the Palace are clear. We will also check nearby buildings and potential overwatch positions for any signs of an ambush.'

It was similar to the types of patrol we had practised at CPTA and Okehampton. I remembered patrolling the farm tracks that formed the entrance to Longmoor. This time, though, if the enemy was present they would not be firing blank ammunition, and neither would we.

'We will leave through the rear gate of the Palace and make our way west into the city,' the lieutenant continued. 'From there, we will follow the main road until we pass Basra hospital. At this location, we will go firm and try to identify any likely overwatch areas that might need investigating. At the conclusion of the patrol, we will return through the main gate where Mr Sparks and 1 Platoon are providing security. Does anyone have any questions?'

There were none.

I felt excited about this first patrol. Before leaving, I had written a quick bluey home about arriving at the Palace and how we were trying to get settled in for the next six months. I had neglected to include how I felt. I didn't want to come across as bullish or gung-ho; the truth was that I was not worried at all at this point. Whether it was training, excitement or youth, I only felt curiosity about and genuine interest in what we were about to do. I was not worried about the possibility of a firefight, booby traps or civil disorder. The only worry I had, if it was a worry, was that I would not live up to what was expected of me. I wondered if the rest of the platoon felt the same way. As Mr Sherwood divided us into what would become our regular fire teams, I looked around to see if I could read the emotions on the faces of the rest of the unit. If any of them were worried they disguised it very well.

Along with Mr Sherwood, Fordy and Drewy, I was part of Sierra Three Zero Alpha. Corporal Parsons' team consisted of Mick, Broz, Thewy and Uzi. They were designated Sierra Three Zero Charlie. Rob, who was in charge of Sierra Three Zero Delta, took Planty, L2, Stick and Elvis. Two teams of five and one of four. The larger fire teams had additional equipment to carry. Similar in size to a 351 radio and battery, they carried ECM (electronic countermeasure) equipment designed to

CHAPTER NINETEEN

disrupt any remotely activated devices in the area. This was not a popular task, as the ECM equipment was much heavier than the rest of the kit. It wasn't a job for NCOs, who were already carrying VHF radios. Elvis carried a Minimi light machine gun and extra ammunition, so he was also exempt. I was carrying medical equipment, and Uzi was carrying a baton gun that fired rubber bullets. In the end, Planty and Broz decided that for this first patrol they would haul the ECMs.

We began our patrol. One team at a time, we sprinted out of the gates and into the city.

Chapter Twenty

Drewy led our team out of the gate. The plan was to 'hard-target' by running in a zigzag pattern to a piece of cover. At staggered and unpredictable intervals, the rest of the team left Basra Palace and 'went firm', waiting for the entire unit to get into position. We conducted our five and twenty checks, looking for obvious signs of disturbance on the ground and checking likely places for devices or markers. We were clear. We were on the ground. It felt different from anything I had ever experienced. I was still breathing the same air, still the same person with the same tastes and abstract sense of humour, but crossing that physical threshold felt like crossing a mental one. This wasn't training any more. It wasn't school or a safe job somewhere in the UK. It wasn't a game. People were depending on me as much as I was depending on them. I didn't know it then, but this mental and emotional shift would stay with me forever.

The platoon patrolled down the street leading away from the rear gates of Basra Palace. To our left was a wide road acting as a partition from the rest of the city. Beyond the road were large houses, once occupied by those favoured by Iraq's ruling party. Many were now derelict or unoccupied. Some had residents, but whether they were long- or short-term, we didn't know. To our right was the external wall of the Palace, about twenty feet high and made of reinforced concrete, almost entirely undamaged even after the Battle of Basra.

We moved forward, spread out to avoid becoming an easy target for automatic fire or explosives. Occasionally, a pedestrian walked past us in the opposite direction. I decided to try my Arabic on the next passer-by.

'*Assalamu alaikum,*' I said to a white-robed man as he walked past me.

CHAPTER TWENTY

'*Salaam,*' was his one-word reply.

There were cars on the road, and more than a few drivers and passengers watched us as they drove by. There was no way to gauge their intent. I saw Mr Sherwood ahead of me. Turning around without breaking my stride, I saw Fordy behind me. We were all looking around, not only for signs of danger but also because these were our first steps into this new environment.

We had to ensure the route out of the Palace was clear. This meant stopping regularly to check for IEDs, or markers that could assist in attacking our forces as they left the base. We were lightly armed and lightly armoured, with only helmets and Enhanced Combat Body Armour (ECBA), which none of us trusted much. We had been instructed to patrol in our berets in order to present a 'softer image'. At least we were light enough to quickly get into substantial cover if needed. We did, however, have our ECM kit constantly sending out disruptive signals to interfere with any remotely detonated devices. There was no defence against command wire devices or small-arms fire, though. That would come down to training and how well we reacted to enemy fire. It was all part of the risk that these patrols frequently had to bear.

Half an hour into our patrol, we arrived at a bridge over the Alkhora River, which fed into the Shatt al-Arab – a huge waterway acting as a natural border between Iraq and Iran. We spread out in our fire teams and went firm to observe the main roads to and from the Palace. Those with night vision equipment flicked the devices down over our eyes, bringing a new green reality to what was previously invisible. The passing traffic was easy to identify. Most cars had a headlight or two. Nothing seemed out of place. There was no erratic or overly aggressive driving. People on foot were where they would be expected to be – on the pavement, not lurking or behaving furtively. Looking higher up, there were no obvious observers in windows or on rooftops. We waited. I saw the officer speaking into his radio handset, sending a report back to our ops room. Satisfied, we moved north-east to join the main road to the Palace and clear the route back in.

We checked the main approach to the Palace and arrived at the gate. The gate was actually a red and white traffic barrier with an FV432 Armoured Personnel Carrier behind it. The driver, a member of the Royal Corps of Signals, rolled it back a few metres as Carlos pushed down on the barrier counterweight. As when exiting the base, we went in as quickly as we could. We saw members of 1 Platoon keeping a sharp eye out. Numerous defensive positions were fitted with searchlights and GPMGs, as well as blast barriers and Hesco bastion blocks filled with rubble and dirt. It didn't look like a Palace; it looked like a war zone. Until very recently, it had been. Only after passing through the gates and looking back could we see the huge arch and iron gates defining Basra's biggest structure.

We had been out for two hours. Not long at all. But even in the night-time air it was above 30° Celsius. I felt sticky from sweat and the dust kicked up during our patrol. I took my beret off and passed it through a belt loop. The warm breeze felt cool against my skin. We walked to the side of the gate's guard house and unloaded our weapons. As we waited, we saw the outgoing force protection company forming up their convoy. Now that they knew the route was clear, they were ready to start their journey home, back to the UK. There were a few waves as we walked past their line of vehicles, and a few words of encouragement.

We returned to our accommodation. Mr Sherwood conducted a simple debrief before taking the fire team commanders to write a patrol report. The rest of us could return to the relative comfort of our room and get ready for our next patrol at 0400. After cleaning our weapons, kit and ourselves, we would probably get three or four hours' sleep. I didn't feel tired at all. Instead, I climbed to the roof of our building and looked back to where we had just been. I watched the red tail lights of the convoy leaving through the palace gates, then went back inside to try to get some sleep.

Chapter Twenty-one

The morning patrol was to begin at 0400, which meant being ready well before the appointed hour. At three in the morning multiple alarm clocks went off and the lights in the room were turned on, hurting my eyes as they adjusted to the brightness. I had managed to sleep, but the anticipation of going on patrol had kept me awake longer than I wanted, so I felt tired and unenthusiastic.

I rolled out of my bunk and asked if anyone wanted something from the fridge. A few requests for bottles of water came my way. Stick asked me to fill the kettle, which I did. A hot drink on a hot night didn't seem ideal to me. Stick seemed to have an addiction to tea, or at least a strong psychological dependence.

'It doesn't matter if it's hot; it still hydrates you,' he told me as he stirred in an unusual amount of sugar.

We had cold rations for breakfast, taken from a box in the middle of our room. We just took what we fancied, and breakfast was over within a few minutes. We then grabbed our patrol kit and headed down to the briefing area next to the ops room. I looked in to see that Pat was on duty along with the operations officer, Lieutenant Moorhouse. I barely knew him. He was 'third in command' or something. I never recalled speaking to him, or him speaking to me. It looked like he was running the show overnight, conducting radio checks and compiling situation reports and observations from the guard towers. I left them to it without interruption.

We were briefed about our patrol. We were to conduct another clearance to ensure that cargo vehicles en route from Shaibah could access the Palace without risk as soon as the sun was up. Afterwards, we were to push into the city to 'prevent crime and disrupt terrorism'. Essentially, it was a patrol to assert our dominance over any hostile forces and deny them freedom of action. It was still dark outside. The patrol was supposed to last four hours, after which we would have the day off, before assuming guard duty in the towers overnight. That seemed good to me. We had seen the city at night, but now we were going to see it during the day.

We made our way out of the base and onto the main road that connected the Palace to the city. There were several small fishing boats floating on the river, their occupants apparently asleep. Not being an angler myself, I assumed they were waiting for sunrise or had already made their catch and were resting. Either that, or they were pretending to fish and actually monitoring coalition troop movements. I made a mental note to mention it during the patrol debrief. Someone should be able to figure it out, I reasoned.

As the sun began to rise, so did the temperature. Soon it was well above 30°. I could feel the heat of the sun on my skin and through my dark beret. As this patrol was about 'hearts and minds', we still did not wear helmets, in order to project a less aggressive image. Our unit, being a mix of three regiments, had three different cap badges on display; four, if you counted the Glosters' back badge. I could see Broz ahead of me and the sunrise glinting off the thin metal badge on the back of his headdress. I hoped my badge looked just as glorious.

As soon as the sun was up, the city came to life. Orange and white taxis came and went, apparently the preferred method of transport other than walking. Construction vehicles headed to countless building sites to repair the battle damage from eight months ago. Police patrols drove past, either waving at us or eyeing us with suspicion from the back of their Toyota pickup trucks. There was a lot of foot traffic leaving the city and heading towards the Palace and the hospital. Workers were on their way to morning shifts, and outpatients were seeking medical care from the city's overstretched medical services.

We continued to assert our dominance by patrolling through side streets and rejoining the main road at unpredictable locations. The platoon never moved as a single group. While parts of the multiple repositioned and moved in and out of cover, other parts provided overwatch, securing those who were moving. Everything happened slowly and deliberately. There was no need to rush or run – it would tire us out, draw a lot of attention and alarm the locals to see armed

CHAPTER TWENTY-ONE

British soldiers darting in and out of cover. Instead, we patrolled in a way that offered visibility and allowed us to evaluate and assess the area we were working in.

On our return to the Palace we went straight to the cookhouse for breakfast – our second breakfast. This large building in the centre of the Palace had to provide meals for the entire coalition garrison and was always busy during mealtimes. Outside of those hours, we had to make do with whatever was available through foresight and good planning – usually an improvised horror bag or several dozen biscuits and a bottle of water.

We were dripping in sweat and covered in dust. We left our armour and equipment outside with Elvis and Uzi, who were having a gasper, while the rest of us headed in. Fine cuisine it was not, but food never tasted so good. We sat down as a multiple in the main hall – the officers had a separate area. Plastic forks and paper plates in hand, everyone inhaled their food. Some went back for more. Over Weetabix and full Englishes, we reflected on our first patrols.

'I think the other company was right when they said it was a quiet and boring tour,' Planty said.

I could see his thinking and hoped the deployment would remain uneventful. If every patrol was quiet and without significant difficulties, soon the city could be handed over to local security forces, and the British deployment could be scaled back.

'Not likely to be a running battle, though,' Mick added. 'Just because it's quiet doesn't mean someone isn't watching. Someone is bound to be taking notes, recording our activities.'

He was right. That reminded me of the fishermen, and I wrote an 'F' on my hand to remind myself to mention it in the debrief.

Uzi joined us and produced a 'heart attack sandwich', a recipe of his own invention – a fried egg between two pieces of fried bread. It looked good.

Hungry as I was, I asked him, 'What's it fried in?'

I genuinely didn't know.

'Fancy one, do you?'

He handed me the rest of the sandwich. Whether it was suitable for vegetarians or not, I did not know. But I was in dire need of calories and salt, and it went down a treat.

We had twelve hours off. 'Time off' is a very loose term on operations; it actually means time not on duty, but there are always tasks to complete and odd jobs to do. Along with trying to get some sleep before our next job, there was always cleaning. We had to mop out the communal areas of the company accommodation, check and service the vehicles that weren't in use and find time to carry out our own personal admin. Some of the guys wrote letters home, some went for a shower and others went to look for a mate from another platoon. Fordy went to the gym. It was too hot to sleep, so I decided to write a bluey and went up to the roof. Wearing only a pair of cut-off combats, I thought I would soak up a few rays while I was there.

The roof was the usual hangout for the smokers, and that included the CSM. Preferring Café Crème cigars, the CSM was sitting on an oil drum, enjoying the view as far as I could tell.

'Hello, sir,' I announced.

'All right?' he answered. 'Just in off patrol, aren't ya?'

The only thing I knew about the CSM was that he was the CSM, so avoiding small talk and the outside possibility of being thrown off the roof, I stuck to the narrative and his line of enquiry.

'Yes, sir.'

'Good lad. Get some scoff?'

'Yes, sir.'

'Did they have a veggie option?'

'Yes, sir.'

I had applied wilful ignorance to Uzi's ingredients for his heart attack sandwich. The CSM took a drag on his stogie and exhaled. The cigar smelt sweeter and fuller of flavour than a cigarette.

'You know, it costs eleven quid for a box of rations for the blokes. You cost twenty-three.'

'I'm sure I'm worth it . . . um, sir,' I replied before thinking about it.

I had been reminded, more than once by now, about speaking to the senior NCOs and officers in a more 'correct' way and the need to 'keep my fucking opinions to myself'. But I must have caught him on a good day, as he simply nodded, dropped the remainder of his smoke into a tin can and went back inside.

I rested my blank bluey on the floor and started to write home. There wasn't much to say, so in no time at all the message was concluded.

CHAPTER TWENTY-ONE

I repeated the process several times, and before I knew it I had a dozen envelopes to send. I went back inside to find Corporal Hill, who was running the company stores along with the CQMS. Their living quarters were also the equipment supply rooms. I walked in and saw radio batteries on charge, piles of spare equipment and stacks of brand-new uniforms.

'What's up, Matty?' Mark said as he saw me come in.

He stopped what he was doing and took a few steps toward the folding six-foot table that acted as the stores countertop.

'Got some letters to send,' I replied, holding the pile up in front of me and fanning myself slightly with them.

'Good timing.'

He disappeared for a moment and returned with a handmade red postbox.

'Just finished putting the paint on. Drop 'em in there, I'll send them out every other day.'

He held the box out in front of me, and I put the letters in.

'Anything else?'

There wasn't. I decided to go back to my bunk and try to get some sleep.

Chapter Twenty-two

Guard duty in the towers, or *sangars*, was very boring 99 per cent of the time. The 'Tango' towers were tall concrete structures that jutted out from the walls of the Palace, surrounding the entire west side of the base. On the east side, the Shatt al-Arab side of the base had two *sangars* built by the Royal Engineers after the Palace had been occupied by Coalition forces. Finally, there was the rear gate, which was basically a tent and a chair, out of sight of anyone. There were also two internal checkpoints that needed to be manned, separating the CPA area from the British garrison.

The internal checkpoints were probably the worst postings. They were only open during the day, and locked shut at night. During the day there was very little cover from the heat of the sun, and a constant stream of IDs to check. At night, we had to guard a locked gate in a locked palace full of friendly forces.

'Shouldn't this be a job for the monkeys?' Elvis commented.

There were only a handful of RMP at Basra Palace, and we weren't sure what they did. They were located with the CPA in another part of the base. But Mr Sherwood reminded us that we were the force protection company, so the responsibility lay with us. Of course, during guard duty, the senior NCOs and officers had the comfort of the ops room to cool off in, while the troops cooked under the desert sun. At least there was interaction at these checkpoints, and time seemed to move.

The towers were another matter. There was no power and no facilities of any kind. Essentially concrete pillboxes on concrete legs, they were substantial but very uncomfortable. During the day, they trapped heat and became extremely hot. At night, the spotlights attracted every insect known to man, so the guard was usually focused more on avoiding being

CHAPTER TWENTY-TWO

bitten by a scorpion the size of a deck of cards, or stopping supersized wasps from buzzing around their faces, than on their duty.

We had to remain in the towers no matter what, so it was a good idea to bring an empty plastic bottle for basic bodily functions. It was also smart to bring something to help break up the monotony of guard duty. Snacks were a popular option. One biscuit per tower made for a delicious countdown timer.

The towers looked out into the desert, except for one, Tango 3, that overlooked a small village. Tango 16, which I really hated, gave me the creeps. Being somewhat superstitious, that place made me uncomfortable. The tower was on the corner of the base, exposed on three out of four sides. The wind came through the firing ports, making a low howl at night. The radio signal was always unreliable when I was on duty, and odd things would happen, like my torch battery dying for no reason or the sound of disturbed gravel coming from the bottom of the winding staircase that led to the fortified concrete pillbox. All these things contributed to the sense of unease I felt whenever I was there.

Luckily, we only manned a tower for an hour before rotating to the next. They were all connected by radio frequency, and the NCOs would drive from tower to tower to ensure that the security arrangements remained satisfactory.

On a hot night, two weeks into the tour, 3 Platoon was responsible for guard duty during the hours of darkness and was due to hand over the next morning so that we could take over the main gate. This task did not require the full multiple to be on duty, so three of the unit would be lucky enough to get some sleep, while the majority of us would go straight from the guard towers to the gate *sangars*.

Looking out of Tango 13, I used my NVGs to scan the area. The tower was close to a village called Abu al-Khaseeb, although we referred to it as Mitan for some reason. I never found out why. It seemed like a peaceful and quiet group of mud-walled single-storey buildings. The villagers appeared to be farmers, using the ample water from the adjacent river to irrigate their crops. The hand-dug irrigation ditches made the area look like an oasis compared to its surroundings. It was a deep green, with palm trees and low shrubs lining the tracks that made up the simple road network connecting Mitan to the rest of the city. It fitted the stereotype of an Arabian settlement.

During the day, it seemed the villagers enjoyed having armed protection so close by, and they would usually be seen waving to us. Patrols from our company regularly passed through Mitan, and the tower could keep a lookout from its elevated position and report to the patrol commander using a 351 radio. True to what we were told, a young Iraqi boy would often come to the towers and shout 'Hey soldier!' then run into town to pick up any requested items, with a mark-up for himself, of course. I was yet to take any of them up on the offer, but a few crates of Zamzam cola, knock-off DVDs, the odd football shirt and pieces of militaria had been delivered within the first few weeks. To be fair, at a time when Amazon was just another start-up, those little entrepreneurs knew their business. They could get you anything.

Looking out at night, it was always quiet unless a patrol was passing nearby. But if we did hear the sound of a vehicle or voices, then probably something was up. I put my NVGs down and checked my watch. I had treated myself to a new timepiece before deploying and had already developed a serious tan line. One day I forgot to wear it and ended up with a bright red wrist where the sun had cooked my pale skin. Now, I wore it on my chest rig, like hospital nurses hang theirs. I wrote the time in the tower logbook and noted 'NTR' – nothing to report. Next, I would head to Tango 10, where Drewy was, then Tango 3, and then finally get two or three hours of sleep before restarting the rotation.

I heard a thud as I looked out of the firing ports, like a bass drum being kicked from far away, but hard enough to make the sound carry through the night air. Then another, and another. As I started to realize why I recognized the sound, the first mortar round landed in Mitan. The explosion threw dirt and mud up and over the towers. The next two landed, and I heard Drewy on the 351.

'Tango 10, contact wait, out.'

I called in as well: 'Tango 13, contact, explosion. Wait. Out.'

It seemed the brief barrage had finished as soon as it had started. That did not mean there wouldn't be a follow-up. Using night vision equipment, I surveyed the village and called in my SITREP.

'Hello Zero, this is Tango 13, SITREP, over.'

The call came back: 'Tango 13, go ahead.'

CHAPTER TWENTY-TWO

I told them what I could ascertain from where I was.

'Three explosions, probably mortar fire. At least one landed in Mitan, other two impacts unknown. Distance from Tango 13 approximately 100m. Over.'

Sergeant Derrick was surely writing it all down, while a runner had been sent to wake the major or Captain Roberts.

'Tango 13, received. Out to you. Tango 10, send SITREP, over.'

Drewy reported in. He was closer to the impacts. Tango 10 was the only tower with permanent searchlights. They illuminated a dirt track of crossroads that joined the agricultural area to a road that surrounded the Palace. Possibly this was an aiming point. We recorded the incidents in the tower logs and maintained our vigils. I didn't feel so tired or bored after that, but I was still looking forward to a couple of hours' kip.

After guard duty we went to the gate. Three of the platoon were able to go to the guardroom, halfway up the arches, and get some sleep. The rest of us manned the gate positions. I had to put on a hi-vis vest and sit inside the Palace to direct traffic once it arrived. That was quite good because it meant I could sit in the air-conditioned office while no vehicles were about. I picked up a printout of the major's report for the previous day and night's activities. It read:

> During last night's mortar attack, Pte Drew was manning sangar T10 and Pte Okuhara was manning sangar T13. T10 was the closest position to the impact of the 3 mortar rounds, which landed near the sentry positions. Pte Drew gave an immediate, clear and accurate contact report to and steer, which enabled a confused situation to be quickly managed by the ops room. His information was corroborated by accurate reporting from Pte Okuhara in T13, who had also been very close to the mortar impacts. Both soldiers remained at their posts and on the net until the incident was closed, passing back and clarifying information in an effective manner throughout.

I asked Mr Sherwood if there was any follow-up information from the QRF who were dispatched to Mitan to check on the villagers and check for damage.

'Luckily, nobody was hurt,' he replied. 'No damage either, really, except for a few chickens. They got blown up, but the village top boy said that they would just clean up what they could and eat them. No harm done.'

I went outside to direct some Hilux trucks carrying scrap wood out of the Palace. I used my PRR to call the barrier guard and 432 driver and waited to send the trucks forward. They went off with a wave as I heard the 432 come to life and ease itself backwards.

Chapter Twenty-three

Compared to the towers, the gate was a relatively decent assignment. It offered shade or air conditioning to keep off the worst of the Basra heat. The main exceptions were the two guard posts overlooking the main approach to the palace: one built into the gate and the other high up on the stone arch that dominated the Palace's architecture.

The downside was that we were vulnerable to anyone determined to attack Coalition forces. While the gate probably had enough firepower to repel a significant frontal attack, casualties among the squaddies would also be likely. Vigilance was crucial as we kept a lookout and controlled access at the gate, checking people as they arrived for work and inspecting vehicles requiring access to the palace.

A small door beside the *sangar*, the forwardmost guard post, was manned by one of the company who acted as a searcher, similar to a police stop-and-search. If someone knocked on the door they would be let in and searched, while another platoon member kept them in their sights. It must have been disconcerting for the casual labourers to be essentially held at gunpoint and searched before entering the Palace, but those were the rules.

Whenever possible, I participated in the searches. I thought it was a good job. Either you had a constant stream of visitors to check, keeping you busy, and allowing me to practise the few words and phrases of Arabic I had learned, or you had no visitors at all (at night, for example) and could take it relatively easy. The world being a small place, I even searched one of my clients from Gloucestershire, who was looking to conduct some business with the consulate. He didn't go into much detail but always came across as a bit shady – which explained his wealth and the ambiguous nature of his accounts back in the UK. I guessed he had contacts in Iraq or the Foreign Office and was looking to score some kind of deal. I remember opening the gate and finding a white guy in a linen suit instead of one of the regular visitors, so I brought him in and went through the procedure.

After checking him, I asked, just to pass the time as he waited for his escort, 'What are you doing here?'

It was then that the penny dropped, and I started to think, 'I've seen you before somewhere, I think . . .' Of course, he didn't recognize someone as junior as me, but before long we were chatting about some of the more senior figures at the institution where I worked. I never found out how things went and never saw him again.

Checking vehicles was much more arduous and dangerous. A lay-by was built to the side of the main gate, and once a vehicle had cleared the barrier it would park in what was essentially a concrete box about the size of a football penalty area, surrounded by tall, thick concrete walls. The searchers could go in, out, under and over the vehicle to check for bombs, weapons or anything suspicious. If something dodgy was found, the call 'checkmate' would alert the guard commander to a potential problem. The call 'bingo' would indicate a positive result.

We regularly found weapons in the cabs of trucks. The drivers insisted they were necessary for their protection around the city. It was a fair point, as Basra was far from the safest city in Iraq. But there was no way they could bring them into the Palace. Normally, the local police would confiscate the gun and write a receipt so it could be reclaimed, but occasionally, especially at night when the cops weren't around, we would seize the weapon and hand it over to the quartermaster, who would then hand it to the RMP. Whether or not the property was ever returned, I have no idea. I suspect that in most cases they became part of the IZP's arsenal.

We were issued an alert to be on the lookout for a white Scania dump truck filled with explosives. If any truck matching that description entered the chicanes on the run-up to the Palace, we were to notify the guard commander so the company commander could be alerted. Of course, while 3 Platoon was on duty, not one but a convoy of white Scania trucks entered the chicanes. We let the guard commander know. I saw Mr Sherwood as he raced to the front gate and got the convoy to stop by firing a flare at the lead vehicle. It was not worth taking any

CHAPTER TWENTY-THREE

risks. If there was a VBIED of that size, it would demolish everything nearby.

Our interpreter, Jacob, managed to get the convoy to reverse out of the chicane, and over the next hour the vehicles were brought into the search bay one at a time and checked thoroughly. Rob's section was on search duty. Rob preferred this task, but I didn't fancy it much. It was usually a dirty job, and when big dump trucks or refuse collection vehicles turned up, someone had to check the cargo area for any security issues. More than once, I remember climbing into the tipper of a truck or crawling under a piece of plant machinery. The convoy was clear, as far as we could tell, and it entered the Palace without incident. At the same time as Rob's searches, I checked the drivers' mates who had to come through the pedestrian entrance. No problems there either. That was until a huge explosion detonated at the end of the chicane. Fortunately, it was not from any of the Scanias but from a taxi.

The concussion wave of the blast was visible, like a ripple of water, and the low, deep roar of the explosion was sickeningly loud.

'What was that?!'

The guy I was searching, an Arsenal fan judging by his shirt, was under the table used to rest personal possessions during searches.

'I don't know.'

I gave him back his things and opened the gate to see if anyone else was waiting to come in. I was fairly certain he was the last, but I didn't want one of those truckers to be left outside while all their mates were in the safety of the Palace. Nobody. I shut the gate and pushed the Arsenal fan towards his truck and waiting driver.

The personnel search bay was adjacent to the front *sangar*, where all my kit was stored. The searcher only ever wore body armour to project that 'softer image' that was the popular style of the time. I raced up the steps and started to get my equipment on. I could hear that the 351 radio was very lively. The network connecting the guard towers and gate obviously had a lot of information to pass on. As I made myself small behind the Hesco walls and wriggled into my belt kit and weapon sling, I could see that L2 was keeping a lookout down the barrel of his GPMG and Mick was doing the same with a powerful pair of binoculars. Once I was set, I joined L2 on the gun and got ready to start feeding it if the time came. We probably all had the same thought: this was the initiation of something much larger.

Outside, a VBIED had detonated at the junction connecting the Palace to the city. The huge explosion killed a score of civilians and damaged the road so badly that it was unlikely any vehicles would be able to come and go using that route until it was repaired. From now on we would need helicopters to bring in supplies. We had been in Iraq for less than a month, and insurgent activity had been building in and around the city. We had been briefed on the increase in anti-Coalition sentiment that had increased the month before, just as we had arrived.

At the start of the month, in Al Amarah, the PWRR had been in an eight-hour running battle with insurgents. Six soldiers were wounded, but British troops managed to regain control of the city by deploying armoured units to the streets. The week after, in Basra, police stations had become targets. The local security forces were taking casualties, and it was only a matter of time before we became targets as well. It was 9 May.

Chapter Twenty-four

On 14 May, insurgents from the Mahdi Army launched concurrent attacks on the southern cities of Iraq. British forces at a checkpoint known as 'Danny Boy' came under sustained attack and engaged with the enemy at the point of the bayonet.

British soldiers were ambushed by Mahdi Army insurgents near the checkpoint as they launched a coordinated attack using small arms, rocket-propelled grenades (RPGs) and mortars. In response, a platoon of British soldiers from the PWRR was dispatched to reinforce the checkpoint and engage the insurgents. The battle involved close-quarters combat, with fighting in trenches. Several British soldiers were wounded and numerous Mahdi Army fighters were killed during the engagement.

On the same day, a patrol led by that angry sergeant from 2 Platoon came under fire. Sergeant Paul-Reeves was hit in the chest, although his body armour stopped the round, somehow. He continued directing his multiple until the insurgents broke contact and melted back into the city. The month of May was becoming busy. We had taken indirect fire on many occasions now, the firing points usually coming from the west, close to the agricultural land that ran along the Iraq/Iran border. These were not attacks of opportunity either, but rather coordinated assaults on Coalition forces, intended to disrupt military effectiveness and wreak havoc on the city prior to the CPA holding democratic elections and the transfer of power back to the Iraqis.

The Mahdi Army was a Shia militia that initially comprised seminary students – men who were training for a life as clerics. Recruited by Muqtada al–Sadr, the militia eventually grew in size by recruiting disaffected locals as well as Republican Guard veterans and some foreign volunteers. They were no ragtag bunch of criminals, but well funded, well trained and well armed, and they always operated when conditions favoured them. Along with its political wing, the Mahdi Army was able to capitalize on destabilizing the cities of Iraq by promising that their candidates for election would provide better conditions than the democratic candidates could. Their campaign had begun the month before, in April. Initially they focussed on attacks in the central and northern parts of Iraq, which were under American occupation. As the influence and capabilities of the Mahdi Army grew, they began to attack British and other Coalition forces as well; they had assaulted the Spanish Foreign Legion in Najaf, killing soldiers and civilians alike. These casualties, along with the Madrid train bombing, caused the Spanish government to withdraw its forces – a success for the insurgents that they were keen to repeat.

Basra became extremely unsettled. Additional forces were put on patrol in order to counter the terrorist threat and reassure the civilian population. The IZP, or Iraqi police, deployed its TSG – Tactical Support Group. Wearing blue camouflage fatigues and carrying military equipment, these police officers patrolled the innermost parts of the city. Regular police officers joined Coalition troops on patrol, and the traffic police enforced a late-night curfew by shutting down the roads in the city.

On 16 May, 3 Platoon was tasked to join an IZP patrol near Basra Hospital. The police had been given information that a known and wanted agent for the Mahdi Army would be near the Palace conducting reconnaissance, preparatory to an attack that would render the city's medical services ineffective. We joined three cops after we had deployed from the back gate. There were supposed to be four, but one had not arrived. The plan was to split the multiple into two teams. One fire team would join the IZP on patrol between the two entrances to the hospital – around a kilometre from Basra Palace. The other patrol, led by Rob, would climb an abandoned building and provide overwatch. Along with Mr Sherwood, Fordy, Drewy and I joined the police patrol. Rob took Planty, Stick and L2 to the roof of a nearby derelict building.

We were looking for a white Toyota pickup truck with a single occupant. That was pretty much impossible; every other car was either a taxi or a pickup. But the IZP had requested support, and the OC of Salamanca Company had obliged by deploying his patrol multiple 'in support of local security operations'. It was a hot night again. It had been

CHAPTER TWENTY-FOUR

getting hotter over the previous weeks, and during the day the mercury would regularly hit 40° or higher. The night offered little respite as the temperature generally hovered around 30°. It was one of those nights. I was carrying the medical equipment along with the ECM. Half of the multiple had been left behind and were resting up ready for another patrol in the early morning. That meant all of the equipment had to be distributed amongst the balance of the platoon.

The police, on the other hand, were lightly armed. Wearing a basic uniform, two carried pistols in holsters and one had an AK47 with a single magazine. They had no handcuffs, radios or notebooks, so I wondered how they intended to arrest the guy they were looking for and how they would report it in. The Iraqi police force at that stage was barely functioning – having been dismantled along with the military after the 2003 invasion. As far as I could make out, the police stations were manned by whoever lived nearest and didn't mind wearing a blue shirt. They seemed barely trained, if at all. It must have been a job of last resort. The casualty rate was very high, and their chances of survival during a contact were pretty low. But they were not there to fight, they were there to enforce what little law still applied. They often seemed to wait out their shifts in the police station and only patrol very nearby. I didn't see this as cowardice, however. It was bloody sensible, all things considered.

We patrolled up and down the length of the road. One kilometre up, one down. The coppers stopped occasionally to check the odd car. The sun had gone down and it was dark. Without torches, the IZP relied on the few functioning street lights to illuminate any suspect vehicles. It wasn't much of a system, but it kind of worked. Whilst they conducted their enquiries, our fire team provided security. I could hear the team on the PRR radio passing the occasional comment, but Rob was out of range and relying on his 349 to stay in touch with Mr Sherwood. I was kneeling behind a broken floodlight on an un-illuminated sports field. It was only five or six metres from the road. The rest of the fire team were in similar positions. From there we could see everything that happened, and we ourselves were very hard to spot in the dark shadows. As the IZP moved off again towards the hospital we got up to change position as well.

Suddenly I was running towards the contact. I don't remember how it started. During a traffic stop, one of the IZP fell backwards from a car he was checking and crawled a few feet towards the pavement. I thought I had heard a shot. Or maybe a burst of fire. As I ran, following Mr Sherwood, he turned and pointed to the wounded police officer on the ground before sprinting forward to join Drewy, who was in a good piece of cover near the hospital gates. The IZP officer was definitely in a bad way. He was the senior man of the three, their equivalent of a corporal or sergeant. He had been leading his team and spoke some English, which had made it slightly easier for us to work together. I swung the patrol pack off my shoulder and went into one of the side pouches to get some first field dressings. His shirt was red from the shoulder down. It was obvious where he had been hit – the projectile had reduced his shoulder joint to fragments and pulp. I ripped open the bandage cover and held it in place.

'I've been… sh–shot.', he told me.

I could see the look in his eyes, as he looked to me for some kind of reassurance.

'You'll be okay', I told him.

I wasn't sure that he would be. His blood had soaked the bandage within seconds. It was like putting a sponge into a bucket of liquid. I felt the warmth and stickiness of the blood between my fingers as I applied pressure and started to secure the bandage in place. Recruiting the assistance of a hospital security guard, I had him place his hands over the bandage as I prepared another. Whack, whack, whack, whack! A pavement block behind me disintegrated as fire came down from one of the rooftops. 'Fuck!' was my involuntary call as I tried to make myself small. I was out in the open, at the side of the road where the casualty had crawled. A few metres away were the gates to the hospital. 'Fuck me!' I shoved the next bandage on top of the previous blood-soaked dressing and took a bungee cord from my kit, thinking I could try to arrest the bleeding that way. I made it into a noose and guided it up his arm to what little remained of his shoulder. Passing up to the collar bone I thought, 'This is not going to work', and started dragging him to the hospital gates with the security guard. Other members of the hospital staff ran out, taking a limb each and running him inside. He was still alive.

I picked up my patrol pack and put it back on, running to the first piece of cover that I could find – a metal newspaper stand. There was

CHAPTER TWENTY-FOUR

no way that would give me any protection, so I needed to rejoin the rest of Sierra Three Zero Alpha as soon as I could. I looked around. Another police officer was lying face down, motionless. I couldn't see any injuries. He was lying half on the pavement, half on the road, and I turned him over to see if he was alive. He was hanging on. I grabbed him under the arms and went back the way I came, dragging him towards the security guards. I could hear them shouting something, either to each other, or to me, or both. There was gunfire. I didn't know where it came from. I just kept going until I crossed out of sight of the contact area and fell backwards, accidentally pulling the casualty over me. I looked down at the man who was now lying on top of my legs and saw that the white training shoe on his left foot was red. I was about to get some more medical equipment out but stopped when the hospital staff dragged him away and helped me up. I felt them pat my kit as they pushed me away back towards the contact.

I had been so preoccupied with treating the casualties that I had lost sight of the entire platoon. But I could hear their comms over my PRR. They must have been very close. There was the occasional burst of gunfire. I could hear the higher-pitched rounds of 5.56mm ammunition, indicating that Sierra Three Zero Delta had started to engage from their overwatch position.

'FORDY!' I called. 'Where the fuck are you?!'

He yelled back, 'Over the fence!'

Between us was the steel fence that separated the hospital from the pavement. I had somehow pushed forward and rejoined the rest of the fire team who were in the hospital grounds, using the fountains and statues in the garden as cover.

The fence was eight feet high.

'How did you get over that?!' I asked myself and Fordy at the same time. 'Jump over! FUCKING JUMP!'

I got over the fence and landed in a heap on the other side as another burst of fire was let loose. I didn't hear any impacts. Were they shooting at me? Were the guards shooting back? I crawled behind a low wall that acted as a partition between the gardens and the doorway to the hospital. Another burst of fire. I wriggled out of my patrol pack again and peeked over the wall. Fordy gave me a target indication of where Rob and his team were firing. I laid my weapon to roughly face the target area and looked through my sights. A single gunman dressed in dark clothing disappeared behind a wall, similar to the one in front of me. It looked like it could have been made from spare building material from the building site to act as an improvised barricade; breeze blocks or thin concrete slabs. I saw where he disappeared and immediately fired two shots into where I thought he would be behind the wall. I didn't know whether my rounds would have enough velocity to penetrate it. At the very least they might convince him not to re–emerge. There was less than 100m between us and the roof of the building opposite. But with a bridge and a river in between us it was risky to try to get any closer. I got back into cover and shifted my position. I was calming down and could see Fordy in cover nearby, breathing hard. That was the first time I had ever seen him out of breath. It had gone quiet. There was no traffic. Everyone who could had retreated inside the hospital. I looked behind me and saw nothing. The car that the IZP had wanted to check was not there. There was only a pool of blood where the police officer had crawled to, and bloodstains leading to the hospital gate. There were discarded bandage wrappers and chunks of broken pavement. And there was silence.

Chapter Twenty-five

Sierra One Zero, 1 Platoon, were the QRF and joined us within minutes. The contact seemed to have ended. More reinforcements arrived in the form of the armoured Snatch Land Rovers of the Royal Military Police. Our platoon had regrouped and pushed to the far side of the river bank, close to the built-up area where we had been taking fire. We took positions along the road, using traffic barriers and the steep river bank for cover. It was quiet now, but it was impossible to confirm whether there would be a follow-up attack. We waited. Behind one of the Snatches, the officers confirmed their next moves and reported back to the ops room. Mr Sherwood ordered us back to the hospital, deciding that there was no need to push forward into a potentially more hazardous situation.

The RMP began to set up a crime scene around the pools of blood and the hospital entrances. They rolled yellow tape onto traffic cones and started taking photographs of the floor. The bright flashes did not seem very tactical. But then again, if someone was watching, the flashes were not giving away our location. It was obvious where we were and what we were doing. 1 Platoon was deployed to provide all-round defence, while 3 Platoon prepared to ascend the building from where the gunfire had come. The RMP wanted to ensure it was clear of insurgents before securing any evidence.

Metal Mickey was the driver of one of One Zero's vehicles. Knowing there was a water supply on board, I wanted to wash the blood off my hands and arms.

'Mickey,' I called as I approached.

He turned and looked at me.

'Yeah, mate?'

I pointed at the cargo panel on the side of the Wolf that I knew contained bottles of water.

'Grab a bottle and help me wash this blood off, will you?'

He looked at my arms. From fingertip to elbow they were dark red, almost brown. I looked at the gore and rested my back against the side of the Land Rover. Mickey opened a two-litre bottle and slowly poured it over my hands and arms. I tried to rinse off as much blood as I could. The clear water turned red before hitting the ground. I looked at my boots and the knees of my combats, also bloodstained. 'That's not going to wash out', I thought to myself. Mickey finished pouring. He said nothing.

'Thanks,' I replied to his silent query, and rejoined my multiple.

'You all right, Matty?' Drewy asked, passing me a smoke.

I took it.

'Yeah, all good. You?'

He inhaled a lungful of smoke and then laughed, infectiously; soon the whole platoon was chuckling.

'We was lucky, boys. We was lucky,' Stick said.

I looked at Planty, whose hand was bleeding. I pointed at him and said, 'Let me have a look, mate.'

He explained that while running from one position to another, he had tripped and landed on a large wooden splinter. There was nothing inside the wound, so I wiped it down with alcohol and dressed it with a bandage.

'Clumsy twat. You'll need to see the medics at camp for some antibiotics, I reckon.'

He nodded, and Rob joined in: 'Lazy wanker was eating some Haribo, leaning against a wall when it all kicked off!'

We all started laughing again as Planty produced some jelly sweets from his pocket and offered them around.

He insisted, 'I was in a good position.'

L2 countered, 'A good position for eating sweeties.'

We continued talking until Mr Sherwood joined us. We moved up to the river and crossed the short bridge in pairs, forming up outside the building from where the incoming fire had originated. It was four storeys high and on the riverbank. A brand-new chain and padlock secured the rusted door to the foyer. The building looked like it had once been a hotel or the offices of a small corporation. Planty, L2, Rob and Mr Sherwood prepared to enter. The rest of us took up positions outside

CHAPTER TWENTY-FIVE

under Fordy's direction. We were to provide security but were ready to be called in if needed.

'Did anyone bring bolt croppers?' asked the lieutenant, probably rhetorically.

Of course, we didn't. We were already fully loaded down. Instead, Rob ripped the chain from the rusted door handle within a few powerful tugs. The door opened, and they looked inside.

Another question from the officer: 'Does anyone have a torch?'

Some of us had LLMs on our weapons, which would have sufficed, but I did also have a large Maglite police-style torch with me. Its size made it a good club-type weapon as opposed to a device for illuminating dark spaces. I took it out of my belt kit and handed it over. Cautiously, the four men went inside.

It seemed risky to go in. As we waited, I thought there was probably a better strategy. But I wasn't the boss. CQB (Close Quarters Battle) had not been part of our pre deployment package. It probably should have been. I certainly hadn't done any of that training since my infantry course, the year before. Without a doubt, they would have discussed and conferred on what to do and how to do it, though, and agreed that a limited push into the contact area was warranted. Soon enough, the team exited the building, declaring it clear.

'Empty shell,' said Mr Sherwood as he picked up his radio handset to send a further SITREP.

Rob filled us in on the rest of the details as we made our way back to the RMP cordon: 'There was blood and bullet casings on the roof. Some bloody rags. But no bodies. Whoever was up there got away before we arrived. Best to let the red caps do their thing and pass the story back to us when they can.'

I looked at my watch. It had been a little under three hours since we first deployed.

We made our way back to the Palace while 1 Platoon carried out a security patrol. The RMP finished up and left.

'Couldn't they have given us a lift?!' Planty asked as they drove away.

As we passed the hospital, I saw a woman dressed in black hitting her head against a wall. She was shrieking and screaming something over and over. It looked like she was going to beat herself unconscious.

Other women, also in black, surrounded her. They didn't move. Nobody intervened. I guessed she was processing some awful grief. None of them looked at us as we went past. Other than that party of mourners, there seemed to be no life in the hospital. It seemed eerie and dark. I looked at the tall sides of the building and realized that none of the lights were on. There were motionless shadows in some of the windows. It felt like they were watching us. Everything was black and white, like a scene from an Edgar Allan Poe story. I looked back to my front and continued patrolling. By the time I looked at the hospital again, the street lights were illuminating the pale walls, the interior lighting was on and the mourners were gone. 'What?' I turned as I patrolled, keeping the hospital in view while walking backwards for a few metres. Then I turned to my front. My mind went back to the task at hand: returning safely to the Palace.

Chapter Twenty-six

We attended a debriefing for our patrol. Mr Evans and Captain Roberts wanted the full picture so that they could report the incident to the battlegroup HQ. There had been several contacts over the preceding days, and the Intelligence Corps were trying to build a comprehensive picture of the situation in Basra. The major informed us about a rocket attack that happened the day before, and linked it to that night's contact. 1 Platoon, who were the QRF for that incident as well, had been dispatched to find and secure the firing point.

'They made good use of their interpreter and quickly found the firing point', the major said, indicated a position on a large map affixed to the briefing room wall. 'They remained on task for approximately five hours until ATO and the RMP were able to secure valuable forensic evidence from the scene.'

That brought us to our contact.

'We're working on int that suggests that these were coordinated attacks aimed at the hospital. With either overstretched or no medical services in the city, medical provision will need to be provided by the CPA, and we simply do not have the resources to treat the whole population.'

Mr Sherwood led the debrief and spoke for the majority of the platoon. Nobody interrupted or corrected anything that he said. He seemed to have a good grasp of what had happened. I gave a report on the casualties, noting that they had been alive by the time they had been received by the hospital security guards.

'Unfortunately, following your contact, the casualties did not survive', the major told me after I had sat back down.

I let out a long nasal sigh and bit the inside of my cheeks; a childhood habit that I used to employ when I felt myself getting upset. There wasn't much else in the debrief. I didn't hear it anyway, but as everyone got up to leave, I did as well, and we headed back to our room. We were all still in our patrol kit, so after getting changed I went straight to the shower to clean up.

There was a limited water supply, and each soldier was allowed only sixty seconds of flowing water from the lorry trailer that comprised the shower block. Twenty seconds to get wet, twenty seconds to wash and twenty seconds to enjoy. I went back to my bunk and grabbed a snack from my kit bag, then fell asleep.

Surprisingly, my rest was untroubled and undisturbed. I woke up feeling refreshed, full of energy and in the mood for corn flakes. The rest of the platoon were up before me and had not tried to wake me as they were getting ready for breakfast. Mr Roberts came into our room and let us know that the RMP would be taking statements from us during the day. I rolled out of my pit and put my blood-soaked uniform back on. My spare uniform was still in the dhobi (laundry), being boil-washed somewhere. There was no way I was going to breakfast covered in gore, so I went to see Mark in the company stores. He had a list of what everyone had on issue. I handed him the soiled uniform and he checked the tags for the sizes. It felt surprisingly liberating to be standing around in my shreddies with the air conditioner keeping me cool. The new uniform arrived, fresh out of the pack. I threw the clothes on and noticed that the sleeves didn't have a UK flag.

'Don't you have one with the Union Flag?'

He shook his head. 'That's all we have, Matty. Sorry.'

I asked him as a favour, 'Can you cut the flags off the old one then? I'll sew them on when I have time.'

He obliged, producing a Leatherman tool from his pocket and handing me the small badges, no larger than a postage stamp.

'Have you seen the company orders?' he asked.

Every day, the 2i/c produced a set of printed orders and distributed a copy to each multiple commander. I hadn't seen them yet because I had only just woken up.

'Nope. Probably about all the action from yesterday, isn't it?'

He slid a copy across the countertop:

Right: The author, nineteen years old, at Wyvern Barracks in Exeter. The photograph was taken during basic training, and by the time my compulsory call-up notice had arrived I had less than a month of experience in the Army.

Below: A mix of cap badges – the D&Ds, the LI and the RGBW at HMS *Raleigh* during basic training. The Rifle Volunteers were made up of infantrymen from south-west England.

Above: Training for the heat of Iraq in the snow of Dartmoor. Broz is closest to the camera.

Below: Arrival in theatre. Saxon armoured vehicles were our main transport. Once at the Palace we transitioned to unarmoured Land Rovers.

Above left: The old Ba'ath party HQ after the RAF had redecorated it. The area became a training venue for troops deployed to Basra.

Above right: Public order training. The author and Fordy, along with two others.

Getting ready to mount up into a Saxon armoured vehicle.

3 Platoon. (L to R) Rear rank: Drewy, Uzi, L2, Lt Sherwood, Rob, Elvis. Front rank: Thewy, Stick, Planty, Mick, Fordy, Author, Broz, Cpl Parsons.

Taking a break. (L to R) L2, Drewy, Rob, Elvis.

A Chinook coming in to land at Basra Palace. Most personnel were dropped off by helicopter after a VBIED had destroyed the junction that led to the Palace.

The author at the front gate.

Right: A GPMG ready to go and the view from the front gate.

Below: On patrol in Basra. A semirural area south of Basra Palace.

Uzi returns to the vehicles after dismounting somewhere near to the Shatt al-Arab Hotel.

Cpl Foster from 2 Platoon on the main road between Basra Palace and Basra Hospital. 3 Platoon came under fire from the abandoned building in the background a few weeks earlier.

Right: On patrol with the IZP (local police).

Below: Taking a break in 'Mitan', a village close to Basra Palace.

Bottom: 3 Platoon and ATO in the marshes. Bomb disposal teams were regularly called out and needed an escort to accompany them.

Left: Cpl Parsons and Lt Sherwood confirm details with an IZP police officer.

Below: The author on his twentieth birthday, preparing a Snatch Land Rover for patrol.

CHAPTER TWENTY-SIX

> During last night's GDA patrol, C/S S30A came under small arms fire in the area on PINK 19. They immediately returned fire in accordance with Card A and effectively suppressed and defeated their attackers. 2 civilian casualties, who were the initial targets of the gunmen, were treated in an efficient and professional manner by the team medic, Pte Okuhara, assisted by LCpl Ford, until they could be evacuated to the hospital. Although they subsequently died of the massive injuries that they had sustained, there is no doubt that this prompt action stabilised the casualties and gave them a better chance of survival than they would otherwise have had. C/S S30A then secured the area and awaited the RMP investigation team; who congratulated the C/S for an extremely efficient and well set up cordon location. Throughout the incident the patrol sent back accurate reports which enabled Coy HQ to co-ordinate and control the situation efficiently.

'Hmmm', I mused as I took in the report. 'Not how I remember it'. But then again I had been so focussed on my task that there was no way that I could have taken in the full picture. That was the officer's job. I remember seeing him crouched behind a wall, speaking into his radio as the rest of the platoon engaged. There had been some playful banter about the officer hiding and letting his blokes do the work, but we knew that he was expected to coordinate as well as fight. We privates only had to focus on one thing at a time. To be fair, he did have a lot on his plate during the contact.

Half of the multiple had conducted a patrol led by Corporal Parsons earlier that morning. To make up for the shortfall in numbers, a few of the HQ multiple had back-filled, giving them an opportunity to get out on the ground. Once they were back in and ready for the next tasking, we were assigned to the gate. Fordy had brought a can of Fanta with him and stuck it in the guard room freezer.

'We'll have that later, yeah?'

I was looking forward to it. It would make a change from water or over-diluted squash.

'About last night,' I began. 'Were you with the casualties as well?'

I didn't remember seeing him.

'Yeah, mate', he answered matter-of-factly.

I didn't ask or try to clarify anything else. By the time he had spoken in the debrief I had retreated to my own thoughts, replaying the last words of the Iraqi policeman – 'I've been . . . sh . . . shot.' I just put it down to perceptual distortion, owing to the stress of the situation. We grabbed our equipment and climbed the spiral staircase to the top of the gate, ready to begin our duty.

I liked being at the top of the gate. Not only was it well fortified, it also had a GPMG, flares, a searchlight and plenty of ammunition. It felt safe up there. It was also so high up that nobody usually bothered whoever was on guard duty, or 'top cover' as we usually called it. It was easier just to make a radio call, and even easier just to leave us alone. There was a bucket on a rope for water and supplies to be passed up and down. In all, it felt pretty cosy. I leaned my body against the sandbags that reinforced the concrete aperture giving us a view onto the main approach to the Palace. I took the binoculars to check the road, whilst Fordy unloaded the gimpie and began to check and oil the mechanism. I could hear the working parts clicking and sliding as he finished up.

'Anything out there?' he asked.

'Nope.'

Below us and around fifty metres ahead was the front *sangar* and traffic barrier. I could see through my binoculars that they were doing the same as Fordy and I. The signaller who drove the 432 was sitting in his compartment with his head poking out. A signaller with a maroon beret sat on top of the APC talking to him. I had seen him around and assumed he was the NCO in charge of that detail. He seemed pretty hostile most of the time. I had bumped into him at breakfast once as I was filling up cups with orange squash. I grabbed the four cups in both hands and began taking them back to my seat.

'Thirsty are you? Need a little bit of squash?' the signaller asked, with just enough venom to know he was trying to be offensive.

'We are in the desert', I answered, not really realizing that he was trying to wind me up.

'We're in the desert, *Corporal*', he countered.

CHAPTER TWENTY-SIX

It took me a few seconds to really figure out what he was getting at, but then I saw he had a single stripe on his uniform.

Another Gloster who was near me, Kav, heard the exchange and said, 'Fuck off you muppet, he's one of mine.'

Kav was a big man. People generally did what he said without too much argument. It seemed that the signaller was unhappy with the 432 driver as well. The heat of Basra certainly brought out the worst in people from time to time.

Chapter Twenty-seven

The closest anyone got to time off while on ops was QRF duty. The Quick Reaction Force provided the 'blue light services' for the company and was designated to respond to unforeseen incidents or to reinforce units out on patrol. They rested in an air-conditioned, blacked-out ready room and waited until needed. If they were not needed they did nothing and pretty much enjoyed a day off. The downsides were that you could never be more than a few metres away from the ready room, had to sleep with your boots on and had to cope with the boredom of inactivity if you weren't sleeping. Typical pastimes included board games, chess, two-week-old newspapers and knock-off DVDs provided by the little entrepreneurs who visited the *sangars* when we were on guard duty.

On more than a few occasions, of course, the QRF had to deploy. There was normally no time for a briefing. We would scramble to the waiting vehicles and try to get ready as we made our way to either the front or rear gate. The patrol commander would get the information via radio, while the rest of us prepared for a 'worst-case scenario' unless told otherwise. It was usually a good idea to assume the worst, as the QRF was not typically required for routine patrol or guard activities.

I can't remember my first QRF shift. It must have passed without incident, and I probably slept through it. I do remember early on in the tour, after our incident at the hospital, that we were deployed to assist 2 Platoon at a cordon they had set up in the heart of the city. They were the closest British unit, sent to assist an American private security unit hit by an IED. Upon arrival, they found two burnt-out armoured SUVs that the Yank security teams seemed to favour. They had loaded their casualties onto their remaining vehicles and made a beeline for the

CHAPTER TWENTY-SEVEN

closest medical facility at Shaibah. 2 Platoon was tasked with securing the wrecked SUVs until they could be recovered. Apparently, valuable kit was still aboard; the insurgent media publishing a victory over the invaders would score valuable propaganda points, which would do nothing to improve the security situation.

With only one multiple on patrol and several junctions to cover, 3 Platoon, on QRF, was sent to assist in creating the cordon. We were out of the base and on our way in minutes, still unsure of the threat level to the platoon on the ground. In many cases, IED blasts were followed by opportunistic, well-concealed attacks. The bad guys knew how we worked and often exploited Coalition procedures to cause disruption or casualties. Joining 2 Platoon, however, put a full thirty guys on the ground. A big target, certainly, but a heavily armed one – something that could not be taken on spontaneously and without at least some level of coordination.

After jumping off the wagon, I linked up with Jim, a friendly Welshman from the Glosters who was also the 2 Platoon medic. Jim had been in the TA for about three years and, like the rest of us, had not expected to be mobilized. He confirmed there were no casualties left; they had been treated and evacuated by their own people.

'I kind of envy them,' he told me as we surveyed the damage.

It was a very 'classic' war scene. The two vehicles were burnt-out wrecks. There couldn't have been anything of value left aboard, despite what the Yanks said. The wrecks were still smoking, the fire brigade having left after dousing them with water for a few minutes and returned to the fire station next door to the Shatt al-Arab Hotel. Most of 2 Platoon were in position, preventing access to the junction, while Iraqi coppers were enforcing a diversion. That left 3 Platoon to patrol the immediate area and disrupt any hostiles who might try to take advantage of the situation.

I asked Jim, 'How are you jealous?'

The private security contractors seemed to get hit all the time, certainly at a higher rate than conventional military forces.

'Well, they do the same as us, really. In fact, I would say they do less. But I spoke to a couple of those guys in the CPA compound, and they are on serious money.'

Now I could see where he was going.

'And what do we get? A grand a month?'

'Something like that,' I agreed.

In truth, as reservists, our wages varied depending on what profession we had left, matching our previous pay so that we didn't end up out of pocket.

He had a good point, however. The private contractors performed a very specific function in Basra which on the face of it did not seem too different from our regular patrols. They were usually well-armed with a variety of weapons, ranging from US-made M4s to AK47s, and everything in between. They were (apparently) well-trained, mostly ex-military types, and all seemed to wear very nice khaki trousers, custom-fitting boots and expensive sunglasses. I, on the other hand, had sewn my uniform back together a few times and wore sunglasses bought from the carousel at a service station somewhere between Okehampton and Hastings. And Jim was right – they earned a lot of money. I would be lucky if I could afford a second-hand car on return to the UK. Those living the American Dream would probably be able to afford a brand-new motor, and a trip to Disneyland to boot.

But their line of work did seem a bit 'murky' to me. Sometimes referred to as mercenaries, the security contractors were usually employed to provide protection to commercial concerns that would otherwise be vulnerable. This could mean protecting executives, or facilities, or accommodation complexes for local workforces. On the face of it, this seemed very sensible, but when I thought about it I realized that the only people with the kind of money required to raise a private security force, or with interests that could afford this very expensive kind of protection, were foreign companies, usually American. Therefore, very little money was going into the local economy. To me it seemed ghoulish that some corporations were fighting over the corpse of the city to further their bottom line. But business is business. The counter-argument, that 'the West broke it, the West should fix it', also didn't sit too well. After all, it was a deeply unpopular conflict that was looking more and more spurious as time went on.

During the QRF shift, the platoon had returned and refuelled the vehicles. We were set and ready to go. We were ready, if required, to be deployed into the city within three minutes of being dispatched. Back in the ready room, Stick produced his folding DVD player and inserted

CHAPTER TWENTY-SEVEN

his latest acquisition, *Love Actually*. A romantic film, more commonly referred to as a 'chick flick', it was good enough to kill a couple of hours, especially seeing as Keira Knightley was en vogue at the time, and we'd already seen *Bad Boys 2* several times.

The privates in the QRF team had to take turns sitting in the ops room to act as runner or liaison between the officers and the QRF. After watching the first part of the movie, Elvis returned and we swapped places. I took my seat in the ops room, where Mr Evans was coordinating Salamanca Company. The signals sergeant, Sergeant Pinnel, was on duty too, along with Pat. There was a box of worn-out old magazines of a mildly pornographic nature next to the runner's chair, and I rummaged around for one that I hadn't read yet. A fair few of them had been sent over by my older brother, but they had now become communal property. Time always passed slowly in the ops room. I was glad I wasn't a signaller and spending the vast majority of the tour dealing with radio calls. But then again, they probably felt the same way about the multiples that had to do guard duty, gate duty and patrols.

It wasn't long before I got bored sitting in the ops room, so I stepped out to grab a broom and began sweeping up the accumulation of sand and dust that formed every few hours. It was marginally better than watching the clock. Marginally. The major looked up from his maps and notes.

'Cleanliness is next to godliness, sir,' I commented.

'Are you a religious man?' he asked.

'When it suits me.'

I hadn't really thought about it too much. My understanding was that the phrase meant that spiritual cleanliness and physical cleanliness were both important to maintaining a healthy life. I was sure there was room for argument from more than one perspective about that particular saying. The phrase also features in a song by an American rock band called The Smashing Pumpkins that was on one of my minidiscs. That was probably how it entered my head in the first place.

'Would you like a brew, sir?' I added as I put the broom back. 'I'll go and put the kettle on. Pat? Sarge?'

I brought in the drinks and handed Pat his cuppa.

'Sweeping, tea . . . Cinderella at your service. Let me know if you need any sewing done.'

Broz came to replace me after a couple of hours, and I went back to the ready room and lay down on one of the beds. A few of the platoon were watching another DVD, but most by now had grown tired of the showcase and decided to catch up on a few hours of sleep. We needed it. All of us had been working hard and operating on sleep snatched whenever we could manage it. I woke up while everyone else was still asleep. Checking my watch, I saw it was very early in the morning. I left the ready room to get some light from the hallway and sat on the floor outside to write a few letters home. I folded them and put them in my pocket. Feeling restless and not particularly tired any more, I stepped out to the QRF vehicles and jumped aboard one of them. I picked up my belt kit, checked it and laid it back down again. Holding onto one of the roll bars, I looked up and saw that the constellations in the sky were exactly the same as those back home in the UK. I knew the light of the closest star to Earth took four years to reach our planet. 'What was I doing four years ago?' I asked myself. I would have been fifteen and had not yet completed my GCSEs. I picked out some of the familiar patterns in the night sky. Some of the starlight would have taken generations to reach Earth. It reminded me of JFK's speech about all of us living under the same stars and breathing the same air. He was right. But even that eloquent and intelligent man couldn't prevent conflict breaking out. I thought back to earlier, when the major asked me if I was religious. I still didn't know.

Later that morning, the CSM came into the ready room and asked Mr Sherwood if he could come to the briefing room. Normally, that kind of message was a job for the ops room runner, not the CSM, so we had no idea what was going on. If it needed the CSM, it must have been important. They came back.

'Matt,' said Mr Sherwood, pointing to me and calling me outside.

I looked at the others quickly while getting up, but was only met with a few shrugs and blank stares. '

Yes, sir?'

I went to join the CSM and lieutenant.

'Job for you. General Stewart is visiting the lines and will stop in to see Mr Evans and Mr Roberts as part of a tour of the Palace. Stand by that table and give him a cup of tea if he wants one.'

CHAPTER TWENTY-SEVEN

I looked at the CSM.

'The OC said you're a chatty little twat, so if the general starts talking to you, you could at least manage a conversation. And you don't have an accent, so he'll understand what you're saying.'

I didn't know how I felt about that. Hardly a QRF task. But it was an 'unexpected' job, so I suppose that fitted the brief. The ready room was still only just down the corridor, so I was close to hand if the platoon was needed to deploy.

'Okay, sir,' I told him. 'Now?'

'Yes, now. You've got time for a quick piss and a smoke if you want but be back here ASAP.'

I went to my station by the table and made sure I had everything I needed to make a quality cup of tea. I had never met a general before. There was a generous number of biscuits next to the kettle, and I made sure to pocket the best ones while nobody was around.

An armoured Land Rover arrived outside the accommodation, and Mr Evans guided the general right past me and into the ops room. They didn't even look at me or break stride. His bodyguard followed behind, carrying an MP5 and wearing civilian clothing. He stood outside the ops room and looked at me. I looked at him.

'Tea?' I picked up the kettle in eager anticipation.

'What did you do wrong to get this shitty job?' he asked, indicating that he wanted two sugars in his brew.

'Apparently I'm a "chatty little twat" and therefore suitable for tea duties,' I told him. 'I don't mind, though. Biscuit?'

He took a digestive. All the Hobnobs were in my pocket. The general emerged with the major and saw me.

'Tea?'

He looked a little surprised. Maybe hot drinks on a hot day were not to the general's liking. The bodyguard was happily sipping from his polystyrene cup, however.

'No, thank you. Actually, yes. Milk, no sugar.'

'Certainly, sir.'

I passed him the cup. 'It was nice of you to come and visit, sir. I'm sure the entire company appreciates you taking the time.'

The major was ushering him towards the briefing room.

'Well, oh, yes, very good. Thank you.'

They disappeared. The bodyguard took a handful of biscuits. When they emerged after a few minutes, the major told me to get the QRF to kit up and to send Mr Sherwood to the ops room. I did as I was told.

'Why have we got to get kitted up? Job?' Uzi asked.

'Some kind of job, I guess. The boss is having a briefing now.'

We boarded the vehicles and started the engines. When Mr Sherwood joined us he informed us over the PRR that we had to escort the general from the Palace to his next location.

'Escort his escort, more like,' Drewy noted as he settled into the driver's seat.

We did seem a little superfluous. The general already had a heavily armed RMP call sign with him. On the other hand, how often does a British Army general get a Territorial Army escort in a conflict zone? Probably never. Nobody saw it as a privilege. Maybe the major did. But he wasn't coming with us. It was more of a pain in the arse for most of us. I heard some grunts and muttering, but I thought it was great. I liked to be on patrol and out of the base. It was certainly better than explaining the rules of chess to Rob again, or trying to remember the answers from the Trivial Pursuit board game we had played countless times. We drove out of the Palace and headed to the Shatt al-Arab Hotel, where the general was based.

We had been to the Hotel numerous times. It was the HQ location for the British military in the south-east of Iraq, whereas the Palace was the HQ location for the Coalition Provisional Authority – the civilian component of the occupying forces. The Hotel was a heavily defended location in the middle of the city, and like the Palace, it sat on the banks of the Shatt al-Arab river. The base was home to the main component of the occupying troops. There were Warrior IFVs and Scimitar CVRTs going through maintenance and first works (pre-patrol checks). The jetty beside the Hotel had the Royal Engineer and Royal Marine river patrol craft tied up alongside. I noticed how much better equipped the troops at this base were than us. We were in unarmoured Land Rovers and carried no heavy weapons. Coming through the gates, we looked less like infantry and more like pirates. We all had *shemaghs* (desert scarves) to keep the dust off our faces as we drove, and dust goggles to protect our eyes. Of course, the stylish leader of our outfit had red-tinted Oakley ski

CHAPTER TWENTY-SEVEN

goggles, while the rest of us made do with the general issue equipment. A few looks were cast our way as we parked up and disembarked. Now that we were here, we had time to do a few admin tasks if we wanted before heading back to the QRF ready room.

As was their SOP, or Standard Operating Procedure, Uzi and Elvis sparked up as soon as they could, and remained with the vehicles so that the rest of us could head into the Hotel. I still had a few blueys in my pocket to drop off at the quartermaster and then went to a small office to see an AGC, Adjutant General's Corps pay clerk. I drew an advance against my wages so that I would have some pocket money for the next few weeks. There wasn't a lot to buy, but a few of the troops from the REME and Signals were running side hustles and selling goods that had been brought to them somehow. Mostly it was cigarettes, Irn Bru and shower gel, but I had heard from someone that Pop Tarts were also on offer somewhere – and they were my main objective while I was here.

Toaster pastries in hand, I went back to the Land Rovers and waited for the rest of the team to mount up. We began to make our way back to Basra Palace, driving through the city and carefully observing our surroundings. We could not afford to become slack in our routine, even if we were starting to feel like veterans. We knew that even the best-equipped soldiers were still at risk, as were the most skilled; the seasoned campaigners and the first-timers were, too, but the complacent were especially so. By now there were regular contacts with the insurgents and daily indirect fire on the British bases. We stopped at obstacles that could be booby-trapped or rigged with explosives, the small bridges that crossed irrigation ditches, for example, or busy junctions. We had to disembark and conduct checks to ensure we could safely traverse any potentially hazardous areas. It made a long journey longer and put us in dangerous positions, such as being stationary or without cover. Where possible, Drewy positioned our patrol in the centre of the road. Our ECM was active to try to disrupt remotely detonated IEDs. But if a device did go off on the side of the road, there would at least be a bit more space between us and the blast.

Our Land Rovers had wire-cutters fixed to them so that if any rope or cord was strung across the road, we would not be decapitated. We watched ahead as we drove to look out for any indications that IEDs had been placed in gutters or on lamp posts. Recently, a Warrior IFV had been disabled and a British soldier seriously wounded when a device made from an ice cream tub blasted stones and pieces of metal through the open driver's hatch. The vehicle was towed to Basra Palace by a REME recovery unit. Uzi and I watched the driver's seat being removed from the disabled IFV and saw the damage behind where the crewman's head would have been. Within a few hours, the whole battlegroup had been ordered to stay closed up where possible. In a separate incident on the same day, a soldier from the Royal Highland Fusiliers had been killed when an IED destroyed the armoured Land Rover he was patrolling in. Apparently, they had no ECM equipment, and their Snatch armoured car only offered the bare minimum of protection. Still, it was better than we had. Our vehicles did not have any armoured protection at all.

Chapter Twenty-eight

While the CPA was based at Basra Palace, Salamanca Company was responsible for manning the base's internal checkpoints. We thought this task would be better suited to the Royal Military Police (RMP) than the infantry, as it focused more on enforcing security procedures than on combat. At least on the guard towers and gates, we were looking out for external threats. On internal duties, we were assigned to checkpoints that separated the two main components of the Palace: the Army and the CPA.

To pass a checkpoint, individuals had to walk through, flashing their ID tags, which came in a myriad of languages. Normally, anyone within Basra Palace's boundaries was on legitimate business and would show their ID as they transacted their affairs.

Vehicles, however, were strictly prohibited entry without the correct paperwork, making this easier to manage. Most vehicles belonged to local contractors removing scrap or delivering materials for CPA employees. The Palace provided many jobs for locals seeking to earn American dollars, the currency used after the invasion. Jobs included fixing walls, emptying sewage, collecting scrap and other menial tasks outsourced to provide income to those in need.

Private security contractors also operated in the CPA area of the Palace, mainly Americans paid to secure US business interests in southern Iraq. Rebuilding and repairing properties in the city were dangerous tasks, necessitating a substantial logistical chain that required round-the-clock protection from the port at Al Faw Peninsula to wherever goods and services were needed. While on patrol, it wasn't unusual to see blacked-out SUVs crewed by private security teams for contracting companies, and the same contractors sunning themselves in the CPA compound when off duty.

While acting as QRF we were told to stand by and wait for further instructions, a not unusual occurrence. Sometimes we had to deploy straight into the city, while at other times we received a set of orders before deploying. On one occasion, the CSM, who was the overnight watch-keeper, sent us into the CPA compound to look for a missing gunner. He had enjoyed some American hospitality and likely needed help finding his way home. Not wanting to involve the RMP, and to keep things 'in house', the artillery had requested that the force protection company look for the guy, which we did.

This time, we were sent to the internal checkpoints, splitting the call sign in two. One of our vehicles went to Charlie One, and the other to Charlie Two. From there, we were to assist in internal security matters.

'2 Platoon struggling with the gates?' Stick asked. 'Nothing much to it. Open, close, open, close.'

He was right. We were a bit confused as to why the internal security gates needed reinforcements. Mr Sherwood did not come with us as he was receiving a full briefing on the situation, so instead, Rob and Corporal Parsons took us out.

We jumped out, much to the surprise of Foggy from 2 Platoon, who was manning one of the gates.

'Need to come through?' he asked, assuming we were heading into the CPA compound.

Foggy was the next youngest in the company, probably only a month or two older than me – a teenager. He had designs on joining the artillery and was so skinny that Fordy reckoned they could probably slide him into the barrel of one of their big guns to clean it.

'Nah, we're here to help on the gates,' Rob said.

'Oh.'

Foggy didn't feel the need for any further elaboration – but we all did. It seemed like a bone task (bone in army speak means 'pointless or without purpose').

Charlie One, the checkpoint we were at, was just a few metres south of the CPA headquarters. This impressive old building was the hub for all civil decisions in the city and is now the 'Basra Cultural Museum'. At the time, it formed the northernmost part of the CPA compound and was usually occupied by various civil and military bodies concerned with the

CHAPTER TWENTY-EIGHT

running of the city. Charlie Two was not too far away, near the rear gates of the Palace, where the other half of the QRF had headed.

We manned the gates and waited until we either received a full briefing or were returned to stand-by.

'Well, it must be something,' Stick mused. 'If we're here, that means there's no QRF for whoever's out on patrol.'

We knew we could be redeployed, but he raised an interesting point. What was serious enough to warrant sending the QRF to reinforce the internal checkpoints? We soon found out.

We returned to stand-by after being out for less than an hour. Even so, the air-conditioned room was a relief from the heat. The internal gates lacked any decent cover from the fierce sun during the day, or any reprieve from the baking concrete ground at night. After checking the vehicles over and replacing our equipment, we got back to killing time by playing board games and re-watching movies.

Mr Sherwood, who had not joined us earlier, gathered us in to let us know what had happened.

'So I guess you want to know why we were sent out.'

We did want to know. Our speculation had landed on the possibility of unpaid locals getting pissed off and forcing themselves through the compound in search of their wages, or even just a 'test run' to see how quickly the QRF could attend an incident within the confines of the Palace.

'The CPA is being closed down, as you know, and control will revert to a local authority – with an elected mayor and officials.'

We knew that, too. What we did not know was that the currency would be changing as well.

'When the CPA pulls out, they will be taking their American currency with them . . . Well, they would like to have done. It seems that rather a lot of it has gone missing. And seeing as Salamanca Company was on internal checkpoints, it must have come through us at some point. The CPA is blaming the missing cash on us.'

The CPA building had a large basement level which acted as a bank for the cash needed to accomplish CPA tasks. The contractors paid the CPA for withdrawals and paid the locals with dollar bills. The old Iraqi money with Saddam's picture on it was not worth much. As part of the change between dollars and dinars, the CPA had packed up piles of money in preparation to sending it back to the States.

The boss added, 'But whoever was working at the CPA has managed to remove that money within the last twenty-four hours. The CPA is blaming the Army. The Army is blaming the RMP, who in turn are blaming the force protection company. You were deployed just in case the CPA wanted to lock down the Palace.'

'How much?' Uzi asked.

Millions. In cash. They would have needed a lorry. Several probably.'

'They would have needed paperwork, too,' Rob added. 'It was more than likely an inside job. A heist. People with knowledge, access and authority would have been needed to pull off that kind of thing.'

Rob seemed unusually knowledgeable about this subject.

For my part, it reminded me of the George Clooney movie, *Three Kings*, in which a rogue American unit tries to steal Iraqi gold.

'Anyway,' Mr Sherwood continued, 'the major has to go to the hotel to offer an explanation, so get yourselves fed and mount up at 1500; we'll be taking him there and back.'

Chapter Twenty-nine

I was driving for a change. Normally, our regular drivers handled this task. It wasn't an official appointment, but Drewy and Stick preferred to drive, just like Elvis preferred to carry the LMG and Broz liked the baton gun. We were all trained for these tasks, but occasionally we rotated duties.

To drive to the hotel, there were basically two routes. One was straight up the middle, through the city in a straight line. While faster and easier, it also carried more risks. The other route involved driving south, leaving the city, and coming back through a village known as Al Dawoodia. It took twice as long, if not more, but once we were out of the city and in the relatively flat open areas of the southern villages and farms, there was less opportunity for ambushes. The roads were regularly patrolled by the RLC and other Coalition call signs, keeping the area clear so convoys could move unimpeded in or out of the city.

I enjoyed driving in the semi-rural and rural parts of Basra. Driving in the city was exhausting, not only for the driver but for the entire vehicle crew, who had to remain extra vigilant and regularly disembark to walk alongside the vehicles or conduct checks on road furniture and obstacles. Driving in the desert was better, but there wasn't much to see – just a vast open expanse of white nothingness, as if an animator had forgotten to draw on a piece of paper. The villages, however, were usually colourful and almost enjoyable to pass through. When we stopped, friendly kids would come looking for a bit of pocket money or some sweets from our rations. The men and women were usually pleased to see us, a different kind of Basran to those who lived in the concrete jungle.

It was odd to see the major in his kit. Normally, he hung around the ops room, but now he was in the back of my Land Rover. He didn't seem to be in a talkative mood. I guessed he was either preparing an argument or livid about being called to account for something that had nothing to do with him. I couldn't see how Salamanca Company fitted into the heist. If we had been told to lock down the gates and failed to do so, I could understand that. And if we had been put in charge of securing the CPA compound, not just the military one, I could see a tenuous connection. Shit rolls downhill, though, and I guessed a few turds had landed on Mr Evans.

We had been to the Hotel only a few days before and were quite happy to be back. We knew the major's meeting would take a while. Since the Hotel was better resourced than the Palace, we were keen to access the internet and send a few emails. Uzi wanted to stock up on smokes again, and we all wanted some better food.

Of course, someone had to remain with each of the vehicles while we were waiting, so Broz and I took the first watch. There was a lot of equipment on board, and if several million dollars could go missing, then it might be even easier for a set of ECM or a load of belt kit to disappear as well.

I took out a pen and a bluey and started to write home about nothing in particular. I had recently received a bluey from a girl I had worked with at one point, and she had included a polaroid photograph. It didn't take long to write, and I put it in my pocket, ready to send. To pass the time, Broz and I talked about when we had joined the TA, at around the same time. Inevitably, the people you join up with end up becoming your closest friends as you go through so much together. Drewy had also been on our infantry course, making us by far the most junior soldiers in the company.

We were less than six weeks through the tour, but it felt like we had been in Iraq forever.

'You gonna join full time after this?' he asked.

'Probably not. You?'

'Maybe. I'm thinking about it. Seems all right to me.'

I didn't know what Broz's job was in Gloucester. It seemed to change regularly. All I knew was that he came to the TA centre on a motorbike and went home on it. Like the Fonz, but less of a rebel. We talked about our time in the Rifle Volunteers and waited for two of the others to come back so that we could make use of the base's welfare area.

CHAPTER TWENTY-NINE

After completing phase one, which is basic training, 'A' Company of the RGBW was sent to RAF Fairford to help with the Royal International Air Tattoo. There were several reasons for this. It was our local recruiting area, so Foz was running a recruiting stand; it was a good way for the volunteers to get a weekend's worth of money; and finally, we had to provide unarmed security to some of the emergency gates along the side of the airfield boundary. At the time, the base was hosting several American units key to the initial stages of the Iraq war, so having a few surplus local troops was seen as desirable.

Broz and I had not had much opportunity to speak to each other before Fairford, as we had been in different sections during training. But over the long RIAT weekend, it turned out we had more than a few shared interests. Music, for example. Broz wasn't a musician but liked similar artistes to me, and similar movies, too. That gave us plenty to talk about. By the time we were on the combat infantrymen's course we had become good friends, although I still had no bloody idea what he did for a living outside of the TA.

Whereas Broz and I always got on, not everyone in the company necessarily did. As in any large group of people, there were personality clashes and intangible factors that meant some people were mates and some weren't. I remembered going to one of the towers and seeing 'Okuhara is gay' scribbled onto the desk holding the radio and binoculars. I was annoyed to be singled out for attention but then laughed, satisfying myself with the thought that someone in the unit was my closeted secret admirer. Over the next few days, a running battle of messages evolved on the table – some defending my honour, others defaming it. I had also pissed off the RLC aid detachment, who now had to provide a vegetarian meal whenever I was on guard duty and couldn't get to the scoff house. Mr Sherwood had been annoyed with me from time to time due to the state of my uniform, which had holes that regularly needed sewing up. I also needed a haircut, and I had been told that if I didn't sort myself out, one of the NCOs would have to make sure I did. It was that kind of thing that put me off the military full-time; although I was doing what was expected of me, in many cases I was doing it differently from what was seen as normal. At least I didn't have to shave yet.

The major rejoined us a few hours after heading into a conference with the brigade commander. His spirits seemed to have lifted, although nobody asked about the outcome of the meeting. Nobody asked the reason for the meeting either. We were just the taxi service. It was now dark, and we made our way through Al Dawoodia and into the southern part of the city.

I was driving at a steady pace, but the lieutenant asked me to speed up, so I did. The problem was that we then regularly caught up with any traffic in front of us. Luckily, there wasn't much, but it happened every few minutes. As the MTO had told me at Willsworthy, I positioned the vehicle well ahead of time and made a long overtake before drifting back in.

'Fuckin' get a move on.'

Still too slow, apparently.

'Be more aggressive with your driving.'

'Yes, sir.'

I suspected the major was in the ear of the lieutenant, who in turn was urging me to get us back to the Palace quickly. I accelerated to around the top speed a Land Rover can achieve on a dirty and damaged road in southern Iraq and started cutting in and out of the traffic 'more aggressively'.

'What the fuck are you doing? I said be more aggressive, not "drive like a dick".'

It was lost on me. 'What?' I could see the major gazing at me in the rear view mirror, reminding me of the day the company assembled when I was late to join them. Even with my eyes back on the road, I thought I could feel him looking at me.

'All right, Fangio, just take it easy and try not to ram the locals off the road.' Apparently, things were starting to look like Mario Kart.

Thewy, who was driving the other wagon, and I were conducting the last parade before handing the vehicles over to the oncoming QRF. He shook his head and laughed.

'What you playing at?'

I told him, 'Mr Sherwood told me to drive more aggressively.'

That didn't stop the laughter or the head-shaking.

CHAPTER TWENTY-NINE

'I think what he meant was, "dominate" the road, not try to ram the other drivers.'

Well, that made a little more sense, but I decided that driving duties might be better left to Drewy, who unlike me didn't seem to attract any complaints. We handed over the vehicles and went back to the accommodation. We were due to be on patrol before first light, so needed a decent rest. I also had to sew up another hole in my combats before Fordy 'ripped off my arms and hit me with the soggy ends'.

Chapter Thirty

Even though we were on deployment, there was still regular training to do. Some basic training tasks served useful functions. For example, when we had to do weapon-handling tests, we could also check-zero our weapons. If we were in between patrols, we could practise contact drills. This was all done locally and was arranged by the 2i/c, who was in charge of company administration. Larger training manoeuvres, however, were handled by the battlegroup. Two months into the tour, we had to attend a refresher on public order training. This wasn't because our previous training had expired, but because intelligence suggested that with local elections just around the corner it would probably be a good idea to have plenty of troops available to deal with possible riots or civil disturbances.

We were deployed to an abandoned Iraqi Army base. It was actually the old HQ of the Ba'ath Party – Saddam Hussein's political party. Most of the facility had been bombed into rubble by the Royal Air Force, but the Royal Engineers had been busy tidying it up so it could become a training area for British forces. Along with a contingent of the PWRR from Al Amarah and some units from the Shatt al-Arab Hotel, we were due to practise dealing with petrol bombs.

We were transported by Saxon armoured vehicles. These large trucks were designed to be battle taxis during the Cold War, ferrying troops or equipment to and from low-risk areas. They were also useful for domestic patrol duties, such as during the Troubles in Northern Ireland. While not heavily armoured, they were still well protected enough to negotiate the more dangerous parts of the city. Being wheeled as opposed to tracked made them manoeuvrable, too, unlike the Warriors, which couldn't navigate a significant proportion of Basra's road network.

CHAPTER THIRTY

Sitting opposite L2 and Stick, I whipped out a disposable camera and took a quick shot.

'Candid moment,' I called as they looked at me quizzically.

Stick shook his head. The Saxon was cool and comfortable compared to what we were used to. Air conditioning had been retrofitted, and we actually had real seats instead of strapped-down equipment. When we arrived at the Ba'ath Party HQ we jumped out and grabbed our gear. Instead of belt kit and webbing, we had our combat jackets and riot armour, which offered some protection against flames and low-velocity impacts. We were armed with batons and perspex riot shields – or that was what we were supposed to be armed with. In reality, we had broom handles that Corporal Hill had drilled a hole in one end of to take a lanyard made of a bootlace. I fancied that a broom handle in the right hands could still leave a black eye, or worse. We also had fire extinguishers, and baton guns which fired 37mm rubber bullets.

Joining us for the next few days was an American Army combat cameraman. He had been assigned to get some images and footage of the 'Brits doing their thing'. How he ended up with a bunch of reservists from the south-west, I had no idea. He just turned up one day, as far as I could tell. But we liked having him around. I loved hearing him speak and always smiled when I heard the American idioms which just seemed to roll off the tongue. I think he said he was from Atlanta, Georgia. Likewise, he was fascinated by British slang, asking us about our words for cigarettes, British meatballs, and saying, 'What the hell is spotted dick?' Uzi seemed particularly knowledgeable in this regard and gave him all the information he could while he and Elvis had a couple of fags. He had trouble understanding Drewy, finding his Cornish accent almost impenetrable. Elvis translated as necessary, but his Bristol burr wasn't much better.

The baton gun shooting detail was very easy. A bunch of old mattresses had been crucified onto some telegraph poles, and we took turns blasting them. I picked up some of the ejected 37mm rounds and examined them. They were hard as fuck. I didn't fancy getting hit by one of those. I wondered how people would react if they were actually fired during a riot. I thought to myself, 'If some British squaddie turns up with a large-barrelled gun, fires it, and someone goes down –which they are guaranteed to do when hit by this solid lump – how are they going to know, in the heat of the moment, that their mate hasn't just been blown away by a large-calibre cannon?' I thought it might make things worse. But on the other hand, 'If things were so bad that rubber bullets were needed, then I'd rather shoot than try to open up negotiations.' I took my place at the improvised range and started firing alongside Broz and L2. The 'visual information specialist,' as our honorary 3 Platoon member introduced himself, took a battery of shots while we were training and encouraged us to pick up the rate of fire,

'Get to gettin'! Yeah! I'll send y'all some copies.'

To conduct the petrol bomb training we had to form into teams of four: one commander and three shields, left, middle and right. The commander would stand behind the middle shield and move the team as needed, while the front three protected their faces by curling an arm around the bottom of the riot visor. Failure to do so, we were warned, could result in the loss of eyebrows and nasal hair.

'That peacekeeping hair will probably catch fire, too,' the sergeant major running the training said, pointing to me.

My hair had got quite long and was in the messy 'peacekeeper' phase. I didn't mind having a bit of length up top, but in the desert heat, maybe he had a point. I decided I might get it buzzed off when I got back to the Palace. I actually knew the sergeant major, a friend of my older brother and a regularly player for the same rugby team. I surreptitiously asked if he could send an extra bottle or two our way so the cameraman could try to get some good images of 3 Platoon in action.

'Yeah, fine,' his answer came out, almost as one word.

During the training, the idea was to let the bomb land while the shields were down on the floor. This would stop petrol from seeping under the shields and onto our boots. After the impact, Fordy would move us forward to a point where we could conduct some other kind of action – using the batons, separating to let a team pass through to arrest someone, or surrounding the rioters to prevent further movement. These actions could then be replicated into larger schemes if needed, up to company strength.

We began. The bottle exploded in front of us. I was on the left, Uzi in the middle and Broz on the right. After the flames finished rolling off the shields, Fordy called, 'FORWARD!'

CHAPTER THIRTY

As one, we advanced slowly, so as not to break the folded corners linking our shields together.

'HALT!'

We stopped and slammed the shields down hard as one. Another bottle.

'FORWARD!'

We were off again. I couldn't see anything. My chin was against my chest, and my left arm was folded under my helmet visor to stop flames or fumes from reaching my face. My right arm held onto the shield handles. All I could see were the tips of my black boots and the bottom of the shield.

'HALT!'

Fordy separated Broz from the line as two PWRR came through with fire extinguishers. They blasted the fire and retreated behind us. We closed up.

'FORWARD!'

Standing off to the side, our US companion clicked away as he followed our advance. I tilted my head slightly and saw he wasn't risking getting too close.

As soon as we got back to the Palace we were dispatched directly to the hospital to provide protection for a chauffeur who had survived a shooting. A candidate for city mayor had been gunned down as he was driven to a venue where he was due to give a speech. He died, but his driver survived. Apparently, the gunmen were wearing police uniforms, so his security while he was undergoing treatment would be provided by the CPA, not the coppers. That was then delegated to the British Army, and then to Salamanca Company. Then to us.

Corporal Parsons ran external security with half of the multiple. The other half went into the hospital. I went inside the main doors with Mr Sherwood. The hospital was pretty much as expected: a waiting room with plastic chairs, a reception and signs indicating the routes to various departments. The difference I noticed from the hospitals I had been to during my short life was that many of those waiting to be seen were dead. And nobody was at reception. I would have said it was like a horror movie, but that would be to compare this harsh reality to fictional Hollywood entertainment.

There was a putrid, sickly-sweet smell in the air. Even without having smelled it before, I knew what it was. Flies buzzed around, landing on bodies and the dirty windows. A man walked past holding a baby whose sickly green colour contrasted with the white linen it was wrapped in. I had never seen that colour in anything or anyone before. He walked through reception and left the building. I watched as he exited and the door swung shut behind him. Looking back, I saw several motionless bodies in a part of the waiting room. They had blankets over their upper bodies and heads. There were long bags in the corridor. They all seemed to have someone in them.

'Matt!' The lieutenant was calling me. 'This way.'

Our interpreter, Jacob, had found where the chauffeur was being treated, and we went to his room. Along the way, Mr Sherwood positioned men from 3 Platoon at stairways and receptions. By the time we got to the room, it was only the three of us.

'He's had emergency surgery,' Jacob began. 'Now he needs to rest. He will be transferred to a secure facility where he can assist the investigation at some point tomorrow.'

Mr Sherwood nodded.

'They say he is not above suspicion himself.'

The lieutenant moved to a window, where it was easier to get a signal, and sent a SITREP. I sat on a plastic seat opposite the casualty's door.

'So are we just going to wait here, sir?' I asked.

We had not really had a briefing, apart from 'provide security'. It seemed very loose and lacking in detail, but achievable.

'1 Platoon will relieve us at midday tomorrow. Until then, yes. We wait.'

That would equate to a 36-hour patrol, including the public order training earlier in the day. Luckily, we had plenty of water. Food, on the other hand, was just whatever we had in our belts.

Our orders were not to let anyone into the room apart from medical staff, and then only if they would submit to a search first. The word had got around the hospital about the British Army being somewhere in the building. Our floor was quickly vacated – nobody wanted to risk being near a target for assassination. A doctor arrived, a short man in a white coat. Jacob explained to him that he would need to be searched. A brief exchange followed between the two, before the doctor threw up his arms

CHAPTER THIRTY

in frustration and walked back out the way he had come in. I looked into the room and saw that the chauffeur was not too badly injured. He was awake and bandaged around the midriff. No blood was seeping through, and he greeted me.

'*Salaam.*'

I nodded. '*Salaam.*'

Maybe it was only a flesh wound.

'Going to the toilet, boss,' I said, after noticing a sign to it at the end of the corridor.

I stepped into it, looked around, and came straight back out.

'On second thoughts, I'm fine for now.'

The facilities consisted of a large hole with a foot plate on either side. Apparently, the hole was hard to hit accurately, despite some valiant attempts and several near misses.

'Is it okay if I switch with Elvis? I'd rather be outside.'

The place was getting to me – the smell, the harsh lighting and the absolute quiet of our abandoned ward. At least outside the hospital, there would be life. And fresh air. Inside the hospital, there didn't appear to be either of those things.

As I went down the stairway I looked out of a window to the building opposite. On the other side of the river, it was the building that we had taken fire from two weeks earlier. It looked dark and empty. I studied the road outside the hospital and realized it was the one we had patrolled as we made our way back to the Palace after the contact. I must have been at one of the windows where I had seen the shadows looking at us. But this was a staircase, so why were all the shadows still and not ascending or descending? I guessed they were watching us, a little like I was watching the empty road right now. I made my way down and outside, boarded the Land Rover, looked out around the hospital grounds and rested my back against the roll bar. I took my helmet off. The evening breeze was humid but at least it felt cool for a few seconds as my sweat dried.

I felt something gently tap me on the head. My hand automatically went up to investigate the disturbance. Bird shit. 'Great. Is that lucky or unlucky? Both, probably.' I grabbed a bottle and cleaned my 'peacekeeping' hair, then got Stick on the PRR and asked him to come back to his wagon and move it forward a few feet. There was an overhang above the Land Rover and the associated risk of being subjected to more incoming bird shit. Stick looked tired. Almost on 'autopilot,' he got in, started up, moved, switched off and left. Normally he was chattier than that. He probably needed a cup of tea.

Jacob came outside for a smoke, although I couldn't see what harm it could have done inside.

'Jacob? Why hasn't anyone moved those bodies?'

He shrugged. I liked Jacob. He had a very French '*je ne sais quoi*' air about him.

'I think they are still trying to identify them and inform the next of kin.'

It seemed like a reasonable answer. It's not as if anyone had insurance to pay medical and undertaker costs, either. The morgue must have been full, and the slightly better-ventilated foyer of the hospital must have been the macabre waiting room for those awaiting identification. I put the thought to the back of my mind and continued my vigil.

Being in that hospital felt like purgatory. Time seemed to stop whenever I crossed the threshold of the building. I felt distinctly uncomfortable the whole time I was there. By the time 1 Platoon arrived, our entire multiple was thoroughly drained. It might have been fatigue, but I felt like the life had been sucked out of me. We did nothing but provide static security all night. We saw nobody and spoke to nobody – not even each other. Now, luckily, we were on QRF for twenty-four hours. That meant we should be able to catch up on some admin and some sleep. After setting up the vehicles and preparing our kit, we all went to the ready room and crashed. No showers, no smokes, no snacks. That could wait. I was asleep before my head hit the mattress.

Chapter Thirty-one

Corporal Parsons had taken the platoon out on patrol while the officers attended an orders group to discuss the arrival of new equipment. Lieutenants Sherwood, Thynn and Sparks were required to contribute their thoughts on the upcoming patrol strategy and the necessary logistics. The 'head shed' needed to arrange for better vehicles with armour, as well as more ammunition. We were only carrying 100 rounds per man, which would not last long in a protracted engagement. Since Mr Sherwood was not on patrol, Sierra Three Zero Alpha was also not on patrol. Instead, we had been loaned to the CQMS to complete the most loathed job in the military: sandbagging. We had a four-ton truck full of empty sandbags and a pile of sand, or more accurately, a pile of dirt. Sandbags are excellent defences – simple, strong and rapidly deployable. However, the downside was filling and carrying them, especially in the desert heat.

Salamanca Company had moved to a new accommodation block. With the elections over, the CPA was no longer required and had left the Palace, leaving us with some premium real estate. However, some areas needed to be fortified. The buildings we were using had served a civil organization, so while they were protected, they did not have the infrastructure an infantry company would need. We needed to build defences around the all-important smoking area, which had plastic lawn furniture and palm trees offering shade for troops looking to relax for a few minutes. We also had to build a POL point for storing spare petrol, oil and lubricants for the vehicles. We were expected to carry out all our own maintenance and only involve the REME if something was completely broken. We needed to sandbag the roof to lessen the impact of any indirect fire. Luckily, a different team would handle deploying the bags, but for now, our fire team, under Fordy and Corporal Hill, were filling the bags and loading them onto the truck.

I threw a filled sandbag over my shoulder, only for the seam to rip and the sand to pour down my back.

'Ah, fuck it! I'm having a break!'

I jumped onto the wagon to get some shade. Drewy joined me.

'Sandbagging. Someone's gotta do it, mate,' he said, looking for a smoke.

He was right. The sandbags wouldn't fill themselves, and there was nobody else to do it.

'Anyway, after this, we're on night patrols, yeah? That'll be all right.'

Drewy enjoyed the night patrols, which were usually cooler and quieter than the daytime routine. Most people were asleep by the time we deployed, so if we did see anyone, it would raise a few questions, and we could react accordingly.

'Yeah,' I answered. 'You driving again? I'll help you first parade after this.'

That would speed things along and give us a few extra valuable minutes to rest before heading out.

Corporal Hill turned up in his Toyota pickup, horror bags in hand. He handed them out as we got out of the sun to see what was on offer. The inside of the bag was still quite cool, so the sooner we ate, the more refreshing the meal would feel. He handed me a bag with a 'V' written in black marker pen.

'There you go, veggie.'

I opened it and found, to my surprise, that instead of the usual sausage roll I invariably traded for an apple, I actually had food. I took out the item. 'Vegetable lattice. Thanks, Mark!' The military-grade vegetarian option was still frozen, but a few minutes on the bonnet of a Land Rover turned it into a delicious snack. It went down a treat. We soon got back to work, shirts off, short-handled shovels out.

That night, the entire platoon headed out to the Iraq/Iran border to monitor traffic. The border was supposed to be closed, but the vast area was impossible to fully patrol, even with an entire battlegroup in theatre. The great thing about the border was getting there. We had to drive through some fascinating geography. After crossing the Shatt al-Arab river, we were in well-irrigated land, unlike the rest of the city. There

CHAPTER THIRTY-ONE

were palm trees and large farms. The people who lived there apparently just wanted to be left alone, and we wanted to leave them alone too. They had no interest in the elections or the new internal politics of Iraq. After the Iran-Iraq War and the first Gulf War, the Marsh Arabs, who were not welcome in larger population centres, had settled away from Basra and largely kept to themselves for the past twenty years.

Some farms looked like small army bases, with watchtowers and outbuildings usually protected by a gun-toting farmhand. They normally waved if they saw us, not to welcome us but to indicate they weren't looking for trouble. We had visited them a few times as part of an ATO escort. Whenever they found munitions caches hidden on their land or old ordnance from the conflicts of the 80s and 90s, one of their number would come to the Palace to report it. The Ammunition Technical Officer would then dispatch some engineers to make the explosives safe or carry out a controlled explosion.

We also had to pass some old battlefields. The threat of mines and unexploded bombs still existed, so other than the road and its immediate sides, the area was very treacherous. In the near distance we could still see the tank berms and trenches established decades ago. There was the odd tank hulk and, according to Jacob, the odd skeleton.

'Nobody wants to risk recovering the bodies,' he told me. 'There are mines and traps from decades ago.'

He took a drag on his unfiltered cigarette.

'The Mahdi Army pays children to go into the battlefields to recover explosives to attack your troops. Many of the children do not come back.'

He flicked the cigarette away.

'How do the Mahdi Army feel about locals assisting the Coalition forces?' I asked him.

He shrugged. We knew that the interpreters were fair game as far as the insurgents were concerned. Many of them slept in their cars in the Palace when they could. But even more of them lived with their families in the city. They were paid more than most locals working for the security forces – I just hoped it was worth the risk.

We arrived at the border and jumped off. This was going to be a 'standing patrol', which meant getting into a place of concealment and then monitoring a specific area. Between the three fire teams that made up the platoon, we could cover three kilometres of border. We were located on a stretch of desert that overlooked two Iranian border posts and the roads that crossed into Iraq. However, we were far enough back not to alarm the Iranians. Recently, some Royal Navy personnel had been captured by the maritime component of the Iranian Revolutionary Guards. While training new recruits for the Iraqi River Police, they had accidentally crossed the unmarked border on the Shatt al-Arab river, provoking a response from the Iranians. After being captured they were made to believe they were to be executed. They were marched into the desert, blindfolded and made to kneel, while the Guards prepared their weapons for firing. After enduring that, the six Royal Marines and two sailors were paraded on national TV, forced to read statements prepared for them by the Islamic Revolution, and finally released after three days of captivity. There was speculation at the time that the British Naval party was not off course and that the Iranians had carried out a raid to secure captives. It was later established that the Iranians were 'mistaken' and the whole incident was just one big misunderstanding. While on patrol we were very keen to avoid any 'misunderstandings'.

We were equipped with the Lion Hand Held Thermal Imager (HHTI) as well as our night vision equipment. The HHTI would make it easier to track any vehicle movements, as the heat of the engine would show up clearly through the digital eyepieces. Anyone travelling with their lights off would still be visible to us. Light on that flat part of the desert travelled for miles, so before we arrived at our LUP (lying up position), Drewy and Stick had driven us to our location using their night vision equipment. We then parked the vehicles at the foot of a slight incline and made our way up the bank to observe the roads, hopefully undetected. It was reasonable to assume that the Mahdi Army, the Iranians or anyone intent on crossing the border would also be using some kind of device to see in the dark.

Mr Sherwood delivered a SITREP using the more powerful vehicle-mounted radio sets. As he remained with the drivers and interpreter at the platoon CP (command post), the rest of us were led by our section commanders to our positions. We were not supposed to engage anyone or anything, as that would risk stirring up a hornet's nest or causing an international incident. Instead, we were to transmit any goings-on back to the CP so it could be relayed to Basra Palace. It struck me that this

CHAPTER THIRTY-ONE

duty did not really have a lot to do with 'force protection', but I wasn't about to complain. Mr Evans had obviously managed to get the go-ahead to expand his area of operations. That would also explain the need for more equipment and vehicles. It also meant more time out on patrol and less on guard duty. We had more time for patrols now that the CPA had left Basra Palace. The 'tango' towers had been passed to the Iraqi security forces, who were now responsible for securing the west side of the base. As a result, our river *sangars* became roadblocks as well, using their position on the Palace's road network to secure our half of the base from the local security forces.

We reported movements. Vehicles were crossing the border in both directions, stopping at the Iranian border posts and making their way either into or out of Iraq. This confirmed that the border was not as secure as it should have been. We scanned the desert in between the guard posts and around them to see if there were any infiltrators using the improvised roads and dirt tracks that were not on any maps. This was unlikely, but it was commonly known that many of the Mahdi Army's associates were hired guns from Iran. They would come over the border, do their work, and then go back, mimicking the tactics of the IRA during the Troubles. In this instance, though, we did not have any assistance at the border from the guards. To make things more difficult, the closer we got to the border, the more likelihood there would be a diplomatic misunderstanding. It meant we had to conduct surveillance and relay the information up the chain of command so they could build a broader understanding of the border and how permeable it was.

Essentially, the patrol was similar to the way we carried out tower duties. Everything we observed was passed back to the platoon commander, who then relayed the information upwards so the Int Corps could build a clearer picture of the situation near and around the border. The patrol was likely a response to the capture of the Navy personnel, and several other call signs from bases in Basra were doubtless employed along the border as well. We were reminded that it was also a 'show of force'. There was no doubt that the Iranian border guards knew we were there and could see us, though how well we did not know. They would have been feeding information back through their own channels and drawing conclusions from their observations. If any task made you feel like a mere pawn in a game of chess, this certainly did.

We returned to the Palace and conducted a last parade, ensuring the vehicles were in good condition. While we had been out on patrol, the new Snatches had arrived. Previously in the employ of the RAF Regiment for internal security tasks at Basra Airport, they had been reassigned to us. The CQMS wasted no time in removing the little RAF flags from the bumpers and spraying on the yellow Wyvern, the emblem of our parent brigade in south-west England. Mr Sherwood helped with the last parade and called us in after we were done.

'We're going out on a clearance patrol tomorrow. As you know, this would normally be done on foot, but I want the drivers to drive the new vehicles and the rest of you to get used to embarking and debussing from them.'

That meant the patrol would take a long time. Longer than usual. On foot, clearance was relatively straightforward. In vehicles, it would require the repetitive task of getting into and out of the armoured troop compartment at the back. At least there would be aircon. The drivers would be pretty comfortable, though a very obvious target if anyone was watching.

'Go and get your heads down,' he concluded. 'Orders at 0400. Good night.'

Chapter Thirty-two

We returned from our clearance patrol. The new vehicles were an improvement but still had a terrible reputation. They were designed for use in Northern Ireland and were almost exactly the same configuration, just a different colour. As armoured patrol vehicles they offered no additional firepower beyond what we individually carried. Those responsible for protecting the Snatch had to stand up in the rear compartment and provide cover with whatever they were using, usually the SA80 individual weapon or occasionally the Minimi light machine gun. There was no facility to mount anything larger.

The rear cabin had six seats separated from the driver and commander by a curtain made of bulletproof fabric, allowing a full section of eight to fit aboard, although we were still working in sections of four or five. After completing our sweep, we were ordered back into the city to conduct a GDA (ground defensive area) patrol to show we still had the freedom to operate in the city and, as always, to 'prevent crime and disrupt terrorism'. We had a quick briefing at the main gate of Basra Palace and went back out. I was in the lead vehicle with the platoon commander, Drewy was driving, and Uzi and Broz were on top cover. I was enjoying sitting in the back while Broz and Uzi kept an eye out. It wasn't overly comfortable, but with a light breeze from the air conditioning it was miles better than the Wolf Land Rovers we had been using previously.

Going on patrol wasn't just a matter of jumping into a vehicle and setting off wherever we fancied. The patrol commander was assigned an area by the OC or one of the operations officers, who would then decide on objectives and the best strategies to achieve them. Once that was done, the patrol commander, usually an officer, would share his orders with the other leaders in the multiple – the NCOs.

Meanwhile, the rest of the unit, privates and a few lance corporals, would be getting the equipment ready: preparing batteries for the radios, checking the medical supplies, collecting and testing the ECM, cleaning and checking our weapons, making sure we had ammunition, rubber bullets, and grenades, loading up on water and emergency rations in case we had to stay out longer than anticipated. If it was a vehicle patrol, we would check over the assigned wagons. If we were on foot we would load up the equipment into patrol gear and test and adjust the fit of packs, webbing and belt kit to ensure they weren't uncomfortable or obstructive.

Once all the preparations and checks were done, we would either go to the cookhouse to eat or, if it was late at night, get some rations from the QM, usually in the form of a horror bag, although sometimes there were nicer things like corn flakes or loaves of bread. A comfort break, a quick smoke, and then the briefing would follow, before mounting up or forming up and heading out into the city.

As we negotiated the streets, Broz came down from the hatch looking really sick. He was pale, sweating heavily, and starting to retch.

'Hold on, mate,' I told him as I got a bag for him to throw up in.

He retched some more. I took his helmet off and passed him a bottle of water. He was suffering the initial stages of heat stress. I used the PRR to contact the officer in the front of the vehicle.

'Boss, Broz is going down with heat stress. We need to cool him down.'

The curtain unzipped, and the officer looked behind to check on us. I opened my first aid kit and started preparing some rehydrate powder to get down Broz's neck before he got any worse. Essentially just a mixture of salt and water, it was the best medicine for this kind of climatic stress. My CamelBak water bottle still had some cold water left, so I let him sip on that while I got his tonic ready. I passed it to him. He didn't seem all there. That wasn't saying much, as Broz was often 'not all there', but this time he seemed quite dazed, as if he had taken a blow to the head. Had he?

'Uzi, mate, did anything happen up there?'

'Nope,' came the reply.

Uzi had been on the same medics' course as I had. After I gave Broz his rehydration powder, I loosened his webbing and opened

CHAPTER THIRTY-TWO

his armour so the air conditioning could work its magic. When he looked more comfortable, I swapped places with Uzi so he could cool off too and keep an eye on Broz. If this patrol caused the injury, it would be best to take preventative action and let them both cool off. While I provided cover, Uzi monitored Broz, and we made our way back to base. It was really hot and humid. Sweating didn't seem to help, and the headwind had more of a hairdryer than a cooling effect. The patrol ended early.

Broz was dropped off at the med centre. We only had a small aid detachment alongside us now: a handful of REME, signals and medical personnel. Other than that, we were self-sufficient. We took Broz's kit and dumped it on his bunk before going outside to the last parade and to clean off the vehicles.

Uzi sighed: 'Heat stroke? Looked like heat stroke.'

'Looked like it. He'll be all right in a day or so.'

'I hope so,' Uzi said as he jumped aboard to grab the used water bottles. 'Someone's got to carry the ECM, and it ain't gonna be me. He might not be good for much, but he's a unit.'

He started throwing the bottles out one at a time, and I picked them up and put them into a black bag. At the front of the wagon, Drewy had the bonnet up, checking the fluid levels and filling up the washer. Uzi got out and slammed the armoured door shut.

'Motherfffff...!'

He opened the door rapidly.

'What!?'

He held up his thumb, which had a very impressive door-shaped dent in the nail.

'That was clever,' I told him sarcastically.

He wasn't in the mood for jokes.

'Give it a rest, you twat!'

He wrapped his hand around his thumb and held it down between his knees, making noises of discomfort. Drewy popped his head around the open bonnet of the Snatch.

'He need a dump or something?'

I shook my head: 'Caught his thumb in the door.'

Drewy nodded: 'That was stupid.'

We closed off the vehicle logs and went back to the accommodation. Uzi was starting to develop a nice blood blister under his nail, which was in turn getting pushed off his thumb by the swelling.

'Can you lance it for me, mate?'

I looked at him: 'Do what?'

He was still annoyed.

'Lance it. Pop the blister. Just heat up a needle with your lighter and push it through the nail,' he said impatiently.

I grabbed my lighter and went to my bunk to grab my patrol kit, which I had not yet unpacked. I opened the first aid kit and grabbed a small needle.

'Okay, I'll give it a go. You sure this will work?'

He shook his head.

'I dunno. Just pop it, will you? It should go through the nail no problem once it's redders.'

I put on one of the gloves from my riot kit so I could hold the needle and began to heat it up. I didn't know if a Zippo lighter was the most hygienic method of heating a needle, but so be it.

'Ready?'

He put his hand on the table and held his wrist. I applied pressure to the thumbnail, and to my surprise, it went through with ease. A spurt of blood jumped out of the aperture.

'All right, mate. You squeeze all the blood out, and I'll get a bandage ready.'

I wrapped the needle up in an empty bandage wrapper and started to wrap up Uzi's thumb.

'Woah, hang on, hang on. I'll do it. You'll make it look like a fuckin' life-threatening injury.'

He handed me the bandage back and went to his own kit. He wrapped some sports tape around his nail and thumb and gave us all an oversized thumbs-up.

'Where's Elvis? I need a smoke. You coming?'

Chapter Thirty-three

We had to head to Shaibah to escort a Royal Military Police (RMP) unit to Basra Palace. Halfway through the tour, we were the only full-strength unit left at the Palace, meaning we received a variety of taskings. Smaller support elements were available, but none had sufficient manpower for protection or patrols. Consequently, escort tasks and training details now fell under Salamanca Company's remit. The RMP were due to meet local Iraqi security forces to assess their training needs. The post-CPA Iraqi police in Basra comprised three departments that were due for training: the city police, the river police patrolling the Shatt al-Arab waterway and the white-shirted traffic police responsible for the city's road network. The Palace, now largely empty, was designated as the police training venue by the local government. It had everything they needed: roads, access to the river, buildings to simulate a neighbourhood and space to learn to drive the recently delivered police cruisers.

Normally, we would have expected the RMP to arrive by helicopter, but a recent accident had resulted in the loss of a Puma medium-lift airframe and the life of one of the aircrew. The desert's harsh conditions were tough not only on personnel but also on equipment. Operating at the limit of its heat endurance, a sudden powerful gust of wind had destabilized the helicopter just as it was landing. The pilots, on their first sortie of the tour, were unable to recover control. The engine, already straining and close to overheating, was at its limit. The subsequent crash caused the chopper to burst into flames, and one pilot was unable to evacuate. While similar helicopters were grounded and inspected, the RAF's remaining transport capability was stretched thin. This meant the Royal Logistics Corps (RLC) had to run more convoys to maintain supplies, and non-combat units had to move themselves around the theatre wherever possible.

We had not practised escorts during our build-up training, as they were not part of the force protection role profile. However, it was not too dissimilar from patrolling, just longer and with more vehicles. Our RMP escort consisted of only four vehicles: two of ours and two of theirs. We had driven ourselves to Basra Airport, the logistics base, and even to Kuwait as a unit of two wagons countless times. We wondered why the RMP couldn't manage it themselves.

'At least we can visit Shaibah,' Thewy said as he prepared his vehicle. 'Get some decent food, buy a clean T-shirt.'

Shaibah still had many welfare facilities. If the RMP were slow to link up with us or late to the RV, we had a good chance of getting some real food on a plate instead of in a polystyrene takeaway box. Thewy didn't drive as much as Drewy and Stick but he was one of the platoon's nominal drivers. Drivers were only permitted a certain number of hours, so if someone exceeded their weekly allowance, another had to take over. Thewy and Elvis usually stepped up, but I had taken the wheel a few times, as had L2. I learned more about driving during Operation TELIC than I ever did driving around the UK in my Ford Fiesta.

We were fortunate that the RMP had other tasks to attend to while we waited for them at Shaibah. This gave us plenty of time to take care of personal admin before heading back to the Palace. We took the long way back, a route that kept us in the desert for quite some time. It was safer, but time-consuming. I looked back and saw the two RMP vehicles in the middle of our convoy. Other than some blue lanterns, presumably for their policing role, their vehicles looked the same as ours. What surprised me was how much better equipped they were than us. They had brand-new ECM and communication equipment, and all of them wore thigh holsters with side arms. We could have used some of that gear. I wondered what they thought of their scruffy escort. We did get them safely to the Palace, so that must have earned us a few points, no matter what else they might have thought.

With reduced air transport capability, supplies also had to be transported by ground vehicles. The destination unit was obliged to provide additional security for the convoy. Slow-moving water tankers and fuel trucks were easy targets for opportunists looking to cause mayhem. Blowing up a lorry full of gasoline in the city would be a major victory for the Mahdi Army. Similarly, if food and water were

CHAPTER THIRTY-THREE

limited and rationed, troop morale would suffer, another objective of the insurgents. Some time after our RMP escort, we linked up with the RLC in the middle of the desert, halfway between Shaibah and the city. The plan was to head into the city, arrive at the Palace, then link up with another unit and head to the Hotel before returning to their place of origin. It was a long, somewhat circular route, much of it through the city. It was advisable to stick to the outer parts of Basra as much as possible, though this was not always feasible.

The heavily armed convoy had half a dozen cargo vehicles and the same number of RLC escorts. Like us, they had Snatch Land Rovers. We planned to arrive at our destination in the early morning, just as the sun was rising. The heat on the river usually caused a thick mist that would obscure the convoy's arrival, but it also made it hard for the escorting vehicles to identify threats. It was a plan, but we weren't entirely convinced it was a solid one. We had to stop regularly at known choke points and disembark to check for IEDs or signs of hostile observation. Each vehicle now had an ECM unit fitted, likely prompted by the loss of the Royal Highland Fusiliers' call sign in July. It was hard, frustrating work, and the convoy never seemed to get above 20mph before slowing down again. Still, an abundance of caution from the RLC was preferable to complacency, especially as the city was still in a state of severe unrest.

I jumped out of the Snatch with L2, and we checked a culvert running under a road. It was an area we were familiar with, having patrolled it many times. South and east of Basra Palace, the area was part of the rural oasis fed by hand-dug canals connected to the Shatt al-Arab. The convoy initially headed east, away from the city, then north to a crossing point over the Basra Canal that the RLC had secured a few hours earlier. From there, it was a straight run across the desert until we hit the first of the suburbs, a place called Abu Al-Khaseeb.

To my surprise, when we returned to our vehicle, another person joined us.

'All right, mate,' L2 said as his head popped up through the hatch, now getting rather snug.

Two people in full kit was a squeeze at the best of times.

'Would you mind telling me who the fuck you are?' L2 added.

'Shit, wrong truck!' the newcomer exclaimed, quickly removing himself.

It was an easy mistake to make. Unless you noted your vehicle registration, all the Snatches looked the same. We had small yellow wyvern decals on our black bumpers, but they weren't overly conspicuous. No doubt his own vehicle would have been very concerned about their missing mate if we had let him stay aboard. He would likely be more careful when embarking from now on.

We arrived at the main approach to the Palace and disembarked to conduct a foot patrol for the last half kilometre. The convoy would have to negotiate chicanes and traffic barriers, prime spots for any devices. But we could barely see a thing. Far from the 'thick mist' briefed to us, today was like walking through pea soup. Visibility was no more than three or four metres. We checked the barriers as we made our way in, using our VHF radios to alert 2 Platoon, manning the gate, to our arrival. They wouldn't see us until the last minute, and we didn't want to surprise them. Surely they could hear the convoy crawling along in first gear. But there had been more warnings of VBIEDs in large Scania dump lorries and refuse trucks. When we had been on the gate we took no chances, so showing a little courtesy to our sister platoon was a favour to both call signs.

Supplying the more remote outposts required extensive planning and resources. The Palace had been a major base but was now merely a military presence on the edge of the city. It still housed the British Consulate, but they had their own security arrangements with privately contracted Gurkhas from Armor Group, a British security company, who wore heavy armour and carried AK47s along with their legendary kukris. There were enough of them to repel a major assault, but they were confined to their part of the Palace and did not patrol or assist with general peacekeeping tasks. This meant Salamanca Company was now essentially securing and operating out of a patrol base, focused solely on its security and that of the surrounding area. Other patrol bases were housed in the city and nearby. The Ba'ath Party HQ, where we had done the public order training, was now up and running as a base halfway between us and the Hotel. There was a prisoner-processing centre near the city, and our parent unit, the PWRR, were stationed slightly north of us in Al Amarah. They had deployed a contingent to a former government facility now known as CIMIC House.

Chapter Thirty-four

CIMIC (Civil-Military Cooperation) House, was the former Ba'ath Party HQ for the Al Amarah region. Unlike the political infrastructure in Basra, this building was left in good condition after the invasion. Similar in appearance to Basra Palace, it was a large estate that used to house the provincial governor, although it was not large enough to sustain a substantial military force. Now it housed a garrison of around 100 British soldiers from the PWRR and the Queen's Royal Lancers. These two regiments, along with reservists from the 52nd Lowland Volunteers, were supplying most of the troops operating from the outposts of southern Iraq. We had trained alongside the PWRR and QRL at CPTA before deploying, and like them, we were now based at an outpost following the dissolution of the Coalition Provisional Authority. Technically, we were subordinated to the PWRR for the duration of the tour. However, in practical terms, Mr Evans received his orders and taskings from the Battlegroup HQ at the Shatt al-Arab Hotel.

The 52nd Lowland Volunteers were fulfilling a similar role to us, providing force protection, while the lion's share of the patrolling duties were carried out by the PWRR. Unlike the Palace, now mostly empty of British personnel, CIMIC House was still at full strength. Lots of Brits, cut off from the main force – an ideal target if there ever was one.

Prior to our deployment, most of the country's problems stemmed from civil unrest. The occupying forces could mitigate these issues with regular city patrols and the provision of basic services. However, in May and early June, the Mahdi Army emerged as a capable fighting force in Iraq, launching concurrent assaults to cause widespread chaos leading up to the local elections and causing many casualties. After the democratic process concluded, they melted back into the cities of Iraq to rearm and awaited their next opportunity to strike. We did not have to wait long. Beginning in August, the insurgents launched a new campaign against the occupying Coalition forces in Samawah, Najaf, Basra and Al Amarah.

On 5 August the Mahdi Army launched a major offensive against American forces in Najaf and British forces in CIMIC House. They also began pushing back into Basra and the southern city of Samawah. It was easy to understand why they targeted CIMIC House in Al Amarah. They had likely been conducting reconnaissance and intelligence-gathering for months. The garrison was well defended but also isolated and entirely dependent on vehicle convoys for re-supply. Compared to Shaibah or the Hotel, there were not many men protecting the base, and the urban landscape made it easy for insurgents to move around and reposition. They could easily set up indirect firing points for mortars and rockets while escaping the notice of local security patrols. They could attack with small-arms fire from any direction and observe the British garrison without exposing themselves to risk. The Tigris River also formed a natural choke point, making British forces easy targets as they came and went from the base. In sporting terms, the insurgents were playing a 'home game'.

Over the next twenty-three days, the PWRR and QRL were attacked hundreds of times with mortar and rocket fire. The 107mm rockets were crude and effective weapons that could be easily set up and fired at Coalition forces. Usually set off from improvised launching mechanisms, the rocket was so simple that it could be fired using a few bricks and a nine-volt battery. The indirect fire was almost constant. The emboldened enemy also assaulted CIMIC House on foot dozens of times but were unable to capitalize on any advances before retreating back into the city. The gunmen, dressed in civilian clothing, were intent on causing as many casualties as possible. If they could affect public opinion back home in the UK they might force a withdrawal of the British military, as had happened with the *Brigada Hispanoamericana* – the Spanish Foreign Legion.

In Najaf, the Americans, who had taken over from the Spanish contingent, also became heavily engaged against the Mahdi Army. Initially targeting local Iraqi forces in the centre of the city, the insurgents soon began to spread out and ambush Coalition units wherever they found them. During the fighting an American Cobra helicopter was shot

CHAPTER THIRTY-FOUR

down, and several US Marines were killed by small-arms fire and IEDs. For three weeks, the US-led forces in Najaf battled against the guerrillas until, as in Al Amarah, they melted back into the city.

Eventually, the Mahdi Army ended their assaults, having taken hundreds of casualties – martyrs, in their terms. The PWRR and Americans had also taken casualties, including fatalities. In Samawah, the Japanese Ground Self Defence Force was on its first ever deployment since being formed after the Second World War. The controversial deployment of the Japanese Iraq Reconstruction and Support Group did not go unnoticed by the Mahdi Army. Ostensibly in Iraq to rebuild the damage done during the invasion, the Japanese Self Defence Force nonetheless brought a heavily armed infantry battalion. Agitators arrived in the city during the attacks on CIMIC House and Najaf, determined to stir up anti-Coalition sentiment. The Japanese soon found themselves dealing with civil disorder and riots. Insurgents warned the Japanese that if they failed to withdraw, there would be severe consequences. Several Japanese diplomats, aid workers and journalists had already been kidnapped, and worse.

In Basra, Salamanca Company was carrying out a comprehensive patrol strategy to disrupt any hostile action. The Palace had been subjected to numerous bombardments from mortar fire and 107mm rockets, but we had yet to make new contact with the insurgents. It seemed as though the Mahdi Army's resources had been withdrawn from the city to focus on the Al Amarah and Najaf areas for the time being.

As part of the patrol strategy, 3 Platoon was assigned to assist in an operation designed to conduct several simultaneous arrests overnight. Intelligence had identified insurgents intending to attack the Palace and those gathering information for assaults on British forces. Workers at the bases, such as cleaners, builders and scrap merchants, were well rewarded if they provided information. They also earned a bounty if they could find useful informants to help create a solid understanding of what was happening in the city. Based on this intel and the efforts of special forces units operating in the city, the battlegroup planned to capture several high-value targets in one night.

For us, it was a break from the regular patrol and guard routine. While a surge force made up of the Warrior-mounted Black Watch Regiment based at Shaibah carried out the raids, 3 Platoon was to provide security, ensuring the roads were closed and acting as cut-offs if anything went wrong or anyone tried to flee. Close to Mitan, it was decided that we would be best placed to provide a security force as this was our area of operations and we knew it well. We simply deployed from the Palace as if we were heading out on a normal patrol, then went firm at the sole crossroads that led to the target area. Early in the morning, before the sun had risen, the Black Watch made their moves all over the city and took their prisoners. It was over in moments. Any attempts to conduct an assault on the Palace were now put on hold while the Mahdi Army tried to figure out which of their fighters and agents they could trust and which had betrayed them. The operation had been a success but was not without loss. A private from the Black Watch was killed by an IED as they returned to Shaibah.

Following the arrests, the city seemed to calm down overnight. We noticed it the next evening as we were manning a VCP (vehicle checkpoint) near the Palace. This wide thoroughfare connected Basra to the neighbouring city of Az Zubayr. We had patrolled this stretch of road regularly since arriving in the city, conducting vehicle checks and securing dozens of weapons, while providing high-visibility security. During the day, the work was hazardous and tiring, with the added threat of VBIEDs and the possibility of being rammed. Many Coalition troops had been killed or injured while taking part in similar activities. The traffic would back up for miles as we checked the vehicles coming into Basra, meaning we would always be outnumbered if any kind of civil disorder broke out. I never remembered hearing any contingency plans, or 'actions on', for things going wrong at the VCP. To make matters worse, tempers flared among the drivers whenever we conducted this task. We knew this was due to the frustration caused by the traffic jam, but we also knew it was a great way to gather intelligence and disrupt terrorist movements. Our interpreters certainly had their work cut out.

The next night, the VCP was a much easier task. The relative cool and lack of traffic made it easier to operate. On some nights we would see no activity at all, calling into question the value of the VCP. In such cases, we would sometimes carry out small local patrols, using the VCP as a start and end point. One fire team could head out on patrol while the other two remained to stop and check any vehicles that came our way.

CHAPTER THIRTY-FOUR

Mr Sherwood sent out Sierra Three Zero Delta, Rob's team. The area around the VCP was almost entirely farmland, fields separated by embankments or irrigation ditches. Farmers had frequently found weapons caches concealed in and around their property, so it was usually a good idea to attempt to locate anything, or at least disrupt any activity. The team headed out but were instructed to stay nearby, so we could still provide mutual support if needed. We also had to consider the effective range of our comms equipment. Rob was carrying a 349 radio, which was powerful enough to transmit a fair distance. But if something happened to him or the radio, then the PRR was all they had, and that would only make 100m in this terrain at best.

Charlie fire team stayed close to the vehicles, providing security for the VCP, while Alpha patrolled up and down, waiting for any traffic. It was very desolate and dark around us. The only illumination we had was what we carried or what the Snatch Land Rovers provided. Either side of the road lay a few metres of desert. There were no street lights and no house lights. Beyond that, the agricultural land began. The further you got from the road, the thicker the vegetation became, as the irrigation ditches deposited water into the paddocks and allotments.

There was a bang.

'What was that? Car backfiring?' Broz asked.

It happened regularly. Single shots were rare in terms of contacts. And it wasn't anywhere near us. It was somewhere off to the left, between the VCP and the city. We had often heard and seen the less than well maintained vehicles of Basra's citizens backfire and belch smoke from various apertures in the bodywork. The unpredictable bangs shocked us at first and sent us quickly into cover, but now we were more experienced and used to the sounds of the city.

'Delta is in contact,' Mr Sherwood told us matter-of-factly, without excitement or urgency.

Rob had reported to him over the VHF frequency.

'They've gone firm somewhere around 100 metres from here.'

That wasn't much of a location status. Both the officer and I were carrying simple satellite maps of the area and checked them, trying to estimate where Rob and his team might be. Ultimately, though, it would be a matter of entering the maze of ditches and trying to link up with them.

'What kind of contact?' Fordy asked.

'Effective fire. A single shot. Possibly sniper fire.'

Drewy muttered under his breath, 'Possibly a pissed-off farmer, more like.' He raised his voice: 'Get off my land!'

The lieutenant wasn't in the mood for levity and folded his map back into his pocket.

'Charlie, remain at this location. Alpha, on me. Matt, you lead.'

I set off with the rest of the fire team following. I had seen which way Zero Delta had entered the farmland, so I thought that would be a good start. Behind me, Mr Sherwood was reporting into the ops room, while Fordy brought Broz and Drewy into line.

Chapter Thirty-five

We headed into the network of walls and paddocks. The layout seemed almost random, and while the local farmers surely knew their way around, we didn't. The locals had worked the land for years and knew every square inch of it. The dry mud embankments formed a maze of high walls that had to be climbed to get from one field to the next. The various canals and irrigation ditches added yet more obstacles to this agricultural labyrinth. Some of the ditches were full of stagnant, dirty water, while others were dry, having not seen a drop of moisture all summer. A single sun-baked track acted as the entrance and exit for the few animals that grazed there during the day.

There was another shot. That made two. Was it a warning shot, or was the intention to kill? Was it someone shooting for fun, or at pests? Were we the pests? We had the right to assume the worst, as we wouldn't get any second chances if someone got hit. I began to hear Sierra Three Zero Delta on my PRR. The reception was patchy and not in complete sentences, but it meant I was probably leading the fire team in the right direction. If I had managed to pick them up over the small transceiver attached to my kit, then we must be getting closer. The terrain would have limited the range of the radios, with the ditches and thick vegetation along the canal banks acting as a sponge for any direct transmissions. Only Mr Sherwood and Rob would have unbroken comms. But if Zero Delta was trying to react to enemy fire, Rob would have told the officer to 'wait, out', while he organized his fire team.

I jumped off a bank and landed on one of the simple tracks that cut through the vegetation. There were palm trees and low, thick shrubs that looked like they belonged in a jungle, not the desert. There were tall reeds, but the ground was completely dry and rock solid, like cement or a metalled road. How anything could grow here, I had no idea. I went firm and waited for the fire team to catch up. It was probably less secure on the track, but as I turned my body in one direction I found I had better reception with Zero Delta. If I turned it another way, it was more broken. I was using the PRR as a direction finder. I conferred with Mr Sherwood.

'What do you think?' I asked.

'I get better reception when facing that direction, so my guess is they went firm over there somewhere.' I indicated my intended direction of travel.

He nodded and said, 'You're up front, you make the call.'

So I made the call and took the team up another embankment, following the improving signal.

On top of the embankments there was plenty of cover. Farm equipment and agricultural debris such as large fuel cans and discarded machinery provided adequate concealment if needed. It would be a secure area for us if we did get into contact. But it would also be good for anyone looking to cause trouble, as they would be exceptionally well concealed and able to move around almost undetected. The tall reeds we flattened as we patrolled through left substantial evidence of where we had been and where we were going. While looking ahead, I made a point to look at the ground, too, for any traces suggesting the presence of an enemy nearby. I reasoned that a farmer or local would probably have avoided leaving any ground sign. Probably. Someone just visiting, like us, would likely be a little heavier-footed.

The radio signal was getting stronger. I could hear Rob talking to his team. Through the snatched transmissions I made out that they had heard voices close to them and that a couple of rounds had impacted the ground nearby, forcing them to take cover. If we were destined to make contact, it would be a very close-range affair, so Rob had ordered his team to fix bayonets. Upon hearing that, I stopped and turned to look at Mr Sherwood. He quietly passed the order for us to do the same. I saw people reach to their belts, draw the sharp weapons from their scabbards and click them into place. I couldn't reach mine. I was carrying it on my back, and the large first aid kit and my patrol pack prevented me from grabbing it. 'Fuck it,' I thought to myself, and carried on patrolling without fixing it. Probably not the smartest idea, seeing as the area was becoming thicker with plant life and mud walls. But then again, it wasn't sensible to put the bloke with the first aid equipment up front either.

CHAPTER THIRTY-FIVE

Instead, I switched my fire select lever from single shot to automatic. If anyone was intent on having a go, I was going to give them a blast of 5.56 instead of skewering them.

We had been searching for the team for around ten minutes before we were finally able to link up. Behind a ditch, they were in fire positions looking in the direction of the perceived threat. To get to them we would have to break cover, dash across an open field, hop over a low wall and fall in behind their embankment. It was a substantial, solid piece of cover they had found. Fordy went first, followed by the boss. Broz followed, while Drewy and I provided cover from where we were. Nobody fired as they made their way from one piece of cover to the next. Maybe the enemy had withdrawn.

As soon as they were in position, Rob and the lieutenant conferred. They quickly planned to withdraw the multiple the way we had come in. That meant I would need to lead us out and try to remember the route. Mr Sherwood had requested a helicopter to come and have a look, but no air support was available. It was very early in the morning and still pitch-dark. The pilots were probably asleep, while their ground crews worked on keeping the airframes in good condition. The only resource available to us was the QRF, but that seemed unnecessary. It would take around half an hour to reach us and could not provide any additional support without entering the farmland. That would be risky and unnecessary.

'Lead us out,' was the order.

Zero Delta peeled off and joined Drewy and me. Once a couple of them had joined us, I started to patrol back the way we had come.

'Pick up the pace,' someone said on the PRR by the time the rest of the multiple had fallen in.

I lengthened my stride a little and sped up, but not too much. I didn't want to begin a haphazard withdrawal, especially seeing as I was the 'bullet catcher', the man at the front.

We rejoined Zero Charlie at the VCP. It was clear no traffic had come through while we were away. They had heard the second shot as well. The three team leaders conducted a quick debrief while the rest of the multiple returned to their positions at the checkpoint. I stayed nearby, took my patrol pack off and threw it into one of the Snatch Land Rovers, whose bonnet was acting as a table for the team leaders' maps.

'So what happened?' Corporal Parsons asked Rob.

'A single shot landed nearby, and we went to ground. When I put my head up for a look around, another one came in.'

'Lucky you didn't get your head shot off. What do you think it was? Farmer? Insurgents?'

It could have been either of those, I thought to myself. It could have even just been some guy having a go, looking to collect the $250 bounty placed on the life of every British soldier in Basra ($500 for a female). If a local could bag a squaddie he would be set for the rest of the year. A small, lightly armed patrol would be a very tempting target, especially in the kind of terrain where it was easy to disappear and reappear at will.

A contact report was sent. We had a small debriefing when we got back to the Palace and gave simple statements to an RMP call sign that had been sent to gather any evidence of crimes or terrorist acts. To me, it didn't feel like a contact at all. I didn't feel I was becoming desensitized, but it just didn't sit right with me. Had it been a contact? It didn't have a deliberate or determined aspect to it. It was not like the explosions that regularly rained down on us when the 107mm rockets and mortar rounds came in. It wasn't like the contact at the hospital or like Sergeant Paul-Reeves' running battle with the Mahdi Army. Two shots. That was it. Granted, they would have been quite problematic if they had hit one of us. But on the other hand, it was impossible to say with 100 per cent certainty that we were even the target. It was part of the nature of rural patrolling. As soon as we left the cities and villages, the small oasis settlements along the Shatt al-Arab were like self-contained countries with their own customs and rules, and they usually did not take kindly to strangers.

We returned to the Palace and got some rest, as we were due out on patrol again before sunrise. Our task was to reach the Kuwaiti border, pick up BBC journalist Ben Brown and drop him off at the British Consulate, which was conveniently located next to our military accommodation block. I had a bit of a soft spot for these trips to Kuwait. We had done a few escorts and long-range patrols to the border before, and once out in the desert it was a laugh tearing across the open flat land in the vehicles. We had done it in the unarmoured Wolf variants a few times, and the headwind was strangely therapeutic.

The border was controlled by the Americans, who had a ridiculous number of troops in the theatre. They had more Military Police at

CHAPTER THIRTY-FIVE

the border than we had infantry in Basra. These MPs were enormous guys, leaning on their Humvees and eyeing everyone with suspicion – especially the Brits, it seemed. Despite my best efforts, they weren't very talkative. The infantry from the 101st Airborne were a different story, though. While waiting for our correspondent I met a couple of American troops, probably around my age. Their names were Field and Halsted. They had a few 'gizzits' for trade, and as always, we swapped rations and tested the optics in each other's weapons.

As it turned out, the Americans did year-long tours in Iraq, and the 101st were just about to start their tour of Baghdad that week. They had been in Iraq for only a few days and were part of a massive convoy travelling from Kuwait to the Iraqi capital. Rather than give them horror stories, I gave it to them straight when they asked about how things were.

I told them, 'I can't say much about where you're going, but the Brits are in contact most days around the city now. Normally, they're fast, well-planned ambushes with very little opportunity to return fire. Best to keep a good eye out and stop any trouble before it becomes a serious problem.'

It was a sound tactic. By looking efficient and switched-on, we hoped to at least make any potential assailants second-guess their plans. Of course, it didn't always work, and most of 3 Platoon were now lifetime members of 'the Contact Club'.

I returned to our vehicles with an armful of MRE burritos – apparently some sort of Mexican or Texan food that Halsted recommended highly. That would be dinner while we were at the gate. He had even provided us with some self-heating elements so we didn't have to eat the TexMex cold. All it had cost me was some grimy British food and a photo op with my SA80. It felt like the most absurd trade deal in history, but I figured it was worth it. With our culinary adventure secured, we mounted up, ready to whisk Mr Brown off to Basra Palace and the consulate. Because, of course, in the middle of a war zone, our top priority was playing chauffeur to a journalist and making sure we didn't eat cold burritos.

Chapter Thirty-six

Drewy and I were manning the last remaining river *sangar* at Basra Palace. By now, every other guard position except for the main gate had been handed over to the Iraqi police. The river *sangar* not only protected the riverside aspect of our area of the Palace but also guarded a small humpback bridge and road junction that acted as the sole entrance between us and the IZP compound. We had erected a makeshift traffic barrier made from scaffold poles and barbed wire to keep visitors out. Anyone wanting access had to wait on their side of the bridge until given permission by Mr Evans, the senior officer at Basra Palace.

Earlier in the day, Drewy and I had been at the main gate when a vehicle started to enter the chicanes and traffic barriers. From our forwardmost *sangar* we saw a white Toyota Crown with blacked-out windows weaving its way through the obstacles. It did not heed the warnings and signs, in Arabic and English, to wait until called forward. It ignored several blasts of the megaphone, despite being given ample time to reverse course. If it had been night, the small red flare we fired at the windscreen would have been easier for the driver to see. Drewy thumbed the safety off the GPMG and fired a burst into the front of the car as it emerged from behind a concrete barrier. I alerted the guard commander, Corporal Parsons, to the incident. The short blast from the gimpie seemed to get the driver's attention. He disembarked, arms in surrender, and surveyed the damage to his vehicle. Probably a write-off. It was a good, accurate burst right into the engine compartment. A passenger, presumably his assistant, got out as well and made the final part of the journey to the main gate on foot, then demanded to see whoever was in charge.

They were brought into the Palace, escorted by some of the Gurkhas employed by the consulate, and were taken away to discuss business.

CHAPTER THIRTY-SIX

A report was sent to the ops room, and Mr Moorhouse arranged a meeting to ensure the consular staff reminded their visitors that there were no exceptions to the security rules in or around the Palace.

'First shots I've fired,' Drewy said as he made the gimpie safe and collected the brass.

The RMP wanted it bagged up.

'Really?' I asked. We were over four months in by now. 'Even during the hospital thing?'

He nodded: 'I never saw anything.'

The rest of the multiple certainly had, and I remembered seeing Drewy as the forwardmost of the fire team. I suppose that even if he had looked up to the top of the building, the angle would have obscured the shooter. And he was so far ahead of me that there was no way he would have seen the coppers go down.

'Lucky you.'

He replaced the belt of ammunition, which now had 197 rounds attached instead of 200.

The river *sangar* was a similar defensive position to the front gate. It had a radio, spare batteries, a GPMG with several boxes of ammunition, a spotlight, rocket flares and smaller .22 calibre flares. There was also a thermal imager and, finally, two bored privates who were required to log traffic on the river and occasionally lift the traffic barrier. That night, those two bored privates were me and Drewy. The bonus of this guard duty was that it only had to be done for two hours before changing over. If those hours happened to be at night, it was reasonably cool and comfortable. During the day, it was sweltering. The traffic barrier would become too hot to touch without a gloved hand, and the sun reflecting off the river would bounce powerful rays of light into the *sangar*, creating a small suntrap.

At times, the view over the river was spectacular, good enough to make you forget about the conflict in Iraq. Across the wide river, the usually still and greenish water would shimmer with light at sunrise and sunset. The opposite bank, where the Marsh Arabs lived, was green and lush. If this piece of Iraq could be picked up and transported to some island paradise or tropical resort, it would have been perfect. Beyond the marshes lay Iran and the battlefields of the conflict of the 80s. The marshes themselves had been the site of Operation Kheibar, a border raid in which Iranian troops used the dense vegetation to their advantage and infiltrated southern Iraq. In response, the Iraqis laid electrical cables in the water and fried hundreds of Iranians as they attempted a similar raid shortly after. It was hard to believe, looking across the Shatt al-Arab, that such brutal warfare had taken place within recent history.

Drewy and I were just chatting as we looked out, trying to kill time until handover. Drewy and his missus had recently split up. He had received a 'Dear John' letter letting him know she was seeing someone else. He took the news reasonably well, although we all agreed that what she had done was unpleasant at best. He decided to burn the blueys from her that he had received up until that point, and a few of us went to the smoking area to assist with their disposal. Before guard duty that evening, he held a polaroid image of her and asked me to light it up with my Zippo, which I did. Once combustion was assured, he dropped it onto the floor and watched the flaming memento curl up and wither before crushing the embers underfoot.

It must have been hard for those men in relationships. As if the stress of the deployment wasn't bad enough, there was the constant worry about those waiting at home. And that wasn't just from concerns about fidelity. Being apart from someone you cared about, but could not make regular contact with, must have been difficult to manage. Money worries, sickness, domestic issues, school, work, and so on. Most of the blokes in Salamanca Company bore these worries admirably. But when Drewy got his letter, I had the feeling that some of those harbouring similar worries would have written home as soon as they could.

As if to snap Drewy out of his melancholy, an explosion not more than thirty metres away propelled us into action. We had not heard the telltale 'pop' of a mortar firing, so it must have come from further away, or been a rocket. We did, however, hear the shower of dirt as it landed over the canopy of the *sangar*.

'Fuckin' hell, Drewy, what is it with you and IDF?'

We had both been on duty early in May when the towers came under indirect fire. We had both been on patrol in Mitan and ended up sharing a ditch while taking cover during a mortar strike, and had been on the main gate when another similar attack had occurred. I stayed low and grabbed the receiver for the 351.

CHAPTER THIRTY-SIX

'Hello Zero, Sierra Romeo One. Contact, indirect fire. Wait. Out.'

Drewy was looking in the direction of the impact. I looked to the river in case it was a precursor to some kind of assault. CIMIC House and the Hotel had both had 'drive-bys' carried by fast-moving boats – something the Palace was yet to experience. I couldn't see anything through the binoculars, so I used the thermal imager. Nothing. Good.

'What you got, mate?' I asked Drewy as I got ready to send a SITREP to the ops room.

'There's an impact point just over the bridge in the IZP compound. Can't see any damage. Looks like it landed next to one of the ponds.'

That was fortunate. Either by accident or design, the round had completely missed any of the nearby structures and landed in the semi-picturesque gardens that were now the training grounds for police recruits.

'Hello Zero. SITREP, over.'

I sent the details, prompting the QRF to be sent to the impact site to assess the extent of any damage. We maintained our vigil from the *sangar*.

Metal Mickey from the QRF came up the stairs holding a huge piece of shrapnel.

'Found this,' he declared, turning it over and around so that we could get a good look at it. About the size of a tennis racket, the metal was thick and jagged. If that had hit anyone, they would not have been cut in two – they would probably have exploded.

'Found this as well.'

He pointed to the wall outside the *sangar*, where a smaller piece was stuck into the wall of the position.

'Shit!' Drewy said.

It was hard to disagree with that succinct assessment. If there had not been a hesco (dirt-filled barrier) between us, then one of us would probably be missing a leg. Mr Sparks now joined us in the *sangar*.

'All okay?' he asked.

'Yes, sir. We'll be handing over in an hour or so.'

He looked around and checked the river for movement.

'Good lads.'

The officer and Mickey rejoined 1 Platoon and returned to the QRF ready room.

The next day, we found out that the British Consulate had lost a business contract that could have helped arrange for labourers to repair the city's infrastructure. The businessman in the Toyota Crown had not taken kindly to being shot at and had terminated any tentative dealings with the Brits then and there. As an act of retaliation, his private security force had fired the rocket into the base so that he did not lose face in the eyes of his competitors. It was designed as a show of force, indicating that he would absolutely not work with the occupiers and would rather attack them than accept their money. His other act of retaliation, or petulance, was to leave his shot-up Toyota at the end of the chicane, restricting the flow of traffic even further. It meant that EOD had to come and check the car, in case it had been rigged to blow. After it had been declared safe, a Royal Engineer armoured forklift was called in to lift and drop it onto the river bank. Stick and I rode shotgun on the outside of the lifter while the operation was completed. The car was dropped onto the riverbank with a satisfying crash and squelch. It started to slide on the soft mud and ended up semi-submerged. The local police were called out from the Palace. They sent a man to the vehicle owner to tell him that he needed to move his car.

Chapter Thirty-seven

3 Platoon was tasked with a night patrol in the city. With only one month left of the tour, Uzi had been eagerly ticking off the days on his chuff chart, awaiting the coming of the Royal Marines to relieve our small garrison. The city had become so dangerous that it was decided a single company of weekend warriors would not suffice should things deteriorate further. The situation in Basra was worsening daily. Basic services were severely lacking, civil servants were often corrupt and the police were untrustworthy. Considering their circumstances, I couldn't blame them; it was likely the most sensible way to stay alive. A recent report on the state of the IZP noted, 'They are not respected by the local population and are seen as ineffective and corrupt.' Indeed, most civil organizations were ineffective. Garbage and sewage were everywhere. Whenever we went on patrol we saw piles of rubbish throughout the city. The insanitary conditions had caused several members of the company to fall ill with D&V after patrolling. There was a lack of running water, most houses relying on overpriced bottled water, despite it being provided for free by the Coalition. Perhaps the CPA had been too quick to disband and hold elections. I wondered what the city was like before the troops had arrived. I doubted Saddam had to contend with this level of civil disorder. If he had, his 'justice' would have been swift and brutal.

Despite the presence of British forces, the city was increasingly contested by both criminal gangs and insurgents. In certain areas, the IZP refused to patrol, forcing the overstretched Army to be deployed there. The handover of civil power from the CPA to a democratic local government had not improved the average Iraqi's life, and the Mahdi Army was keen to exploit the unrest. They knew it was just a waiting game, and they had all the time in the world. Once the Coalition left, they could easily take control. For this reason, we were tasked with heading to the small market of Manawi al Basha to conduct a GDA patrol, reassuring the local population that security still existed in Basra, and attempting to disrupt any hostile actions against the base.

To support the local operations, Mr Evans had received reinforcements from the Royal Horse Artillery. A battery had been sent to Basra Palace to take over the force protection role and cover the arrival of the Royal Marines, who were due in less than a month. This meant Salamanca Company was now focused on tasks outside the Palace walls rather than the guard duties we were originally deployed to handle. The three platoons that comprised the fighting part of the company were now better equipped with new ECM, grenade launchers and armoured vehicles. However, we remained a small, isolated unit dependent on the larger formations at the Hotel or Shaibah for re-supply. It was during one of these routine runs to Shaibah that our HQ multiple was ambushed.

Two Snatch Land Rovers were escorting two four-ton trucks to the logistics base. An explosion destroyed the lead vehicle, reducing the driving compartment to a flaming wreck. The driver and commander were killed instantly – a gunner from the RHA and a craftsman from the REME. Small-arms fire followed, pinning the remaining British forces down and forcing them to withdraw. Aboard one of the trucks, Salamanca Company's CQMS, the convoy commander, was hit. A heavy 7.62mm round penetrated his body armour. The wounded colour sergeant landed on top of Corporal Hill, who was trying to drive his truck out of the contact. With only one escorting vehicle left, the convoy eventually broke contact and returned the way it had come, picking up the survivors from the lead Snatch before withdrawing. A QRF from Shaibah soon arrived on the scene in Warrior IFVs, with a Lynx helicopter providing top cover. The Snatch and the bodies of the men inside were retrieved and taken back to the logistics base. By now, twelve British personnel had died on Op TELIC IV, and many more were wounded.

As we prepared to go on patrol we saw the RHA return to their accommodation next to ours. A lone gunner, who had not been on the escort, sat on the kerb, his head resting on his knees, after someone had delivered the news that his friend had been killed. Uzi and I continued our work, preparing our vehicle, as we saw other members of his battery join him. One sat beside him and placed his arm around him, while others

CHAPTER THIRTY-SEVEN

sat cross-legged nearby in the desert sand. We didn't say anything. We had already received the news of the contact while being briefed for that night's patrol. Corporal Hill had returned and reported to the ops room, giving all the details he knew before resuming his duties and taking over the running of the quartermaster's supplies. A friendly ex-regular called Gerry from 1 Platoon was reassigned to help him, with Staffs being assigned to 1 Platoon to cover for him.

We jumped off the roof of the Land Rover after fitting the ECM and comms antennas. Thewy walked past, shaking his head as he often did. He always seemed to reflect on the deployment, drawing absurd conclusions that caused him to laugh and shake his head in disbelief. I could sympathise with his assessment. In the space of three weeks, four soldiers had been killed, all of them mounted in Snatch Land Rovers, and we were about to head out into the city in the same vehicles.

'Last supper?' he said, inviting us to the cookhouse.

'Sure, why not?' Uzi replied.

We had a couple of hours to finish our preparations, so getting a hot meal instead of a horror bag seemed like a good idea. Everything seemed to be in hand.

Drewy joined us as we headed off. He was with the REME aid detachment assigned to help us. His Land Rover wouldn't start, and he wanted a new battery. Instead, he had been given jumper cables and a portable booster pack.

'Hang on,' he said as he left his wagon behind.

The bonnet was up, and the engine was ticking over, trying to inject some fresh life into the dying power unit.

'Fuckin' REME wouldn't give us a new battery,' he complained. 'If we have to stop and go firm anywhere and it won't turn over, I'll be fuckin' raging.'

That would certainly be a problem. At over three tons in weight, the Snatch would be hard to push start – especially under fire.

We sat in the cookhouse and talked about some of our earlier patrols and contacts. We talked about escorting a pair of nervous signallers in the city and linking up with bomb disposal engineers after an explosives cache was found and needed to be blown up. We also recalled the pleasanter task of driving to the American base at Camp Doha, Kuwait. The US military certainly knew how to go to war. Their base had a cinema, internet cafe, billiard tables and a swimming pool. It had a bus service, a cookhouse that was always open and musical instruments anyone could play. With a few hours to spare before we needed to return, Uzi and I had gone for a dip in the pool but, lacking swimming attire, were soon asked to leave by the management. Visiting the PX, Uzi stocked up on smokes, and L2 bought an impressively large CD player with a dustbin-sized subwoofer for the platoon's room.

'I wish we were based there,' Thewy said.

We all agreed. It seemed the Yanks had a job for everyone and didn't need to rely on locals for support.

'I could see myself as a bus driver, doing the rounds and dropping off the ladies at the pool,' he said, and mimicked his 'funky bus driver' dance, which had been a work in progress since the arrival of L2's entertainment system.

We filled up on food, ready for the patrol. I had a double helping of Black Forest gateau, which seemed to be feature regularly on the British Army menu, no matter where we were in the world. Stick reminded us of nearly being stranded in the desert a few weeks back. During a long-range route clearance between the Palace and the logistics base, Planty saw what he thought was part of an IED on the desert track. Slamming on the brakes, he reversed straight into Stick's following vehicle, damaging the radiator. But at least we were safely away from any suspected device.

We had disembarked and checked to see what we were dealing with. If it was an IED, it was unlikely to be operated by a command wire. We could see for miles in every direction. If someone wanted to hide, watch for approaching security forces and detonate a bomb, they would need to dig a hole and live in it. Possible, but highly unlikely. The Iraqi desert in the south of the country was flat, white and featureless. There wasn't really any sand either; it was just hard-baked ground. So anyone who was out there would definitely have had some seriously impressive camouflage and concealment skills.

I later found out the desert had a name – the Al Harajah – and that, unlike the sandy deserts of western Iraq, it was composed of rocks, stones and salt flats, giving the ground its distinctive white appearance. It was nothing like the sandy yellow deserts often depicted in movies. We often had to enter the Al Harajah, since, being flat and open, it was an ideal location for the logistics base and the airport. Anytime we took

CHAPTER THIRTY-SEVEN

part in an escort, supply run or clearance we found ourselves in this vast white emptiness.

Mr Sherwood volunteered to have a closer look at what we were dealing with. I didn't think it was a good idea and told him so.

'It's not a job for an officer.'

So I went instead. If it was a bomb and it was going to go off, I thought it was unlikely I would hear or feel anything. Looking at what I could see from a few metres away, it didn't seem very large. It was metal, white and had some grey parts. I used my SUSAT (telescopic sight) to get a better look. That didn't help much. So I got closer and found that the suspicious object was actually the tail fin of a British 51mm illumination round, likely fired from a mortar during training or to provide light to a convoy transiting the desert at night.

I told the boss that it was tail fin, not connected to anything, and that I thought it would make a fine receptacle for some Pimm's with a splash of lemonade and a sprig of mint. It was not an IED, nor was it likely to be.

'Better safe than sorry, though,' Planty said.

He was right. Improvised explosives had caused numerous casualties to Coalition forces in both Iraq and Afghanistan. But now we had a new problem.

'Not a good place to crush the radiator,' Elvis noted, looking at Stick's wagon.

If it was impossible to repair, we would have needed to wait for a Chinook to become available and pick us up. It was lucky that Elvis had been on patrol with us. Being a plant engineer, he had a reasonable understanding of machinery and vehicles. He looked at the damage, then sucked his teeth as if he was about to give an absurdly expensive quote for a new part.

'Probably be able to fix it with what we have in the back. Can't say it will last for long.'

Somehow he managed to stop the radiator fluid from dripping out, and we nursed the stricken vehicle back to base.

'Time to go, then,' Rob said as he stood up, gathering his disposable utensils and making his way out of the cookhouse.

We all followed. The sun was starting to set, and we had less than an hour to double-check the vehicles and attend another briefing. After that, we would leave the main gates of the Palace and head into the city again.

Chapter Thirty-eight

Following a route that traced the shoreline of the Shatt al-Arab, we headed into Manawi al Basha. Our two vehicles were due to patrol the market before heading back towards the Palace to sweep the perimeter. It was a dark, hot night, but now that we were well into September it felt cooler – somewhere in the low 30s, as opposed to the oppressive summer temperatures we had previously endured.

Broz and I were on top cover, with Drewy and the boss up front. Following behind, Rob and Stick's patrol left a reasonable gap so that we did not bunch up and present an easy target. During training for the deployment we had not covered much in the way of mounted patrolling, as it was expected that we would be conducting static security for the whole tour. What we needed to know we had to learn 'on the job' and during our downtime. But five months into a six-month tour, we all felt confident and capable.

Being on top cover had the advantage of experiencing a constant breeze. In the evening it felt quite pleasant. It wasn't the same as having the roof down on a roadster, and the scenery wasn't exactly the green and pleasant land of Gloucestershire, but it was a lot better than the front cabin of the Snatch or, even worse, sitting in the rear troop compartment. It was also the most exposed and dangerous position. There was no protection once you were standing out of the roof hatch – except for your own personal body armour. It was a conspicuous position and vulnerable to both small-arms fire and explosives. It was also the only position that had the capability to return fire. Snatch Land Rovers were unarmed and had no firing positions from inside the vehicle. Despite it all, I liked being on top cover.

I had my night vision down and over my left eye, with my *shemagh* covering my face to stop dust and bugs from getting into my mouth

CHAPTER THIRTY-EIGHT

and nose. Broz looked the same, although he did not have night vision, instead wearing a pair of regular-issue dust goggles that gave him a 'Desert Rat' kind of look. I could see the two on top cover following us looked exactly the same, except that Elvis was carrying the patrol's firepower, a Minimi light machine gun. There was idle chatter over the PRR – nothing really worth talking about. More than likely, the two crews were staying in communication just to reassure themselves that the radio link was still working on what was proving to be a less than reliable form of comms. More than a few of the radio headsets had become unserviceable due to bad connections, which were now seen as a common fault. The wireless push-to-talk switches had all seemed to stop working. It meant that to talk we needed to use the PTT on the main transceiver. Shouting was definitely a more reliable way to communicate with each other at this point.

The road left the river bank and curved gently to the left, past a large Ferris wheel that had probably not been used in years. Every time I saw it, and the park it was located in, it reminded me of the opening sequence of *Terminator 2*, in which rocking horses and playground items are all on fire following a nuclear explosion. The park gave me the same disturbing feelings as James Cameron's sci-fi classic – although this was real life, and Arnie was not coming to save the day.

Within less than a minute we were inside the market. There was no illumination except for what our vehicles provided. The market was empty, and the buildings behind the empty stalls were dark and lifeless. It was late at night, and after a hot and tiring day of trading, the stallholders and their families must surely have been trying to rest and prepare for the following day. This was nothing unusual. Every part of the city was usually empty at night. During the day, this would have raised alarm bells. If people were not present when they were expected to be, it could indicate that perhaps they had been warned to stay away or knew something we did not and had therefore decided to stay at home. At night, however, this was not the case, and pre-contact cues were few and far between. Every contact that 3 Platoon had experienced had been at night, and there had been no obvious indication that something was about to happen.

Our small patrol entered a straight part of the road going roughly east to west. Tamooz Street joined the market to the rest of the city and beyond, with Az Zubayr being the final stop along the thoroughfare. During the day, the road was full of trucks coming in and out of Basra and was usually the responsibility of the white-shirted traffic police. At night, they would normally block the road in places, creating VCPs and enforcing a curfew. We would occasionally see them at their checkpoints when on patrol. Most of the squad would be asleep or hidden out of sight, while a couple of them sat in a police car, watching for any traffic or pedestrians. Whenever we drove past we would normally get a friendly wave and a smile. Tonight, however, there were no coppers on Tamooz Street or anywhere around the market.

Mr Sherwood decided that we should push further into the market district. He let us know over the PRR that we would head across to the next block, which was the Alquasm Market. This market was on the other side of a small river that joined the Shatt al-Arab. In fact, it was the same river that we had used for cover when we were in contact at Basra Hospital some months earlier. This area was known as Al Ashar and was outside our patrol zone, although we had been through numerous times when conducting escorts or transiting to the Hotel. It was effectively an island, surrounded entirely by rivers and canals with only a few crossing points. This was only clear when you looked at it on a map, however. When driving, the geography of the area appeared identical to the rest of the city. It was an ideal ambush point, as any routes out of Al Ashar could easily be covered by hostile forces.

As our vehicles crossed into Alquasm Market there was an explosion. The noise reached me after the flash of light, and the blast knocked me to the side, causing me almost to fly over the open hatch. Drewy put his foot down, and all of a sudden I was thrown the other way as he swung the vehicle to the side, pointing us south and towards the Palace.

'CONTACT!' shouted Broz as he started shooting.

I picked myself up and looked to see where he was firing. My night vision had been blown from my helmet, held in place on my cheek by its lanyard. Before I could identify any targets I saw another explosion behind us, only metres away. It detonated in slow motion and looked white – not like the orange Hollywood fireballs so often seen in films. It was close. The first explosion had been between our two vehicles, which were only 20 metres or so apart. With two targets to fire at, it was a miracle that neither of the vehicles was hit. Instead, a wall was now

CHAPTER THIRTY-EIGHT

disintegrating onto the road. The second rocket must have hit a piece of street furniture, as it seemed to explode low, without hitting anything obvious.

Within moments small-arms fire started. The AK is an extremely loud weapon that fires 7.62mm bullets at an extremely high rate. There were bursts of fire coming from all around us, indicating that the ambush consisted of more than one group. Forcing myself to focus and return fire, I tried to look for who was shooting at us. I pressed the safety switch and looked over my sights. All around, I could hear the sounds of battle. Broz and the other vehicle were firing. I could hear bursts of fire from the Minimi as the powerful V8 engines pushed us out of the contact. I was suddenly very frustrated. I felt like I was the only member of the patrol that wasn't doing anything. Maybe I was – the drivers were driving, the top cover was shooting and the commanders were commanding.

I saw a figure running on the other side of the river bank that separated the market from downtown Basra. Two others joined him, and I could see they were looking at us. They were in dark clothing, except for the white shoes or trainers they all seemed to be wearing. I could see they were repositioning. I could see they were armed. I could see the sickle-shaped magazines protruding from their weapons. One was carrying a tube on his shoulder. Was this the guy who had fired the RPGs at us? Did he want another go? To me it looked like they had broken cover and were trying to set up a shot at the rear of our vehicles as we made our way out of the contact and back to Tamooz Street, which had a long straight section. It would not be difficult for him to miss for a third time.

Broz continued firing. I could feel his ejected bullet cases hitting my chest while I took aim. The evasive driving was causing my sight picture to move wildly, but I had the three in my sights. As soon as the SUSAT's needle was on one of the three, I fired. It wasn't a single well-aimed shot, but it was the best I could hope for. I fired five or six rapid shots. He went to ground. Did I hit him? Did Broz hit him? Was the other vehicle also engaging? Was he taking cover? Before I could fire again, we turned hard left onto Al Saadi Street and broke contact. I struggled to regain my balance and immediately began looking out for any follow-up. I could hear on my PRR that we were making our way rapidly back to Basra Palace. There was now only the sound of the engines – as well as a ringing in my ears. I turned to face forward. I continued to look around, but then remembered the feeling of the ejected bullet cases against my chest. Were those bullet cases? I quickly looked down to make sure that I hadn't been hit and looked at my fingers to make sure that they weren't covered in blood. I hadn't been hit. Nobody had been hit. But it had been close.

The QRF linked up with us, and we disembarked, providing an all-around defence. It didn't take long for the ops room to recall us to the Palace. Whereas the QRF suggested heading back in with four vehicles, the major wanted a report so that he could arrange for some better-armed units from elsewhere in the city. As we drove back, I couldn't help but think about how such a well-armed and coordinated ambush had known we were coming. They must have seen us leave the Palace. Then they must have seen us join the road beside the river. That was stupid. It was a one-way road. Of course, they knew where we were heading. Unless we were going to do a three-point turn and head back, they would have had plenty of time to get themselves set up and ready.

Back at the Palace, we jumped out of our vehicles. One of the team bent over and was sick. Rob put his hand on the back of his neck and massaged him, while Stick grabbed a bottle of water and poured it down the back of his shirt to cool him down. The rest of us unloaded our weapons. We were debriefed by Mr Evans and once again gave statements to the RMP about what we had been up to. Drewy was furious. Rightly so. He had wanted a new battery for his wagon. L2 had to calm him down.

'Leave it, mate, don't bother.'

He was intent on finding the REME technician who had given him the booster pack instead.

'It's done. It's over.'

Drewy was verbalizing a lot of 'what ifs': 'What if we dismounted and couldn't restart the motor?' 'What if I stalled it and couldn't get it going again?'

He had done a really good job, and to be fair, we were all thinking what he was saying. It was either good luck or bad shooting on the part of the RPG that had kept our platoon from being wiped out.

Part V
THE RETURN

Chapter Thirty-nine

Six months and several days after arriving in Basra, we were preparing to leave. We had been given the option to stay for an additional two months as part of a platoon that would escort the ATO (Ammunition Technical Officers) during their bomb disposal tasks around the city. With the massive IED threat, they had their work cut out and were always on call. Although several volunteered, none were from 3 Platoon. By then, we were all ready to head back. The marines had arrived, and we were busy handing over the accommodation, ECM and vehicles.

Wearing his coveted beret, Craig Jones, a marine who had been in training at Oakhampton while we were there at the same time, caught my eye. I went over to him.

'You made it, then, mate?' I extended my hand. 'Last time I saw you, you were getting ready to yomp over the Tors. Things are a bit different here to Dartmoor.'

He nodded: 'So we were told.'

He was looking at a folding camp chair I was packing up. I had nicked it months ago and used it as my La-Z-Boy for most of the tour.

'You want this?'

It didn't seem right to bring questionably appropriated stuff back to the UK with me.

'Yeah, all right.'

He pulled some dollars out of his pocket.

'No, no, you just have it, mate.'

'You sure?'

I was sure.

'Yeah, just take it.'

I folded it into its shoulder bag and handed it over.

'Let me introduce you to my guys,' he suggested.

CHAPTER THIRTY-NINE

The section of eight bootnecks was moving into our room. They looked tough. But then again, except for the occasional battle with insurgents, I mostly just knew the world of finance. These guys were professional hard men. Even Craig looked tougher than me, and he had been in the year below me at school.

'This is Matty,' he announced as we went in.

'All right, mate?'

I got a few nods.

'Me and Matt were at school together. Now he's just finishing up his tour.'

'Small world,' said one of the marines.

He was right. The odds did seem pretty remote.

'What's the city like?' another asked.

I tried my best to answer their questions but knew from experience that it would be hard to provide satisfactory answers. We had done the same thing when we took over the Palace's force protection role. I brought them a box full of uneaten rations, along with some bits and pieces that weren't coming with us: spare batteries, tubes of toothpaste and things that make life in the desert a little bit easier. After a few 'good lucks' and 'take cares', I left them to it and went back to 3 Platoon to get ready to leave the Palace for the last time. While most of the company was going back to Shaibah, for a good meal and air-conditioned tents, Uzi and I had been chosen to accompany the baggage to Basra Airport to ensure it didn't go missing.

'This is shit,' Uzi said as we sat around with nothing to do. 'Out of the entire company, why us?'

We had arranged the company baggage by platoon as ordered and now had nearly twenty-four hours to kill before Salamanca Company joined us at the airport. We had managed to find some plastic chairs, but the heat of the un-air-conditioned terminal had made the plastic go soft, so if one sat in the chair, the legs would inevitably collapse. Instead, the bergens we were watching over became our makeshift beds and sofas.

'I'm going to get some scoff,' Uzi announced abruptly.

I was listening to music on my minidisc player and re-reading a manga book.

'What?'

I unplugged one of my earpieces.

'I said I'm going to get some scoff. So you wait here.'

I turned a page, half wondering if I would ever have the ability to draw like the artist in my book.

'All right, well, bring something back for me.'

Thinking ahead, I had brought a load of snacks and some water bottles, so I made myself at home while Uzi went in search of his evening meal. What I had not brought with me was any insect spray. Flies were buzzing all over the place and were extremely interested in sampling the salt in my sweat. I found my bergen and took out my mosquito net. Using the plastic furniture, I built what looked like a four-poster bed with curtains and waited for my colleague to return.

Uzi brought back an absolute feast. Somehow he had managed to snaffle a whole loaf of bread, some little pots of jam, a paper plate piled high with chips, and slices of cold meat.

'Nice scratcher,' he said as he passed a plate of cold chips through the mozzie net.

He also produced a can of bug spray. However, it did not have the push button to discharge the gas, only a small plastic nozzle that connected to the pressurised contents inside. So instead of single well-aimed shots at incoming bugs, Uzi resorted to letting off clouds of gas that covered the immediate area with insecticide.

'All this shit can't be healthy,' he said as he released another dose that produced around 80 per cent cloud cover. As an antidote to the chemical attack, he lit up a cigarette and lay back on a pile of luggage, now temporarily bug-free.

The rest of the company joined us the following morning. After a lot of waiting around, we eventually boarded an RAF Hercules and left Iraq behind, bound for Bahrain and then a civvy airliner to the UK. There were rumours of a stopover in Cyprus for some much-needed R&R, but no such luck. From the Middle East we were non-stop to Brize Norton, Oxfordshire.

We landed at Brize on a cold, wet October morning. Everyone was still in their desert fatigues, but very few seemed to mind the chilly air. Collecting our equipment, we were immediately bussed to the mobilization centre at Chilwell to be discharged from regular service back into the reserves. There was no ceremony or welcome. It was simple and businesslike. We handed back our weapons and body armour.

CHAPTER THIRTY-NINE

Expensive pieces of equipment such as the night vision sets, PRRs and LLMs were also returned. We spoke to some clerks about money matters and finally changed into civvy clothing. Everyone looked like they were dressed for a day at the beach. We made our way to the NAAFI for some 'real' food, while the officers went to the officers' mess. It was the last I saw of them.

Aside from our contingent, the NAAFI was full of reserves who had been deployed to other parts of Iraq. There was no room to sit at most of the tables, and all around, people were enjoying their first pint in months or some high-calorie, greasy food. Considering that most of our diet in theatre was based on chips and white bread, I was surprised to see that most people were filling their faces with similar items, burgers, butties and such. I had a pizza, which by NAAFI standards is cheese on toast but circular in shape. It tasted great.

The payphones had a huge queue. Smiling fathers were speaking to their kids and loved ones. Boyfriends spoke to girlfriends and husbands to their wives. It was good to see. Those with mobile phones stood around in the car park in their unit T-shirts, making calls and seemingly immune to the cold air. I called home. After being dropped off in Gloucester, which is not far from Brize, I planned to stop over at my father's.

We were all happy to have made it. It had been a tough tour. Many of us felt like we had achieved something. Whether we had or not, strategically, is open to debate. But we had undoubtedly achieved things at a personal level. In the bar the sole topic of discussion was what people were going to do tomorrow. We would finally be home and in our own beds.

Chapter Forty

I was met in Gloucester by my father. His car was parked right outside the gate to the TA centre.

'Can you give Stick a lift to the station?' I asked him.

Stick, who was heading home to Bath, decided that the quickest way was by train, and the quickest way to the station was a lift, even if it was only walking distance. After six months in the desert, even a short walk didn't appeal to any of us. Anyway, it was the least we could do. I knew that if he had wanted a lift all the way back to Bath, that could easily have been arranged as well.

As soon as I arrived at my father's house I went for a soak in the bath. I just lay there until the water went cold. I wasn't in the mood for talking. Anyone who wanted to speak to me would just have to hang on. They could wait. I took a deep breath and bit the inside of my cheeks, then exhaled slowly – a childhood reaction to stress and difficulties. But I wasn't stressed. I was enjoying the quiet and the calm. It felt like a new experience, but of course, it wasn't. As I soaked in the tub, I didn't think about Iraq, Basra or the past six months. I thought about nothing, because nothing came to mind.

The following day, I returned to the family home in the countryside. It was strange to hear the cows in the neighbouring fields first thing in the morning. Their lowing woke me up, and it was impossible to get back to sleep. I got up and went downstairs. Just like when my call-up papers arrived, I turned on the TV and decided what to do with the day. It was a Thursday, and everyone I knew – family and friends – were at work. The girl I had been writing to was studying until the evening. So I had a whole day off before needing to head back to the TA centre for the local media on Friday. They wanted to run a special edition welcoming back the city's soldiers. In exchange for some war stories,

CHAPTER FORTY

anecdotes and photo opportunities, they had agreed to provide pizza and beer. That seemed like a fair exchange. And it was something to do. We were also ordered to have fun later that month. A weekend of adventure training in Taunton had been arranged, complete with camp beds in the drill hall and a tenner for every man in the company. 'Sounds great,' I thought to myself. 'What's in Taunton anyway?' I guessed the plan was for everyone to get pissed and sleep it off in the TA centre.

The Glosters of Salamanca Company arrived to meet the press at our small base. Some simple bunting and decorations had been put up in the drill hall and bar. 'The Readers of *The Citizen* Welcome You Home,' read a yellow banner with black lettering. Waiting for us were a few journalists and photographers from the local rag, along with Eddie Fry, the admin officer, and Major Wood. Compared to the journos and admin staff, we looked tanned and lean. We each had our photo taken and were then asked about our experiences. A similar sort of interview had been conducted before deploying, but I didn't recognize any of these correspondents. Before we had deployed, they had run a special as well. Luckily, everyone from that edition was now safely back home.

'Can you tell me who you are and what your role was?' one of the journalists asked me.

I explained that I was an infantryman, just like everyone else, but had also had some medical training.

'Oh! Did it come in handy?' she asked.

'How do you mean?'

She was writing shorthand notes on a pad as she spoke.

'Well, did you have to use your first aid skills?'

'First aid?' I asked myself. 'Oh yeah, sure . . . you know, being on foot patrol can be hard work. Blisters and things, you know? And one time my mate shut his thumb in the car door . . .'

She carried on scribbling.

'And what differences did you notice most between Gloucester and Basra?'

In truth, the two cities were worlds apart, but I didn't want to say that. The wrong occupation in Basra was basically a death sentence, as was the wrong political opinion. In Gloucester, things were arguably a little more easygoing.

'Well, yeah, very different. You know, girls weren't allowed outside without a bloke escorting them. They certainly couldn't enjoy a night out or a glass of Pimm's either.'

I moved to another member of the press and spoke about some of the equipment and vehicles we had been using. He had some photos that had been given to him by the Army, and I looked through them, highlighting where I was and what was happening in the image. Eddie Fry was nearby, making sure that we didn't over-elaborate on anything. The subject changed back to patrols and combat.

'What was it like, being on patrol? Did you see any action?'

I answered as best I could: 'What was it like on patrol? Hot. Uncomfortable. Tiring. As for action, I think we all saw action, mate.'

Towards the end of my interviews, Eddie announced, 'Right. Pizza, beer.'

It wasn't even eleven in the morning.

'Five o'clock somewhere!' said Kav as we made our way to the waiting food and drinks.

We finished up answering a few more questions while dining on our complimentary Italian cuisine. Simple, less formal questions like 'What did you miss the most?' or 'What are your plans now that you're home?' With most of the unit slowly getting pissed, the major set us up for a group photo and ushered us outside. It all seemed bizarre. Waiting wives and girlfriends started their cars as we exited the drill hall, and took their other halves home. Nobody was in the mood to hang around.

Deciding to enjoy a walk with a lower risk of getting shot, I reflected on the interviews. The questions I had been asked, the answers I had overheard and the answers that I had given. None of it conveyed a sense of what Basra was really like. For me, anyway. Looking back, I realized maybe we were all guarding our responses and just providing *The Citizen* with enough to fill out their special edition. Nobody spoke about being in contact; people being killed or wounded; the privations suffered by the population. Nobody spoke about himself as a hero either, or claimed to have opened fire or thrown a grenade. Instinctively, it seemed that everyone had just let the journos ask their open-ended questions and filled in a few blanks where they needed some extra details.

CHAPTER FORTY

The following day, I picked up a copy of the paper. We were front-page material, with a multi-page insert. 'Impressive,' I thought. I sat at home and read the special edition. 'Heroes' Welcome. They're Back from Iraq!' I opened the pages and set the paper down on the coffee table. 'I won't let daddy go away again . . .' A picture of Metal Mickey and his son, Ryan, took up most of the first page. 'Brave Territorial Army soldiers were reunited in Gloucester yesterday after returning from a six-month tour of duty in Iraq. The regiment was based at Basra Palace – a less volatile area than central Basra – but it still came under attack from mortars and rockets.'

'Yeah, and the rest,' I thought to myself.

'They had an area around the Palace to protect but came under attack from rocket-powered grenades by militia.'

'Outstanding journalism.'

'Children would crowd around the soldiers and ask for dollars. Some would come up to the gates and try to sell torches, flags, and football strips.'

'No mention of the copious amounts of porn and slabs of Pepsi that provided those kids with a regular income, then,' I thought as I laughed into my morning brew.

The extra edition concluded with, 'Your TA needs you! If you have been inspired by the courageous actions of our boys in Iraq, why not join the TA? The Eastern Avenue-based unit needs new recruits to swell the ranks.'

It was certainly true that in recent years the TA had shifted from focusing on the defence of national interests to becoming more of a manpower reserve to supplement the Army in operations abroad. With a reduced full-time military, the TA definitely needed us. In 1996, John Major's Conservative government passed legislation allowing the Secretary of State for Defence to call out individual reservists as well as components of the Territorial Army. Five years later, Tony Blair's Labour government used this legislation for the first time in response to the 9/11 attacks and the invasion of Afghanistan. It was used for a second time in 2003, for the invasion of Iraq. In total, nearly 10,000 reservists were deployed in some capacity on Operation TELIC, accounting for around one-fifth of the UK's deployed personnel. A law that I had never heard of had changed my life forever.

I closed the newspaper, folded it carefully, and put it away in my desk. I would probably want to read it again later. But not now. I decided that I would head into town and catch up with some of my colleagues from work. A few of them had sent me blueys, and I wanted to thank them for taking the time to write. I needed to figure out when I was expected back as well, although I knew it wouldn't be until after the New Year. Two months off. Perfect.

Chapter Forty-one

Cheltenham was a great place to unwind, especially after the intensity of deployment. The girl I had been seeing lived in the town, towards the posh area, though she vehemently argued she herself was in no way posh or privileged. She was definitely a rebel, often fixing fluorescent clip-on dreadlocks into her hair and favouring dark clothing that seemed more suited to *The Matrix*. She enjoyed heavy metal music, tarot cards and, for some reason, the ongoing saga of *Footballers' Wives* – a programme about the trials and tribulations of a fictional Premier League football club's WAGS.

It was easy for me to visit her, and even though she was supposed to be a student at the local university, she didn't spend much time studying. Instead, she was more of a socialite and very popular on the alternative scene. She had even secured a modelling contract with an American wrestling competition scheduled to visit the UK that winter, and would be working ringside for one of their stars.

Despite our opposite lifestyles, we had a lot in common. And although she wouldn't admit it, she was extremely intelligent. I had met her just before deploying, during one of our weekends off while training at Okehampton. She knew a lot of my twin brother's friends, other students, and we had started talking while out in town. Things went well between us, and we spent a lot of time together, though we never 'became official', as she put it. That arrangement suited us, and now that I was back, we had picked up where we left off.

Down in Taunton, where we were ordered to have fun, each member of the company first had to sit through a decompression course to be assessed for signs of stress or psychological illness as a result of the tour. Reckless behaviour, such as speeding, heavy drinking or drug use, was highlighted. I had been picked up by the coppers that morning for speeding, but that was because I was being a dickhead in my new car rather than suffering from PTSD.

The decompression course was a mix of useful information and what felt like obvious reminders. As we sat in the drab room, listening to a psychologist drone on about the importance of mental health, I couldn't help but let my mind wander back to some of the lighter moments in Iraq. For some reason, I thought about patrolling Mitan, when we came under indirect fire. Once we were sure everyone was okay, the lieutenant ordered us to move out, double time, and get to a new position. As I was leading I set the pace pretty damn fast and somehow kept it going for the best part of two kilometres while carrying around 40lbs of kit. Of course, those following did not want to come across as unfit either, so the whole platoon repositioned in record time. I laughed to myself when I remembered looking at the out-of-breath faces after we went back into cover. The glares coming my way were not looks of admiration. Stick was put on point after that.

The dull PowerPoint presentation and unenthusiastic speakers made it seem more like a 'tick box' exercise than a genuine concern for our welfare. It seemed as though most of the blokes, like me, were thinking about something else. I looked around the room. It was only the grunts. The officers presumably debriefed their experiences somewhere else. The tour before us had been able to do their decompression at Akrotiri in Cyprus. That would have been better than Taunton.

At that time there was very little aftercare offered to service people, especially reservists, following a deployment. This was partly because Op TELIC was hastily put together, with an emphasis on military results rather than personal safety. Additionally, in late 2004, the operation was still in its early phases. The peacekeeping work had only just begun, and our political leaders seemed unsure about the direction they wanted to take – more troops, fewer troops, more kit, less kit? When we deployed we had less equipment than a company of soldiers in Northern Ireland during the Troubles. No serious armour and no serious firepower. We were using Saxon vehicles from the 80s and wearing body armour more suited to training than ops. Some of us even wore green DPM (disruptive pattern material) uniform components. However, upgrades were now being delivered to the Army in the form of new armoured vehicles, PPE and more reliable weapon systems. This was, of course, at great expense to the taxpayer, which partly explained the apparent dithering in Westminster regarding the nature of the

CHAPTER FORTY-ONE

deployment. Now that 'regime change' had been achieved, Iraq and the Army seemed like a better investment than ever.

Halfway through our decompression seminar, the padre came to have a word. He was a tall old man with a calm presence, fitting the stereotype perfectly.

'Remember,' he began, 'the Lord walks with you, even through the darkest valleys.'

I did not have much to say to the good reverend; none of us did, and before long we were in our civvies, each handed our promised tenner, and off into town. Naturally, the night out became a platoon thing, each platoon doing its own thing before dissolving into sections and then pairs around the pubs and clubs of Taunton.

Most of the company managed to find their way back to the TA base sometime in the morning. I was probably one of the first to arrive, along with Stick, Broz, and L2, as none of us were particularly heavy drinkers. Planty had gone missing – again – but it was his local haunt, so we trusted that he had found his way back home on autopilot. Others didn't reappear until breakfast time, having made their own arrangements or having pulled an all-nighter somewhere. The hair of the dog was on offer to anyone needing a medicinal solution to any lingering effects from the night before, but most opted for coffee and a Full English. It was one of the last times Salamanca Company would all be together. As we sat around the drill hall there was a sense of camaraderie that would be hard to replicate, and I knew it. I wouldn't feel this again in the world of finance or in following my career goals.

True to his word, the week after, Rob invited me to his place of work and introduced me to some of his staff. They were very nice, very talented and surprisingly chatty. Rob was pleased with himself, clearly proud to show off his naive military friend and introduce him to that particular type of adult entertainment. It was a nice gesture, albeit an expensive one.

When I returned I met up with my girlfriend. We went to a café in Cheltenham, one of her favourite spots. She looked great as usual, her dark attire contrasting with her neon-green dreadlocks.

'So, how was it?'

We spent the rest of the evening talking about everything and nothing, the way we always did. Even though moments like these made all the difference, we left it at that.

Chapter Forty-two

I wasn't due back at work until the following year, but I had been attending drill evenings with the RGBW, although I had avoided any of the weekend training. I was keen to pick up where I had left off and go for a commission. Since I was young, the same age as most University Officer Training Corps cadets, the admin officer had managed to get me enrolled into Bristol UOTC, and I was due to start training there in the spring. I had driven down one evening and introduced myself to the staff who ran the unit. I then spent the rest of the drill night watching Steven Spielberg's *Saving Private Ryan* with the rest of the officer cadets. I thought the film was of questionable value, but it was certainly more comfortable than PT. After the movie, there was some light discussion about the decision-making processes that Tom Hanks' character went through, but more talk about the many apparent inaccuracies and bits of movie trivia.

The following week, back at Gloucester, I was called to see the major in his office.

'Sit down, please. Take your beret off.'

I hadn't been back long enough to get into any trouble, so I was curious to find out why I had been called in. The OC handed me a plain white envelope with no name or insignia on it. I opened it and took out the letter. It read:

> From Major General CH Elliott CVO CBE, Colonel Commandant The Prince of Wales's Division, Headquarters Infantry:
>
> Dear Private Okuhara,
> I am writing to say how delighted I am to see that you have been commended in the latest Operational Awards List for

CHAPTER FORTY-TWO

your outstanding service in operations in Iraq. I send you sincere congratulations on behalf of all ranks of The Prince of Wales's Division. This is excellent news and you should feel very proud. This award marks your professionalism and commitment and is not lightly given. My warmest personal congratulations on this richly deserved award.

Yours sincerely,

It was then signed, in a fashion more artistic than legible.

I put the letter back into the envelope. The major was looking at me, expecting me to say something. I must have been looking blank.

'Did you check the Part One orders in the drill hall?' he asked.

Part One orders were a weekly communication from Rifle Volunteers HQ, and I hardly ever looked at them. Nobody did. Normally they contained procedural details that didn't seem to apply to the soldiers of A Company all that often. He handed me a copy. Three of Salamanca Company were to be commended for their actions on Operation Telic IV. Two were sergeants, and one was a private – me. The Part One orders did not offer any citation of what I had done to earn this accolade, but I could guess.

'Your award will be delivered here. You can have it given to you privately if you wish . . . the Lord Lieutenant can award you, if you prefer? We can forward it to the brigade for something larger?'

I put the envelope in my leg pocket and closed the button.

'Can't you award it to me, sir?'

We were due to have our annual company mess function within a few weeks to celebrate our safe return. I thought that would be as good a time as any. Other company awards were due to be given out at the same time, so it seemed to make sense.

'I can, if you want me to,' he responded, indicating also that it was time for me to get out of his office so that he could focus on more important matters.

I stood up, put my beret back on, saluted, and left.

I went back down to the drill hall and checked the Part One orders. I wanted to make sure that it wasn't an elaborate wind-up and that I hadn't been handed a spurious copy of orders in some kind of hoax. Foz and Kav were beside the orders and both shook me by the hand.

'Well done, mate.'

I must have been looking a bit dazed. I certainly felt it. I wasn't expecting to be awarded any kind of accolade.

'What's it for?'

I gave them the condensed as opposed to the King James version.

'It was for that contact in May. On the 16th.'

There had been a few contacts in what had been dubbed 'mad May' by the battlegroup we were attached to.

'When that IZP copper got shot and I tried to stop him bleeding to death. And that other one that I dragged to the hospital.'

Foz's platoon had been in contact the day before so it made sense that he wasn't overly familiar with what my platoon had been up to. As one of the section commanders, he had been escorting his guys through the RMP interviews and writing up after action reports.

'Oh yeah, I read that in company orders. Good skills.'

I soon shook myself out of it and joined the rest of the company for some PT. Running alongside a new recruit called Carl, who also had designs on becoming an officer, I was quizzed by him about the UOTC.

'Can't really say all that much about it, to be honest,' I told him.

Carl was older than me, I guessed in his late twenties or early thirties. He lived in a townhouse in Cheltenham and had a well-paid office job. He definitely had an aloof air about him, like an officer from the Great War – or Lieutenant Thynn from Salamanca Company.

'I only went for one evening to make introductions. They didn't seem to have any military training planned for that night either. Anyway, the normal route is to go through some prep for the Officer Selection Board. Eddie just threw me in there so that I can get a bit of exposure to the management side of the military. You're better off asking him or the major, I think.'

I wanted to change the subject. I was by no means an expert on that sort of thing, but I did know that a few strings had been pulled to get me enrolled at the UOTC.

The Permanent Staff Administration Officer (PSAO – pronounced 'Pay-so') had told me, 'You're still wet behind the ears. If you want to be an officer, you will need to learn more about the Army. And yourself.'

He was right. I never felt that I was particularly suited to the military, despite my genuine interest in it.

CHAPTER FORTY-TWO

The following weekend, I was at the Artillery Grounds at Whiteladies Road in Bristol to train with the UOTC. It was my first weekend with them. There were plenty of cadets – around forty or so. That was more than the RGBW could pull together for most weekend training schemes. We drove up to the Prince William of Gloucester Barracks in Grantham. Along the way, the coach stopped for an (apparently) obligatory McDonald's takeaway at a service station. Apparently, if you produced a military ID there was a discount to be had.

'You coming?' one of the cadets I had been chatting with asked, as he got out of his seat.

I came along and just ordered a milkshake.

'Aren't you having anything to eat?' a cadet queried.

I explained, 'No, I don't really like McDonald's and there isn't anything for veggies anyway.'

A few eyebrows were raised.

'You can't be a vegetarian in the Army, mate. Well, definitely not the infantry.'

I slurped my milkshake and nodded a non-committal agreement with their observations. I wasn't prepared to have this conversation yet again.

The other officer cadets knew that I was from the Territorial Army, not a student, and that I was there to learn parts of the reserve officer training curriculum. They knew because they had been told by their own admin staff and because I had done the same as I made small talk about what degrees they were taking and whether they had any further military ambitions after graduation. There was a whole host of beret colours, indicating which cadets and under officers were being sponsored through their studies by particular regiments. I had my RGBW beret on for now, but was disappointed to read, in Part One orders that week, that the Glosters were to be stood down and absorbed into a larger formation. This was a bitter disappointment. As a transition, the RGBW was to become the RGBW LI (Light Infantry). Then, after the unit was integrated into the LI, the Devon and Dorsets would also come on board, forming a new large regiment simply called The Rifles.

We arrived in Grantham for a weekend of basic training. It was all quite easy and straightforward. Even the newest officer cadets needed very little in the way of instruction. It was almost identical to the training weekends I had done when I was a brand-new recruit – with a bit more emphasis on people management. Out on the training area, one group went through camouflage and concealment, whilst another did harbour routines. A third group went through how to deliver a set of orders, and a fourth, through the basics of a section attack. The four activities took up most of the day, and when we finished we were able to use the officers' mess at the barracks as opposed to the NAAFI. It was a lot more comfortable than anything I had experienced so far. The bed wasn't exactly soft, but at least it wasn't a camp bed or one with a plastic mattress. And whereas I used to share a room with the entire platoon, this time I only had one roommate, who was good enough to wake me up in time for breakfast.

The next day, we were given the task of conducting a reconnaissance patrol; or rather, the under officers, who were third- or fourth-year officer cadets, took the role of platoon and section commander and were given the task of arranging the reconnaissance of an enemy airfield. The airfield was a disused runway from the Second World War, part of the adjoining training area. Looking over the shoulder of the under officers, it seemed to be a straightforward job. They checked the maps and made notes. They talked amongst themselves and tried to create unique tactics and unpredictable approaches to the area. They decided that they would take the platoon north, split into three sections and conduct the recce from two directions, whilst the third section acted as security for the FRV (final rendezvous). I was put into the third section.

'Seeing as you're only new, you can go in with the other first years,' I was told as the sections were finalized. 'You can carry the LSW as well.'

There were a few laughs. Nobody enjoyed carrying the Light Support Weapon variant of the SA80, but honestly, I didn't mind. If I was in the FRV I wasn't likely to fire it. This was confirmed by the generous allotment of five rounds of ammunition per cadet. So I wouldn't be cleaning it much even if I chewed through the whole magazine. Anyway, it was definitely lighter than everything that I had been carrying in Basra. I just nodded and decided to relax into the patrol.

So far I hadn't needed to apply myself too much, although learning about the orders process in greater detail was definitely interesting. At the FRV we went into all-round defence and waited for the other two sections to return. Forming part of the old airfield taxiway, our FRV

CHAPTER FORTY-TWO

was made up of some abandoned buildings and worn-out car tyres that were overgrown with several years' worth of weeds. It was quite an obvious area, so would be easy for the other sections to find in the dark. Tactically, though, it would also have been easy for an enemy force to locate and neutralize. The officer cadets weren't especially tactically aware, however. Even the under officer who was nominally the section commander seemed to be taking things a little bit too easy. I guessed, correctly, that he had done almost identical exercises before.

'Yeah, it's good being at the FRV. We don't have to do anything,' he whispered to me. 'We'll just wait for the other two sections to patrol past us and bring up the rear. Should take around an hour and a bit.'

'That's quite fast for a CTR,' I told him.

Stick, who had come from the Rifle Volunteers recce platoon, often talked about the skills needed for that kind of work. In Iraq, we had occasionally done reconnaissance tasks, but I had not done a CTR (close target reconnaissance) since my days at the Infantry Training Centre. Even then, it took pretty much an entire night.

* * *

Now I recalled an occasion in Iraq when we had needed to revert to our green DPM jackets, which were harder to see in the dark. We had to insert ourselves into an abandoned building to watch a specific road near the rear gates of the Palace. Getting everyone in position, without drawing any attention from the city below us, took over an hour, and that was before we could get the comms set up and start reporting back our observations.

Leaving the Palace through the rear gates, we were immediately in a wasteland of unfinished and half-destroyed buildings. The area was completely unlit, and at night it was pitch-black. Moving through the terrain without disturbing the loose ground and causing noise was hard enough, but doing it in near-blackout conditions was even harder.

We were occupying the shell of a three-storey building. As far as we could tell, by the lack of any significant activity, we had managed to get in unnoticed. This meant that for the next few hours we could provide detailed observations of that part of the city. Concerns had been raised about the number of new residents arriving and their proximity to the

British base. We wanted to watch them watching us, and identify likely positions for observations.

Just as we were getting settled in, the building was illuminated – not by a torch or searchlight, but by an overloaded power unit. The locals had managed to attach an unbelievable number of makeshift power lines to the one live electricity outlet in the area. It just happened to be directly opposite us, and it caught fire while we were trying to remain unnoticed. If the power unit didn't burn itself out, there was a good chance the locals would try to extinguish the blaze, or the fire brigade would be brought in, no doubt ascending the building we were occupying to tackle the fire.

We all lay prone on the floor, hoping not to provide silhouettes which would draw attention to us. After about ten seconds the white sparks turned into yellow flames, and the junction box, presumably after charring the wood it was attached to to the point of uselessness, fell away. Those of us with night vision quickly used it to assess how much attention was coming our way. It was about two in the morning, and in the stifling night-time heat nobody had really paid any attention. Maybe that kind of thing happened regularly. A few men were leaning out of windows and looking over balconies, probably thinking about a new way to power their homes now that the entire block opposite was without power. No doubt, by the time first light came around, some knowledgeable electricians would be coming to assess the damage, along with keen recyclers looking to take advantage of the highly valuable conductive metals in the cables and power unit. It was time for us to leave before they got here. Getting back out without any indication we had been there took just as long as getting in.

* * *

'Was that fast?' asked the under officer, having listened to my account, with an air of doubt and superior knowledge thrown in for good measure.

'It usually only takes an hour or so. Afterwards we'd stay up and write patrol reports before bed.'

I nodded and thought to myself, 'I should have gone to uni like my twin brother and joined a UOTC. This is a piece of cake. And I'm getting paid.'

CHAPTER FORTY-TWO

We carried on making conversation in our section. I looked out towards where we were expecting the rest of the platoon to return from. Nobody else seemed overly bothered, and there was quiet conversation going on all around.

'How long have you been in the Terries, then?' one cadet asked.

'About two years. Not long.'

A few second-year UOTC students had been in the same amount of time.

'I've been in three,' the section leader said, and added, 'Hoping to do my board and get a reserve commission before I graduate.'

I nodded.

'Well, yeah, good luck with that. Which regiment?'

He wanted to go into the RLC, Royal Logistics Corps. I didn't ask why. They were definitely a good choice, with lots of opportunities for those who weren't looking for a combat role.

'Where do you want to go?' he asked.

'Well, I guess it will be The Rifles,' I told him, 'when they finally get formed. When I started out, I wanted to be in the Glosters, but they won't be around much longer.'

'Well, in a bigger regiment there's more chance that you'll be able to do something like Iraq or Afghan if you wanted. I don't think the small county regiments even deploy anymore.'

I carried on looking out, waiting for the rest of the cadets to return.

'I suppose you're right. It looks like the first section is coming back now. We should get ready to move.'

Chapter Forty-three

The company came together for the annual mess night, with the officers in uniform as tradition dictated. I couldn't wait to wear my own mess dress one day; the bold reds looked very impressive. I wondered if the uniform would change to dark green once we became The Rifles, and I mentioned this to my date as we took our seats at the end of the first table.

The mess was held in the drill hall, which served as the main indoor space for almost every activity in the Territorial Army. The building in Gloucester was quite old, making it a fitting venue for the annual function. In the corner was a small bar used only for special occasions like this. On the walls were displayed large wooden plaques detailing the Glosters' achievements over the years. While we ate off standard Army folding tables, Mo, the storeman, had dressed them with fine tablecloths and regimental silver, hiding the grubby old worktops. With a top table for the officers and three lines of tables extending from it, the room was nearly full. Most of the company attended, many with dates. Those without mess dress wore black tie, and the women were in their best dresses.

I arrived at the TA centre in my new car, the one I had been pulled over in a couple of weeks earlier. I had saved money while I was away and, with no bills to pay, treated myself to something sportier than a Ford Fiesta. It was probably more car than I could handle, but it was mine.

'Fuckin' nice car,' a slightly drunk Bons said to me. 'Going for the young officer stereotype already, are you? Nice car, no cash?'

He was right. A friend of mine, the son of a doctor, had recently graduated from Sandhurst into the Royal Artillery and bought a TVR as soon as he could. The car's unreliability and expense were beside the point.

CHAPTER FORTY-THREE

'It's all about image in the first few years,' he had commented.

He did have a nicer motor than me, though at least mine required no horrendous monthly repayments.

'I'm not there yet, and I'm definitely a long way off,' I told Bons.

If I was going to complete the entire syllabus at Bristol, it would take up to three years.

'But if I'm going to be driving over to Whiteladies every week and weekend, why not do it in style?'

Bons raised his pint and winked.

We sat down to our meal, making polite conversation with those beside and opposite. Much of the talk revolved around Operation TELIC and Op Fingal (in Afghanistan), which had also seen some of the Glosters deployed. Before and between courses, speeches and toasts were given. Sitting opposite, I noticed Broz and his date had drained more than a few glasses. The officers' port decanter was gradually emptying, and the sergeants' table held an unbelievable number of empty pint glasses.

After dessert was cleared, the chairman of the mess, the most junior officer, announced, 'The company awards will now be distributed.'

The first award was a local one. The company 2i/c, also a troop commander in 21 SAS, had donated a trophy to A Company, awarded to a soldier voted for by his peers. Rightly, the trophy went to a survivor of the ambush in Afghanistan which had claimed the life of one of the Rifle Volunteers. The applause turned into a standing ovation, embarrassing the recipient to the point of absurdity. Awards were then given to those who had taken on extra responsibility while so many of the company were away, and one was given to the most promising new recruit.

'Private Okuhara, your award, confirmed by Air Chief Marshal Sir Glenn Torpy, will now be presented to you, at your request, by Major Wood, Officer Commanding A Company, The Rifle Volunteers.'

I made my way to the front of the mess. The top table was occupied by the company officers, all standing for the presentation. The major handed me the award while the chairman of the mess carried the certificate and some paperwork back to my seat. There was applause, but I didn't really hear it. I had wanted the major to give me the award because this would be less formal than receiving it from a dignitary or staff officer. On the other hand, I didn't want it to happen in secret either. The mess rose from their chairs holding their glasses, and some banged on the tables.

I could feel myself turning red. Luckily, the room was quite dark, the candles on the tables only adding to the ambience.

Along with a citation and certificate, I was handed an envelope. Once I had sat down I moved my coffee cup aside and read the contents. One piece of paper was a memo detailing the award, noting that it had been entered onto my service record and providing details of the physical item itself. There was also a letter, which read:

> From General Sir Kevin O'Donoghue KCB CBE, Colonel of the Regiment, Regimental Headquarters, Gloucester
>
> Dear Private Okuhara,
> I was very pleased to see in the Joint Commanders Operational List Number 24 that you have earned an award for your recent successful tour of Iraq. On behalf of all members of the Regiment, I would like to congratulate you on this well-deserved accolade. Over the last four or five years, which have been exceptionally busy and challenging, the British Army has performed with great dedication, discipline, and professionalism. You have, by your committed service, enhanced still further the fine reputation of both the Rifle Volunteers and the Royal Gloucestershire, Berkshire and Wiltshire Regiment, and I am delighted that your efforts have received recognition. Well done and many congratulations.
>
> Yours ever,
> K. O'Donoghue

Our AGC clerk, Claire, was sitting opposite me. She asked if she could read the letter, so I passed it over to her. After reading it, she put it carefully back into the envelope and returned it.

'Wow,' she mouthed, so as not to interrupt the next award being given to Mo, the storeman, who had arranged a family day while we were deployed. He was given a pewter statue of a British Army soldier, along with a letter of thanks from the OC.

After the final awards and speeches, the local Army cadet drum corps marched into the drill hall, resplendent in their white custodian helmets

CHAPTER FORTY-THREE

and red coats. Led by their drum major, an adult volunteer with four stripes indicating his rank, they paid their compliments to the OC and officers before performing an excellent routine. They had obviously practised hard and, as far as I could tell, never missed a beat. I later found out they had been practising every week while the Glosters were in Iraq so they could welcome us back with their performance. Their rehearsal room and drill hall were in the building opposite ours, which used to be the base caretaker's cottage. Along with the Corps of Drums and Bugles, there was also an ACF, or Army Cadet Force unit, that had been following our progress in Iraq through local and national press. They had kept various newspaper articles, clippings and other items of interest, and collected them into a binder to be kept in the company interest room for those wanting to read about Op TELIC and the contributions of the Rifle Volunteers.

I decided to take some time away from training to enjoy a few weekends doing civvy things. I didn't want to become 'army barmy' like some of the blokes. I often wondered why they were part-time soldiers instead of full-time; the work so clearly suited them. I had heard that some of Salamanca Company had decided to join the regular Army once they had finished their time off. As for me, some of my friends had started regularly going to the cinema on Fridays, followed by a decent meal, so I decided a few weekends doing that would be a nice change.

That month, one of the admin staff left me a message asking if I was going to be coming into the TA centre or going to the UOTC. I hadn't been to either for a few weeks. Normally she left messages to encourage people to keep volunteering, but she suggested there was some important news and that, unless it was impossible, I should come to Eastern Avenue. When I arrived, straight from work and wearing a suit instead of DPM, I saw that the entire company was in the drill hall. I joined them and fell in with my platoon. It wasn't long before the CSM brought us to attention and presented us to the OC. We stood at ease.

'I'll come straight to the point. By now many of you have heard, but I regret to inform you that Corporal Hill has passed away.'

He paused, letting that sink in.

'It is not my place to describe the nature of his passing. It is a private family matter, but the company is doing all it can to support Mark's family during this very difficult time.'

I couldn't believe it. After all he had been through, what had happened? I didn't know. I looked around and saw the news had hit everyone hard. His closest friends in the Glosters already knew – Kav, Foz, Bons, Pat. I could see them on parade, listening to the major.

'We need three more pallbearers.'

I heard the last part of the officer's address without catching the first part. We came to attention and were dismissed.

The operation had affected Mark. Outwardly, he was a tough but friendly guy, huge in size and personality, seemingly indestructible. The kind of soldier you always wanted on hand. After returning from TELIC, he and his family had gone on holiday. It was to be their last trip together. I spoke to others in the company and some mutual friends he worked with. What I heard was said in confidence, but I am certain nobody would object to the following observation: mental health is too easily overlooked, especially among men and in the military. It can be a killer, affecting every part of someone's life like a chronic illness or physical disability. These issues have taken the lives of many soldiers and continue to do so.

I went home, looked at some pictures I had of Mark, and recalled our conversations – from cutting flags off a shirt for my new uniform to ensuring that the only vegetarian in the British Army got fed. The entire company looked up to him. He had spoken to my family when he bumped into them one day and said more complimentary things than I could possibly have deserved. I had a lot of good memories of him and not a single bad one. When the day of his funeral came, the church couldn't accommodate everyone. Coaches had to be arranged so that the hundreds of mourners could say their farewells and lay Mark to rest.

Part VI
THE END

Chapter Forty-four

I had left the world of banking to pursue a new career. I had moved to Cheltenham and had recently completed the UOTC syllabus, several interviews and a few short courses. With that behind me, I had been very busy, leaving little time for reservist activities. My new role, in a national police force, required me to travel extensively, from the tip of Scotland to the Cumbrian coast, to Portsmouth on the south coast, and everywhere in between. Despite the hectic schedule, I was enjoying being busy and earning decent money. My girlfriend appreciated the extra income too. Now that I had a few days off, my plan was to relax with her and enjoy some quality R&R.

I turned on the TV and picked up that morning's mail. Settling down, I opened a large brown envelope. Most envelopes these days contained bills, but this one had a covering letter from '43 (Wessex) Brigade, Jellalabad Barracks, Tidworth'. 'Oh shit! Not again.' It had been a few years since I had been to Iraq, and the commitment was winding down. But the UK still had a substantial number of troops in Afghanistan. British forces had entered Helmand Province in 2006, five years after the post-9/11 deployment, stirring up a hornet's nest of hostile activity. Some of the reservists I knew from Salamanca Company had already been deployed, and one had been killed.

The letter read:

APPOINTMENT TO TERRITORIAL ARMY (GROUP B) COMMISSION. MR MATTHEW OKUHARA.

Mr Okuhara is appointed to a TA General List Section 'B' commission in the rank of 2Lt (on probation) with effect from 21 Oct 08.

CHAPTER FORTY-FOUR

I checked the *London Gazette* as well. Sure enough, the details were there. 'Only took me one war and four years,' I thought to myself, taking a triumphant swig of coffee and nearly burning my mouth in the process.

I had taken part in the parade that marked my transition to officer but wasn't expecting any follow-up paperwork on top of what I already had. The arrival of an innocuous envelope full of documents brought back vivid memories. 'If I have to go again, I'd rather volunteer than be surprised with another call-up,' I decided. 'I don't think List B officers can be deployed anyway . . .'

I had to come to an arrangement with my new employers. They would only allow me to pursue reservist activities in a 'non-deployable' role. To their way of thinking, there would be a conflict of interest in the event of a serious incident. There were some useful activities I could take part in, but they usually involved travelling to private schools or regional training centres, and administrative tasks. If I was going to make the most of this appointment, and not waste my time, I would need to start participating in activities, earning qualifications and seeing what I could do. With that in mind, I decided to see what was on offer for a very, very junior officer. The other option was to look at other reservist roles and specialist training. But having only just achieved this long-held goal, I was not inclined to start job-hopping quite yet.

As I drove to Okehampton, memories of my experiences there a few years earlier came flooding back. I remembered the way even though I had never driven the route myself, and I didn't need a map or satnav. Salamanca Company had started small-unit training at the camp, preparing for the worst-case scenarios we would face in Iraq, as Major Evans noted.

As a unit, 3 Platoon had seen more than its fair share of worst-case scenarios; we were definitely the unlucky multiple. Salamanca Company's call signs had all fought hard, but in truth, combat is all about luck. You're either lucky enough to avoid it or unlucky enough to find it. That's how I saw it, although I'm sure Lieutenant Sherwood would disagree. He would say it was all about 'preparation, planning, and performance'. Without a doubt, that officer knew his stuff. I heard he had been promoted to captain and was now a Forward Air Controller (FAC) with operational experience bringing in RAF Harriers and USAF close air support in Afghanistan. He had made his point angrily about prior preparation and planning after a patrol we had to abort on TELIC.

I remembered it well. 1 Platoon had dropped us off in the Blue sector of Basra. The entire city had been colour-coded: Pink for the Palace, Green for the Hotel, Yellow for the rural area where Salamanca Company regularly operated beside the Shatt al-Arab, and Blue for the village areas that bordered Green. Green was a highly dangerous sector comprising the main roads through the centre of the city and was often patrolled by Warrior IFVs as well as more heavily armed units.

Deployed as a full multiple, the idea was for us to patrol on foot from Blue to Pink in preparation for a large convoy arriving at the Palace. The convoy was critical. As helicopters were still grounded following the loss of an airframe, the RLC had planned a massive re-supply to last the Palace until air operations were available again. The 8km route clearance was planned to ensure the safe arrival of bombs, bullets and beans.

We disembarked from the wagons and went into all-round defence. Mr Sherwood, as always, had been clear about how he wanted to manage the deployment. Prior to and en route to the drop-off, we had gone through our 'actions on' – the actions we would perform in the event of a worst-case scenario. As usual, we conducted radio and equipment checks as well.

Lieutenant Sherwood came from a UOTC background. Theory and success made up 90 per cent of the Officer Training Corps scenarios, but those kinds of scenario were no use for what was to come. After being deployed, a communication issue meant the entire multiple was unable to maintain any kind of contact with the ops room. The radio checks, boosted by the vehicle radios on the same frequency, gave the officer the impression that all was well. The truth, however, was that our radios had dud batteries. The soldier in charge of picking up fresh batteries had either not done so or somehow swapped duds for duds. I never found out which. Either way, now that we were out of radio contact with the ops room – and any other friendly call sign – it would be an 8km run through the city to the nearest British base, the Palace.

Negotiating the city whilst essentially cut off was quite a different experience. If we got into trouble, nobody would know. If we were about to walk into trouble, nobody could warn us. If we took casualties, nobody could evacuate them. If we needed help, nobody would hear us. It really cemented the concept of having a sound comms plan – something I went on to double- and triple-check every time I developed a strategy and delivered orders myself.

CHAPTER FORTY-FOUR

Cautiously and as quickly as possible, we made our way through the city and back to the Palace. Every few hundred metres, Mr Sherwood would make a radio check. He had enough juice in the 351 to be heard by the NCOs carrying smaller 349 radio sets, but that was it. We were approaching the hospital, around a kilometre and a half from the main gate, when the machine gun nest on top of the gate picked up his radio check. We had run for around six kilometres in 40° heat, stopping periodically to swallow a mouthful of water and check the comms. The platoon commander was far from happy, singling out the dud battery culprit for chastisement in front of the entire multiple.

'All you had to do was get some batteries from stores!'

Mr Sherwood pointed at me; 'He's got to check the medi-kit'. He pointed at L2: 'He's got an incident pack to prepare.'

The incident pack was a patrol pack full of equipment useful for civil contingencies, such as mine-marking tape, flares, and so on.

He went on: 'We have ECM, support weapons, and ammo to sort out . . . all you had to do was get some charged fucking batteries!'

I think it was the only time I heard Mr Sherwood swear. I could see the bloke he was shouting at looking extremely contrite. He probably wanted the ground to swallow him up. I wanted to look away. At least we were safely back, but the patrol had been aborted.

I recalled that patrol as an example of worst-case scenarios and contingencies for my own training. Now, though, it did not seem that I would be going through anything similar at any time soon. My next objective at Okehampton was considerably more mundane.

Okehampton had not changed at all. It had been a few years since I last visited. The cattle grid at the entrance to the camp felt all too familiar. I was there for a course run by the SASC to qualify for running small-arms training. Becoming a Range Safety Officer (RSO) was the first step. The course, known as RMQ (range management qualification), was the first one for which I didn't need PT gear; everything was classroom- or shooting range-based. Apparently, it was boring as hell. But I didn't care, because now, as a one-pip wonder, I had a small Bath Star on the front of my uniform. It could have been the world's dullest or most unnecessary course for all I cared.

On my way to the training building, a signaller from a TA unit who looked like he had been volunteered for some menial task stopped what he was doing, stood to attention and saluted. I returned the compliment, and he got back to lifting whatever he had been told to lift. It reminded me of Basra Palace, when I had been sandbagging with Drewy. 'Someone's gotta do it,' I thought. And as I had learned from experience, 'That someone is usually a private.' I remembered taking a break in the back of a four-ton truck, getting a reprieve from the hot Iraqi sun, and Mark bringing me a half-frozen 'vegetable lattice', or whatever it was. It must have been the only one in Iraq, and somehow he had found it for me.

I joined the others in the lecture room. Most attendees were NCOs from the TA, and for some reason there was even a bloke from the Royal Navy Reserve. I took a seat and got out my notepad. Quiet talk filled the room, with no sign of the SASC officer and NCO who were running the training. I remembered the room well. Uzi and I had done our OPTAG medic training here. I recalled stepping outside to watch trainee marines practise helicopter work, and unsuccessfully trying to light Uzi's cigarette, nearly setting his nose hair on fire in the process. I had heard that he was now a full-time soldier. The job had suited him well in Iraq, and he had decided to transfer out of the infantry and into the Army Air Corps. But I had lost touch with him. The last time I saw him was at Mark's funeral. The whole company attended, and the wake was held at the TA centre in Gloucester.

Eventually, I had also lost touch with the rest of 3 Platoon. I had gone to L2's wedding with Planty and Drewy the year before and driven to see Fordy over in Somerset. Now L2 was living abroad with his wife, and as far as we knew, Planty had disappeared off the face of the earth. Nobody had heard from him. He always seemed a little detached and otherworldly. Someone joked that he had probably gone home to the planet Zog.

Some of the senior NCOs had established a loose 'association' for Salamanca Company, but it was mostly online, with occasional events around Dorset. I had never attended one but heard that The Fox and Hounds, where we had visited as a complete company, was a regular haunt. Maybe this is just how things are for reservists drawn from a wide area. Getting together for reunions and balancing busy lives – it all seemed as though going to Basra and back was the beginning, middle and end for Salamanca Company.

Chapter Forty-five

Operation TELIC, conducted between 19 March 2003 and 22 May 2011, saw the loss of 179 British personnel, 136 of whom were killed due to hostile action. The reasons for British involvement in the Iraq War were controversial and not widely understood. Even those deployed were not fully aware of the conflict's objectives. For my part, I recall reading about the need for 'regime change' and the 'axis of evil' that Saddam Hussein was supposedly part of. Claims of weapons of mass destruction, non-compliance with UN weapons inspectors, the Iraqi regime's support of Al Qaeda and reports of human rights abuses: these were all cited as justification for the invasion.

In hindsight, the conflict is better understood, and it is generally accepted that there was a certain amount of dishonesty from the Bush and Blair administrations. It is widely recognized that the invasion caused significant political instability, leading to long-term repercussions in the region. Even those who voted for military action would have done well to read *For Whom the Bell Tolls* by Ernest Hemingway, in which these words appear: 'Never think that war, no matter how necessary nor how justified, is not a crime. Ask the infantry and ask the dead.' Those who vote for or support conflict invariably do not take part in the action and, in many cases, are not even held accountable.

As a 19-year-old at the time, however, the ins and outs of politics did not concern me. When I was called up, my thoughts were not on the legalities and complexities of the conflict. Instead, my focus was on my loyalty and ambition as a member of the Royal Gloucestershire, Berkshire and Wiltshire Regiment. I do not mean to sound jingoistic or detached from the realities of conflict, imagining it all as a grand adventure. Rather, as an unlikely soldier, I wanted to be the equal of everyone I was deployed with, given that my name had been called.

When I joined the TA I did not expect to be sent to Iraq, or anywhere at all. I freely admit to having been naive about the military; perhaps I felt like I was just 'playing soldiers' at times. But I was also genuinely interested and enthusiastic. After all, it was the first major decision I had ever made in my adult life. Within a year of joining, I had achieved a number of other 'firsts' – some of which nobody would want to experience, and others that were hard-won and worth treasuring as memories forever.

Operation TELIC was one of the largest deployments of British troops in many years. Due to the conflict's nature and longevity, more resources were committed to Iraq than, for example, the Falklands or the Balkans. The deployment was so extensive that the military's reserves were called up in vast numbers for the first time since the Suez Crisis in the 1950s. This mobilization included thousands of reservists from various units, some serving in combat roles, while others provided essential support in logistics, medical services and intelligence. This trend has continued, and the Territorial Army, now known as the Army Reserve, regularly deploys alongside its full-time counterparts in various capacities.

Reflecting on the operational environment, unlike other deployments such as al-Amarah, Shaibah or Umm-Qasr, Basra, Iraq's 'second city', was an environment marked by its political significance and its complex civil landscape. Our deployment involved not only combat operations but also efforts to stabilize and rebuild the local infrastructure that had been destroyed or neglected in the run-up to our arrival. We interacted with local communities, often through interpreters (at great personal risk to them), to gather intelligence and build what little trust we could.

It has been twenty years since I was part of Op TELIC. That is as much time as it took for me to be born, go to school, graduate, join the TA and then head out on an operation and come back. Many of my deployment memories, however, still feel recent. I remember the camaraderie and the shared experiences, the heat, the smells and the dust. Everything. Despite the challenges faced by our company, we successfully deployed to Basra and returned home with everyone alive. Changed. But alive.

The psychological toll taken by the deployment was significant. Many soldiers, including myself, grappled with the transition back to civilian life. Some people negotiate that sort of hurdle quickly, whereas others can be affected for the rest of their lives; the experience of

CHAPTER FORTY-FIVE

combat, the loss and the constant state of alertness leave deep imprints. Support networks, both formal and informal, play a crucial role in helping veterans navigate these challenges. Over the years, I've come to understand the importance of mental health support for veterans and the need for ongoing care and attention to issues that arise long after the deployment ends.

The use of reserves in such great numbers did not go without controversy. In analysing the deployment of the TA specifically, the Royal United Services Institute noted that the threshold for calling out reserves was much lower than it had ever been before. Many of those deployed, including in Salamanca Company, had to sacrifice their careers, families and daily lives to 'answer the call' – failure to do so without reasonable excuse could lead to criminal prosecution. There were questions around whether the regular Army was able to accept such large numbers of reservists into service so quickly. However, as many people say, in the tried and tested cliché, 'It's what we signed up for.'

Operation TELIC was an important chapter in my life and the lives of many others. It was a time of learning, growth and, as Broz said, 'the experience of a lifetime'.